North, America's GREATEST Whitetail Lodges & Outfitters

Willow Creek
GUIDES

North America's GREATEST Whitetail Lodges & Outfitters

Over 120 Prime Destinations in the United States and Canada

BY PETER FIDUCCIA
AND
JAY CASSELL

Willow Creek®
PRESS

Library of Congress Cataloging-in-Publication Data

Fiduccia, Peter.
  North America's greatest whitetail lodges & outfitters : over 120 prime destinations in the United States and Canada / by Peter Fiduccia and Jay Cassell.
    p. cm. -- (Willow Creek guides)
  ISBN 1-57223-308-7 (pbk. : alk. paper)
  1. White-tailed deer hunting--United States--Guidebooks. 2. Hunting lodges--United States--Guidebooks. 3. United States--Guidebooks. 4. White-tailed deer hunting--Canada--Guidebooks. 5. Hunting lodges--Canada--Guidebooks. 6. Canada--Guidebooks. I. Title: North America's greatest whitetail lodges and outfitters. II. Cassell, Jay. III. Title. IV. Series.
  SK301 .C38 2001
  799.2'7652'029673--dc21

2001003222

Acknowledgments

WE WISH TO EXTEND OUR THANKS to Tom Petrie and Andrea Donner for their encouragement and guidance on this project.

C o n t

e n t s

© Peter Fiduccia

Peter Fiduccia with a buck he took near Tilden, Texas.

© Jay Cassell

Jay Cassell with a buck from Alabama's "Black Belt."

INTRODUCTION

There are approximately 55 million white-tailed deer in North America. They inhabit Mexico, most of the Canadian provinces, plus the lower 48 states (you won't find them in Hawaii or Alaska). There are roughly 15 million hunters in the United States out of a total human population of 275 million. Clearly, there are enough deer to go around!

If you are one of the millions of deer hunters in the U.S. today, then you are part of an American tradition that began before white settlers ever set foot on the continent. It is a tradition that will remain a part of our heritage as long as whitetails continue to roam our land. And with more deer now than before the "settlement" of North America, it's hard to imagine that tradition ever changing, despite recent anti-hunting movements.

Deer hunting has changed over the centuries, however. Native Americans used to hunt with bows and arrows, and white settlers hunted mostly on the lands surrounding their homesteads. Today's hunters, however, have innumerable opportunities to hunt whitetails in their local forests, on farmlands, and on state and federal lands throughout the continent. Whether you hunt whitetails locally or within an hour or two from home, the day will come when you will want to plan a hunt in a different state or Canadian province — perhaps a trip of a lifetime for a trophy buck. If that is your desire, then this book is for you.

The lodges and outfitters profiled in this book primarily offer fair-chase hunts. There are those who put you in a position where you are likely to have the opportunity to take a trophy, and those who simply offer you the land to hunt, where your skills and experience are more likely to produce a kill. We did not rate the lodges, as tastes are personal. Instead, we've tried to give complete, pertinent information to help you determine which lodges are worth a further look.

This book will help you expand your whitetail horizons, and hopefully help you add to your life list of hunting experiences. In the process, you'll also learn more about whitetail hunting, and how they do it differently than the way you do at home. Ultimately, that will make you a better hunter. We hope this book takes you to places that fulfill your whitetail dreams.

HOW TO
USE THIS BOOK

THIS GUIDE IS ARRANGED first by region — East, South, Midwest, West, Canada East, and Canada West — with each region organized by state or Canadian province. You'll find that the majority of the lodges are in the Northeast, South, and in Texas, regions where whitetail hunting has a deep tradition. Relatively new areas for whitetail hunting, such as the western states, don't have many lodges and outfitters devoted specifically to whitetails. Most are in the business of hunting mule deer and elk, with whitetails of secondary importance. The western lodges in this book devote more of their time to whitetails than many of the others. (For a listing of lodge and outfitters that specifically hunt elk and mule deer, as well as other big game such as bear and cougar, see the Willow Creek Guide to *Big Game Lodges and Outfitters*, by John Ross and Jay Cassell.

You will also find a variety of lodges and outfitters who hunt in different terrains and use different tactics and techniques to hunt white-tailed deer. As you flip through these pages, have some criteria in mind for choosing a lodge. Location, price, trophy deer, accommodations, terrain, region — all should factor in to your final decision. Also, ask yourself some of the following questions about yourself (and your hunting party).

What kind of hunter are you? Are you dead-set on getting a trophy buck or nothing? Are you just as happy getting a medium-sized buck, or a doe? Does hunting inside an area surrounded by a high fence bother you? Or do you want a wilderness hunt, where you head deep into the backcountry where it's you against the elements? Do you care if the temperature dips below zero degrees on a regular basis? Do you mind or enjoy hunting in snow (if you like to track deer, you can't beat a couple inches of snow on the ground). On the other extreme, would you rather hunt in warm temperatures, where insects can be an issue, but where you can hunt in shirtsleeves and tennis shoes?

Do you want to go on a hunt that is challenging physically, where you had better be in good shape or your chances of getting a nice deer will diminish accordingly? Or are you happier sitting back in a tree stand or ground blind, or moving slowly, simply soaking in your surroundings? Is getting a deer of secondary importance to the actual experience of just being in the outdoors, hunting?

Do you prefer to stay in plush accommodations, where you sleep in a comfortable bed each evening, where the food is five-star rated, and there's plenty of it; where you can relax in a sauna after a long day afield, then go to the great room and perhaps watch some television, or sit back and smoke a good cigar at the end of the day, trading hunting stories with other hunters in camp. Or is a tent camp or a motel in town more to your liking? How about a lakeshore housekeeping cabin? All of these options present themselves in this book.

As far as hunting itself is concerned, do you like to hunt out of tree stands, overlooking well-used game trails or food plots? Or is still-hunting your favorite tactic? How about rattling or calling? Glassing and stalking? Do you like to participate in organized deer drives? Do you enjoy driving around on dirt roads in a Chevy Suburban, glassing likely areas until you spy a buck that's worth stalking?

Ask yourself all these questions and more. The last thing you want to do is go somewhere where you're not happy, where you don't enjoy the style of hunting, the weather, the terrain, or the accommodations. We've tried to detail the lodges in these terms (terrain, cost, accommodations, hunting techniques, etc.), but once you have decided on a lodge, call the outfitter and talk with them. Ask questions — if you hear something over the phone that you don't like, then perhaps that outfitter isn't for you.

References

Once you have narrowed your search and have chosen a lodge or outfitter, get a list of references from one that you're considering. Any outfit that balks at giving you names and numbers of past clients is obviously trying to hide something. Take your search — and your hunting dollars — elsewhere. Call the references and ask questions. Always ask references to give a name of someone at the camp who didn't take a deer — that's a person you want to talk to! It will certainly tell you something about the lodge or outfitter if a deerless hunter has high praise for an outfit anyway.

Obviously, an outfitter is not going to send you to a reference that is going to say negative things. But that's not why you're calling. You're calling to find out more information about the outfitter or lodge, about the hunting, the accommodations, the atmosphere in camp, and the other hunters. Any information you can glean from the conversation will help. After all, it's your money and your time. You want to make certain that you end up going to the outfit that you want, and that you have planned every element of your trip down to the last detail.

Vital Statistics

Each lodge or outfitter entry has two elements: one is made of text describing the hunting, the atmosphere, often the owners, the accommodations, etc.; the other is a quick listing of important facts about the lodge or outfitter, called "Vital Statistics." These lists are designed to give at-a-glance information about each lodge. Most of the headings are self-explanatory, but a few require clarification. A "Yes" in the Draw Blood Policy means that if a hunter hits a deer but does not recover it, that deer is considered the hunter's, and her or his hunt is finished. In some trophy hunting situations, the hunter must pay for the deer as well.

Boone & Crockett information is also included for some listings in an effort to determine the trophy quality of the bucks available at certain lodges. Pope & Young information is substituted for those lodges that bowhunt only. Many lodges and outfitters do not gather rack size information and judge their hunts on the larger hunting experience. Some lodges do take many good bucks, but for whatever reason, they do not make "the book." We've included Boone & Crockett information where it helps, but it is up to the reader to determine whether this type of information is important to the overall booking of a hunt.

Lastly, under "Vital Statistics," we've given complete contact information, including very useful web sites that can help you research your choice even further.

Great Resources

The following contact information for some relevant organizations is provided to expand your resources. Many can provide rich troves of information for whitetail hunting.

BOONE AND CROCKETT CLUB

Old Milwaukee Depot, 250 Station Dr.

Missoula, MT 59801

Ph: 406/542-1888

Fax: 406/542-0784

Email: bcclub@boone-crockett.org

Web: www.boone-crocket.org

Established by Theodore Roosevelt and other concerned sportsmen to promote hunting ethics, foster the concept of fair chase, and help establish wildlife conservation practices which led to the recovery of big game animals in North America. The Club documents the records of North American big game and exhibits its national collection of heads and horns in Cody, Wyoming.

BUCKMASTERS

Box 244022, Montgomery, AL 36124-4022

Ph: 800/240-3337

Web: www.buckmasters.com.

Dedicated to the ethical pursuit of white-tailed deer, and with a magazine, *Buckmasters*, devoted to deer and deer hunting. Buckmasters is also a record-keeping organization for white-tailed deer — uses a full-credit scoring system that does not deduct anything from the rack of a deer. Buckmasters also runs Project Venison, which provides venison to the needy. Call extension 270 for more information.

NATIONAL RIFLE ASSOCIATION

11250 Waples Mill Rd., Fairfax, VA 22030

Ph: 703/267-1000

Fax: 703/267-3909

A nonprofit organization dedicated to protect and defend the Constitution of the United States, especially the right to possess and use firearms for recreation and personal protection; to promote public safety, law and order, and the national defense; and to train members of law enforcement agencies, the military, and private citizens of good repute in marksmanship and the safe handling and efficient use of small arms.

NATIONAL SHOOTING SPORTS FOUNDATION

Flintrock Ridge Office Center, 11 Mile Hill Rd.

Newtown, CT 06470-2359

Ph: 203/426-1320

Fax: 203/426-1087

Email: info@nssf.org

Web: www.nssf.org

A nonprofit educational, trade-supported association that sponsors a wide variety of programs to create a better understanding of and a more active participation in the shooting sports and in practical conservation.

POPE & YOUNG CLUB

15 E. 2nd St., Box 548

Chatfield, MN 55923

Ph/fax: 507/867-4144

Email: pyclub@isl.net

Web: www.pope-young.org

A North American bowhunting and wildlife conservation organization dedicated to the promotion and protection of our bowhunting heritage and North America's wildlife.

WHITETAILS UNLIMITED

Box 720, Rhode Island St.

Sturgeon Bay, WI 54235

Ph: 414/743-6777

WU is a national, nonprofit conservation organization. Its purpose is to raise funds in support of education, habitat enhancement, and the preservation of the hunting tradition for the direct benefit of the white-tailed deer and other wildlife species.

Consulting & Booking Agents

There are two ways to look at booking agents. The first is that agents know and are connected to a lot of hunting outfitters, and they can book you with the operation that best suits your hunting and budgetary needs. They have more than likely hunted with each operation they represent, or at least toured the facilities. They know the owners and guides, and what sort of guests they typically serve. They have also talked with some of the clients who have visited the operation.

The second, more negative view, is that some booking agents will try to convince you to book with one of their outfitters, no matter what your personal preferences. They have exclusive relationships with one or more outfitters, and commitments to provide a certain number of clients to each. Some will do their best to fill that quota. If an agent is the sole representative of a lodge, you can bet that his priority is filling those camps with guests. Sure, he wants you to be satisfied, but your needs may be of secondary importance.

However, most booking agents (including the ones listed in this book) are reputable and are concerned with pleasing both the lodges and its guests. They understand that if you come away from a hunt satisfied, then they are likely to get repeat business. If your hunt doesn't go as it was represented, as sometimes occurs, reputable agents will often return a certain percentage of your money. Agents are generally current on international travel and airline regulations, and they will provide you with a wealth of practical information that can make your hunt go smoothly.

Usually, you pay the same price whether you book through a lodge directly or through an agent; the lodge pays the agent roughly 15 percent for your business. Even if you choose to work with an agent, you should also talk directly with your prospective outfitter. Be leery of an agent who tries to prevent you from doing so. Call the outfitter, and ask about the operation until you're satisfied. It is unethical to attempt to book directly through the outfitter once you have already contacted their agent, and most outfitters would refuse to book you without the agent anyway.

Selecting an agent is somewhat similar to selecting a lodge. Call some agents and see what they have to offer. Ask for references, just as you would with an outfitter or lodge.

ADVENTURES WITH VOYAGEUR VENTURES, INC.

8356 50th Ave. N.
Minneapolis, MN 55428
Ph: 877/240-9112
Email: chrislemke@voyageurventures.com
Web: www.voyageurventures.com
Whitetail hunts in Kansas, Minnesota, Michigan, North Dakota, South Dakota, and all Canadian provinces. Contact Chris Lemke.

CANADIAN WILDERNESS ADVENTURES

159 Cypress Ct.
Saskatoon, Saskatchewan
Canada S7K 5C3
Ph: 306/934-4860
Email: dsenebal@Sk.sympatico.ca
Web: canadianwildernessadventures.com
Booking agency for quality whitetail hunts across Canada. Contact Darrell Senebald.

CLASSIC ADVENTURES

561 Sumerlin Cir. NW
St. Michael, MN 55376
Ph: 763/497-3333
Whitetail hunts arranged across North America and Canada. Will tailor hunts to your needs and prices. Contact Jay Thomas.

H & H HUNT'N

Rt. 1, Box 219
Lipan, TX
Ph: 904/659-8452 or 940/769-2764
H&H offers high-quality, affordable hunts in Colorado, New Mexico, Texas, North Dakota, Utah, and across the U.S. and Canada for whitetails and a variety of other species. Contact Michael Hendrick.

HUNTER'S QUEST INTERNATIONAL

6819 Woodland Dr.
Dallas, TX 75225
Ph: 214/692-8769
Email: Wendell@huntersquest.com
Web: www.huntersquest.com/hunts.html
Trophy whitetail hunts arranged in Alberta and Saskatchewan. Bear and moose too. Contact Wendell Reich.

OUTDOOR CONNECTION

26 Tatnic Hill Road
Brooklyn, CT 06234
Ph: 800/992-1649
Email: outdoor@snet.net
Web www.outdoorconnection-ct.com
Outdoor Connection specializes in custom high-quality whitetail hunting trips in Kansas, North Dakota, South Dakota, Michigan, plus most Canadian provinces and Mexico. Contact Thom Phelps.

R.C. OUTFITTERS

RR 2 Box 345
Dallas, PA 18612
Ph: 570/477-2202   Fax: 570/477-2202
R.C. Outfitters is a booking agency with reputable clients in Montana, Saskatchewan, Alberta, Manitoba, Kansas, Oklahoma, Minnesota, Maine, and Texas. Contact Bob Ciravolo.

SHOSHONE WILDERNESS

PO Box 634
Dubois, WY 82513
Ph: 307/455-3245
Email: info@shoshonewilderness.com
Web Shoshonewilderness.com
A booking agency for quality big game hunts across the United States and Canada. Features trophy whitetail hunts in southern British Columbia, Alberta, Saskatchewan, Montana, Wyoming, Idaho, Texas, Kansas, South Dakota, North Dakota. Contact John Andre.

STEVE'S OUTDOOR ADVENTURES

PO Box 1481
Hermiston, OR 97838
Ph: 800/303-1304
Email: steveshunts@steveshunts.com
Web: www.steveshunts.com
Offers trophy hunts for whitetails in 26 states, plus Alberta, Saskatchewan, and British Columbia. Steve West.

TIMBERLINE OUTDOOR ADVENTURES, INC.

408 South Freedom St.
Ravenna, OH 44266
Ph: 800/580-1856
Arranges hunts for whitetails (plus bears, elk, goats, moose) in Alberta, British Columbia, Manitoba, Saskatchewan, Quebec, other provinces. Rich Sopko.

TROPHYSEEKERS WORLDWIDE

6588 Mountain Dr.
Chambersburg, PA 17201
Ph: 717/352-7119
Email: tseekers@innernet.net
Web: www.trophyseekers.com
Whitetail hunting in Illinois, Iowa, Kansas, Nebraska, Missouri and across Canada. Bow or gun. Tony Ruggeri.

UNITED STATES OUTFITTERS, INC.

PO Box 4202
Taos, NM 87571
Ph: 800/845-9929   Fax: 505/758-1744
Web: www.huntuso.com
Tell USO what you want to hunt, and where, and they'll work out an arrangement whereby they put your name into the whitetail lotteries in the states you'd like to hunt. If you don't draw a tag, nothing is lost except the application fee. Contact George Taulman.

WEST TEX-NEW MEX HUNTING SERVICES

P.O. Box 2305
Roswell, NM 88202
Ph: 505/622-6600
Email: letshunt@zianet.com
First-class whitetail hunts throughout the Southwest

(Texas, Oklahoma, New Mexico, Arizona). Other big game hunts also offered. Contact Jess Rankin.

WORLDWISE HUNTING CONSULTANTS

PO Box 3051
Ft. Leavenworth, KS 66027
Ph: 913/680-1638
Email: contact@worldhunt.com
Web: www.worldhunt.com
Worldwide Hunting Consultants offers high-quality hunting trips in Texas, Virginia, West Virginia, Arkansas, Louisiana, Kansas, South Dakota, Illinois and throughout Canada. For whitetails, other species. Contact Ron McConnell.

WORLD CLASS HUNTS

588 First Pentecostal Church Road
Longville, LA 70652
Ph: 877/932-4868
Email: hunts@beci.net
Web: www.worldclasshunts.com
First-class whitetail hunts (plus exotics, alligators) in Louisiana and Texas. Contact Dale Folds.

WORLD WIDE BIG GAME ADVENTURES

Specializes in whitetail hunts in southern Saskatchewan. More than 190,000 acres available.
Contact Edmond Smith IV at 334/401-8778
Email: edsmith@onion-group.com
Web: www.wwbga.com

WORLD WIDE WILDERNESS

144 2nd Ave.
Saskatoon, SK
S7K 2B2 Canada
Ph: 306/664-1616   Fax: 306/244-6657
Email: World_Wide_Wilderness.com
Whitetail hunts in prime ares of Alberta, Saskatchewan, plus the lower 48 states. Also books other big game hunts across North America. Contact Bob Lozinsky.

TACTICS

ONE PART OF EACH LODGE ENTRY is about hunting tactics, which include stand hunting, drives, still-hunting, calling, and rattling. The following addresses each of these tactics. A final section on reading whitetail body language has also been added to this chapter, as we feel the information will be helpful to all whitetail hunters.

STANDS

by Jay Cassell

Last season, I used climbing tree stands more than I have in all of the past 10 years. One reason is that I got permission to hunt some new property near my home, just before the opening of bow season. I didn't have time to scout the area and put up a permanent stand, as I would have liked, so I just took my climber into the woods each day and set up in areas that looked promising.

Using a climber helped me learn the new property in a hurry, which is one reason for using a climber. Another reason is that when you aren't seeing anything out of your permanent stand, you can watch a different spot with the help of a climber.

The following routines help me get into the woods, up a tree and settled, fast. Most of them apply not only to using climbers, but to permanent stands as well.

Quiet and Quick

The biggest drawback of climbers is that they make noise. You clank your way into the woods, pull this bulky thing off your back, attach it to a tree by turning bolts and nuts, then scrape your way up to a vantage point. Climbers do make noise, but you can reduce it. I always strap an extra bungee cord or two around my stand, which keeps the two pieces together and prevents them from banging as I walk. For setting up at the base of a tree, I replace wingnuts with large, accessory-type knobs; they are quieter and easily turned with gloved-hands. If you drop them in the leaves, you won't lose them. When you go up the tree, go as quietly and rapidly as you can, but do it while keeping an eye out for deer. If you're silent in your approach and setup, you'll be surprised at how many deer may be nearby.

The Right Tree

When I hike through the woods with a climber on my back, I search for trees that overlook frequently used deer trails. I also look for a tree that's at least 10 yards off my chosen trail; if you set up too close to a trail, deer will peg you in a hurry. Search for a straight tree, one whose diameter is right for the size of your climber (mine is about 14 inches). Rule out trees that are crooked, that lean, or that have an abundance of broken branches. Additionally, find a tree near others that will break up your silhouette.

If you find a tree you like, hunt it that day. If you plan to hunt out of the tree again, consider coming back and putting up a permanent stand. Keep in mind that you want to get to it as quickly and as quietly as possible the next time. Find the best trail leading to the tree, one that you can move along quietly, with concealed movements.

Have a Routine

No matter if you're hunting out of a climbing or permanent stand, it's helpful to devise an efficient routine and stick with it each time you go afield. If you know where your gear always is — big or small — you have fewer chances for making mistakes. My climber routine is this: Before I start into the woods, I strap my safety belt around my waist. The part of the belt that goes around the tree is in my left pocket, ready to be pulled out as soon as I get into the tree. My trigger (for bowhunting) is in my right pocket. A rope for hauling up my bow or rifle is attached to the top part of my climber. (If I'm heading to one of my permanent stands, the rope is already there, hanging from the base of the stand.)

When I get to my tree, I take the climber off my back, undo the bungee cords (these go into my pants pocket), undo the nuts, and attach the blades of the climber around the tree. I next tie my rifle or bow to the haul rope, then climb into the stand, put my feet in the straps, attach my safety belt, and start to climb. A handsaw is in the right outside pocket of my daypack in case I need to saw off any tree limbs. Gloves and hand-warmers are in the left outside pocket.

When I reach my desired height — normally 20 to 25 feet — I tighten my safety belt. Once I'm secure, I attach a bungee cord between both parts of my climber, which ensures that the bottom platform won't fall away should I take my weight off of it. My second bungee goes around the top blade.

Next, I take a screw-in step and insert it into the tree. I hang my daypack on the step, then turn around, strap the release around my wrist if I'm bowhunting, then pull up my bow or rifle. I notch an arrow or chamber a cartridge, then settle down.

Coming Down

To descend, do your climbing routine in reverse. Take your time, and don't step on your bow or rifle when you get out of your stand.

SAFETY FIRST

The following is from a report issued by the New York State Department of Environmental Conservation after the 2000 hunting season:

Although firearms-related incidents have declined significantly, falls from tree stands continue to be an increasing concern. Three hunters died last year in falls from tree stands. Unlike firearms injuries, there is no reporting system to track injuries from falls and because they do not fit the legal definition of a hunting accident, these incidents do not appear in official hunting injury records. However, based on anecdotal information, tree stand-related injuries appear to be increasing as use of tree stands increases. DEC is taking steps to address this problem through an emphasis in Sportsmen Education courses and in public information provided to hunters.

Hunting out of tree stands is serious business. I personally have three friends who have fallen out of their stands. One friend, Al, fell asleep in his stand and simply fell out. He wasn't wearing his safety belt, and he paid for it. Luckily, there was deep snow on the ground and he landed right in the middle of it. A few bruises, but he was fine.

Another friend, Dan, slipped while climbing up to his stand. (Climbing up and down are, statistically, the most dangerous times of tree stand hunting, and demand extra care. Don't go up to your stand if it's icy, and wear your belt while going up, even it it's cumbersome to do so.) Dan, who was not wearing his belt, fell down the tree. He only went 10 feet, but one of his screw-in steps dug into his leg and opened a wound from his knee almost to his crotch. Dan lost a lot of blood, but survived. His stand was luckily near a road, and he was able to get help before it was too late.

My friend Leaf wasn't so lucky. As the police told me, they found him lying at the base of his tree stand, next to an 8-point buck that he had obviously shot with his bow. He had fallen from his stand, landed head-first on some rocks at the base of his tree, and died instantly. His wife had called the police when he didn't return that evening; they put together a search party and found him the next morning. Apparently, Leaf shot the buck, went over and gutted it where it fell, then dragged it the 50 yards back to his stand. He apparently climbed back into his stand to gather his gear, slipped, and fell to his death. He wasn't wearing a safety belt.

Lessons? Sure. One slip and you could be history. Use a good safety belt *always*, and always use common sense. Don't go up your tree if it's icy or extremely windy, and don't go up a tree if you're sleepy. It's just not worth it.

DRIVES

by Peter Fiduccia

On the last day of the 1994 New York deer season, I resigned myself to the fact that my chances of shooting the big buck I had been hunting exclusively the entire season (I estimated him to be in the 160 class) were looking less than promising. Typically, I hunted the deer by using my traditional strategies, which included calling, rattling, and rub-grunting — all of which, for one reason or another, left the buck unscathed. I decided my best chance of getting the buck at this point in the season was to organize a drive.

While I'm not crazy about organizing huge drives involving eight or more hunters, I do enjoy driving bucks with groups of four hunters or less. These small drives are not only much more challenging, but are also extremely effective, especially for big bucks.

The tactic of small deer drives, in any sense of the word, is at best a paradox. In all my years of deer hunting, I have come to realize that deer, especially bucks, aren't really driven anywhere. Instead, they often go only where they want to, rather than where you want them to. There-in lies the key to successful small drives.

When planning a small drive, the number one factor is to pay meticulous attention to wind direction. Next, always be aware of where the buck would prefer to go rather than where you want him to go. Another factor is intimately knowing the terrain you're hunting and trying not to drive too large a section of ground. In addition, always keep a buck's instinctive traits of doubling back, circling, and staying put uppermost in your mind — and the rest becomes somewhat easier.

One of my favorite small-drive strategies requires two hunters. I call it "Decoy & Drop Drive." The best time for this drive is between 9 am and 1 pm, as it tries to ambush bedded bucks. A two-man drive works in all types of terrain, but is especially effective along mountainous ledges where hunters can cover as much or as little ground as they desire. It also works in large standing patches of corn, thick swamps, and in heavy evergreen forests.

I have had the most success with it in and among the ledges of a mountainous piece of property I hunt in southern New York. The first hunter begins the drive by walking with the wind in his face, parallel to the ledges in an obvious manner, not taking advantage of the available cover. Basically, he wants the deer to see and hear him, but does not want to alarm them into breaking out ahead of him too soon. In fact, by moving slowly and stopping, Driver #1 naturally encourages the deer to try to escape once he has passed them.

The second hunter waits at least a half-hour before he begins to follow the exact route Driver #1 took. The key to this drive is that Driver #1 must walk slowly through the area, stopping often. In fact, the drive is much more effective if Driver #1 stops and sits for several minutes before moving on. Each time he begins to walk again, he should sharply snap a twig from a tree or make some other obvious noise showing he has once again begun to move. Although Driver #1 could certainly jump a deer himself, this tactic has proved most successful for Driver #2.

The reason for this is that big bucks will often remain bedded until the first driver passes. Most times, because of the slow pace of the drive, bucks become too nervous to remain where they are. They get up and head back toward the direction Driver #1 came from. Or, while watching the direction Driver #1 went, they methodically pick their way up or down the mountain perpendicular to the path of Driver #1.

Any of these escape routes puts the deer in view of Driver #2, who is quietly following Driver #1's backtrail, and taking advantage of all the available cover as he moves forward. This gives Driver #2 ample time to see and shoot his quarry.

This drive capitalizes on a whitetail's instinct to play cat-and-mouse games with its pursuer. Out-waiting the first driver is instinctive. Slowly skulking off and watching the direction of the first driver after he has passed is part of the whitetail's instinctive ploy to a clean escape. Many times, when I have been Driver #2, I have had bucks literally walk toward me or up or down the mountain while looking over their shoulders toward Driver #1. They never knew I was there until it was too late. They usually offer me easy shots because, unlike big drives where they are encouraged to run, they are moving confidently and slowly away from one pursuer, thinking they have evaded a lone predator and not realizing they are about to be intercepted by a second predator.

This drive also works in standing corn. A deer is reluctant to break from the corn cover into the open and will often try to readjust its bedding area in the corn rather than leave it all together — again offering Driver #2 ample opportunities and easy shots.

An off-shoot of the two-man "Decoy & Drop Drive" is the three- or four-man decoy drive. The terrain is critical to this drive's success. I have found this tactic works best in large woodlots where I am familiar with known escape routes, bedding areas, and break-out points from the cover to open ground, which leads to other cover.

The drive begins with Driver A taking a stand ahead of the single driver who will be initiating the drive. Driver A is the point man, and must be on stand a good half-hour prior to the drive's beginning. Driver B begins the drive by walking slowly through the woodlot in a wide, zigzagging fashion. Although he could certainly get a shot at a deer, he is primarily the decoy. Again, Driver B stops often to look and even sit for several minutes. Once Driver B has gone for about 20 minutes, he is followed by Driver C, who walks behind him but zigzags in only half or one-quarter the width of Driver B's zig-zagging pattern. Driver C must walk very slowly and take advantage of as much cover as possible. When Driver B anticipates reaching the end of the woodlot, he patterns his movements to end up on the opposite end of the woods from Driver A. Then he takes up a stand and waits for deer being moved to him by Driver C.

Unlike the first drive I described, the deer on this drive usually move out quicker. At least, that has been the experience of most of the drivers who take up the A position.

Driver A's deer are usually moving at a fast walk and, in some instances, a trot. This could be because Driver B's scent is more prevalent since he is zig-zagging rather than walking with his face against the wind throughout the entire drive. Traditionally, deer that wind danger quickly break out and move ahead of the oncoming driver before trying to sneak back around him. Driver C usually gets shots at deer concentrating on one of the two ends. Driver C also gets a good opportunity when he takes up his stand at the end of the woodlot, between A and B — all of whom are now waiting for deer being moved out by Driver D.

Driver D is an added twist to this drive and acts as the fourth driver. He stimulates deer (that have out-waited and outwitted Drivers B and C) through their own sheer nervousness to finally make a move. Driver D moves forward at a very slow rate (as if still-hunting). He takes three or four steps, stops, and waits a good five minutes before proceeding. He repeats this tactic throughout his entire drive. Optimally, Driver D is still driving long after Drivers A, B and C have taken up their stands at the end of the woodlot. Driver D's success comes from spotting deer the other drivers did not see sneaking ahead, behind or between them. Often, these deer are trying to get back to bedding areas from where they were jumped.

On the last day of the 1994 season, I used a three-man version of the drive described above. My wife, Kate (Driver A), started the drive at 10:30 am by taking up a position where the heavy woods ended and opened up to second growth and then into a large field. A hunting companion, Vin Monti, acted as Driver B. Half an hour after Kate took her position, Monti zig-zagged through the thick woodlot as I picked up the rear, twenty minutes later, as Driver C. Even though the deer were heavily pressured during the previous three weeks, this small methodic drive sent deer out to each of us. Kate saw two does and a small buck as they exited the woods into the heavy second-growth cover. Kate decided to pass on the small 6-pointer, hoping a bigger buck would come through. Monti saw and heard several deer cautiously moving ahead of him, although he was unable to identify what they were. As I slowly walked my route, I saw two bucks — both passing within 30 yards of me.

Unfortunately, neither was the buck I was hunting for, and with a week of the late archery and blackpowder season directly following the close of the regular firearms season, I chose to pass up both 8-pointers.

As with all drives, safety is an overriding factor and should be discussed in detail before any drive begins. In fact, I like to sketch out the drive to make sure everyone knows where they will drive and where they are to stand. Most important, we always clarify each hunter's zone of fire.

The point is, small drives work in either large or small patches of ground. All they require is reasonable knowledge of the area you're driving, keeping the wind in your favor, and using basic hunting skills. Add some unorthodox strategies like the "Decoy & Drop Driver" and you've got the basic ingredients for deer driving success.

THE STILL-HUNTING ADVANTAGE

by Jay Cassell

The buck never knew I was there. I had been pussy-footing down an old logging trail, pausing every five yards or so and stopping every 20. I was standing next to a large hemlock watching the road in front of me, my body partially obscured by branches, when I saw movement off to the right. A deer was walking down a trail that intersected the logging road 40 yards ahead.

Nose to the ground, the buck was obviously following the scent of a doe. Caution was the last thing on his mind. When he reached the logging road, he skidded to a stop, turned, and looked right at me. Too late. I took him with one shot to the heart/lung region.

Still-hunting. It's a highly effective way to hunt whitetails, especially if you do it at the right time, in the right place, and the right way.

The Right Time

When you still-hunt depends in large part on the weather. On still days with crunchy leaves or icy snow on the ground, still-hunting is out of the questions. No matter how quiet you try to be, you'll still make too much noise and spook any deer long before you can get within gun range. It's better to remain in a tree stand on still days, and still-hunt on windy days when gusts conceal your leaf crunching, or on damp or rainy days when ground cover is wet and won't make noise when stepped on. Whitetails also tend to bed down on rainy and windy days, so your best chance of getting a shot at a buck is to go find one quietly on foot.

The Right Place

No matter what the weather, I like to still-hunt when I'm in new territory. While I like to use a tree stand when the situation is right, I don't immediately know where to put up a stand when I'm in unfamiliar country. Still-hunting lets me learn the property, plus it gives me a better chance at a deer than just putting up a stand in any old tree.

In damp or windy conditions when deer are usually bedded down, I head to the thickest cover I can find. Rhododendron stands, hemlock groves, cedar swamps, thickets, steep ledges — any place a buck is likely to bed down is where to go. When hunting such spots, wear camo if the law allows and move as slowly as possible. Deer pick these spots not only because they're sheltered, but because they can detect approaching danger from a long way away.

When hunting tough-to-reach cover, pay attention to the wind. Even if you're wearing a cover scent that's consistent with the area's vegetation, moving into an area with the wind at your back dictates that you stop and figure an alternative route. The brush may be ridiculously thick, or the ledges perilously steep, but common sense says you should try to circle around and approach from downwind. Being lazy and simply barging ahead will only ensure that you won't see deer; they'll scent you and be long gone before you're even close the their bedding areas.

The Right Way

If you think you're going too fast, you are. Serious still-hunting means going painfully slow — so slow that it's almost boring. But you're doing this for a number of reasons. With each step, you have a different perspective of the woods. A bedded buck can come into view with just one or two steps. Take five or six, and that buck will detect your movement and be gone before you even know he's there.

You're also moving slowly because you want to be quiet. Take each step carefully. Watch where you put your feet. If you suspect there might be a stick under the wet leaves you're about to step on, put your foot down slowly. Gradually increase the pressure, first placing your weight on your heel, then rolling it onto the rest of your foot. If you can, put your foot on a rock that won't tip, on moss, on snow — anything that you're certain won't make noise. If you're in an area where you know your footsteps will be silent, then don't watch your feet as much. Instead, watch the woods around you, at least 100 yards out or more where you are likely to see a buck. Train yourself to look as far as you can, and you'll start spotting deer you wouldn't have seen otherwise.

As you move through the woods, be aware of where the large, silhouette-breaking trees are located. Pause by them. The last thing you want to do is pause out in the open, because that's exactly when a buck is going to come walking into view, and see you. Pause by trees, boulders, blowdowns, anything to break up your silhouette. And do it no matter where you are, even if you think you're in an area where you know a buck won't be.

Always Be Ready

A number of years ago I was hunting in New York's Catskill Mountains. I was way down the mountain, hunting virtually inaccessible ledges. With a lot of hunting pressure up top of the ridges, I figured deer would be down low in more inaccessible areas. It was nearing the end of the season, there was snow on the ground, and it was late afternoon. The snow was somewhat crunchy so I was moving extra carefully, placing my feet on rocks whenever feasible.

Climbing down to another ledge, I stopped next to a boulder. Generally when I stop, I don't move for at least 5 minutes, usually 10. Just as I was about to end my break and move forward, I heard crunching off to my right. Sure enough, a doe and yearling appeared, moving along my ledge. To my surprise, they came within 10 yards of me, then stopped and started to paw the ground, looking for food. They didn't see

FINE POINTS OF CALLING:

ALARM/DISTRESS SNORT

Usually, a deer makes this snort when it is severely frightened. Having winded, seen, and probably heard the hunter, it blows several snorts and stomps its foot and flees. Hunters can use this call to roust deer from heavy cover, swamps, ledges, and so on. The first step is to stomp your foot hard several times and put out excess amounts of interdigital scent. Deer use excess interdigital scent (produced by a gland between the deer's toes) to warn other deer of danger. Then blow the alarm distress call several times (WHEW. . . WHEW. . . Whew . . . whew . . . whew . . . whew . . . whew, whew, whew). The first snort is loud and has a fair amount of force. As you continue the call, make the intervals between snorts shorter and the calls less powerful. This type of snort call will make any deer too nervous to remain where it is. By trying to sneak away, the deer may present the hunter with a shot.

me even though I was so close I could practically swat their tails. While I was tempted to quietly say "Boo," I stayed silent and motionless. I wanted to see what would happen.

I soon heard more crunching off to my right. Then antlers came up over the lip of the ledge. It was a 7-pointer, just 30 yards away. He looked at the does and froze, his widening eyes riveted on me. He had me, but he didn't move. Obviously the presence of the does so close to me had him confused. What would he do? I figured I'd better do something, because he'd probably bolt any second. Ever so slowly, I started to raise my rifle. If I could get it just halfway up to my shoulder, I could take a snap-shot and get him.

It didn't work that way though. The retractable scope cap snapped on the zipper of my camo jacket, both the doe and yearling heard it and looked right at me, and then all hell broke loose. Throwing the gun to my shoulder, I looked through the scope and immediately saw brown. But it wasn't the buck! It was the yearling running to my left, blocking my view of the buck. Within seconds it was over and all three deer disappeared over the ledge. I took no shot at the buck because the only shot I had was a running kidney shot. It was too risky in that situation.

Did I learn a lesson? Unquestionably! Whenever I stop somewhere now, I never, ever hold my gun low on my body, no matter how tired I am. Port arms is my rule now. And so is that time-honored piece of advice — always be ready, because you never know.

CALLING ALL DEER

by Peter Fiduccia

Hunters across the continent have had tremendous success in simulating deer vocalizations and antler-clashing buck fights to attract both bucks and does. All deer are vocal animals, and respond readily to calling. In fact, studies have shown that whitetails make 13 different types of vocalizations. Learn how to imitate these calls, and you'll discover how quickly deer will respond to calling and rattling — if they are done correctly.

The secret to being a successful caller is confidence. Knowing that your call sounds authentic and believing it can lure in deer are critical to your success. Confidence can mean the difference between seeing and actually bagging game. A few years ago, a friend and avid hunter, Chuck Jermyn, first used deer calls. He was skeptical, as most novice callers are, and that first year Jermyn didn't get a deer. In his second season, after practicing all summer, Jermyn called in several nice bucks. Practice helped him gain confidence that paid big dividends.

Hunters can effectively replicate several different types of deer vocalizations. Snorts, blats, bleats, grunts, whistles, and barks can all be used to lure deer to your stand, as can rattling. The four calls that will bring you the most success, however, are also the easiest to learn. They are the alarm snort, the burp grunt (doe and buck), the loud blat, and the social bleat. Some variations of the snort include the alarm/distress, the alarm, the social, and the aggressive snort. The alarm snort is the one most frequently heard by hunters. When a hunter encounters a deer unexpectedly, the deer may respond by blowing a single snort, then run several yards, stop, and blow a second single snort. "Whew . . . Whew." It is alarmed, but has not been able to pinpoint why. The deer is trying to locate and isolate what the danger is. A hunter who knows what this call means can attract the deer back to his location. By blowing back at the deer with an alarm/snort call, you have played on the deer's curiosity, and it may pick its way back toward the location where it first encountered the danger. When you jump a deer that blows an alarm snort, wait until it has blown the second snort. Then, place the call in your mouth and blow hard once, hesitate about two seconds, and blow the call again. Do not blow the call a third time until the deer snorts back at you. Once the deer answers you, respond to it with two more snorts. Keep doing this as long as you hear the deer approaching and snorting.

A number of years ago, my wife Kate shot her first buck while still-hunting toward her tree stand. As she approached the stand, she saw a deer moving through the trees ahead. She tried to position herself for a shot but stepped on a branch in the process. The deer heard the snap and blew an alarm snort. It ran off several yards, then blew a second snort. Kate blew back at the deer, and the buck answered. Each time the deer blew two snorts, Kate blew back two responses. The buck, curious to see what had frightened it, kept coming closer to Kate

SOCIAL SNORT

Skittish deer make this call when they hear, but do not smell or see the perceived danger. The deer makes a single snort. It wants to be answered. If it is another deer it is hearing, it will listen for a single return snort — low and without much force. To relax a nervous deer that has made a social snort, blow a single soft snort — whew. This will usually reassure the animal that the noise it heard was another deer. It will generally relax and continue on with whatever it was doing before it became nervous.

FAWN BLEATS

The fawn makes several vocalizations. Some will attract siblings and other does; others will attract bucks. The wide range of fawn calls includes the whine, the feeding bleat, a mew, and a low-pitched noise I can only describe as a growl. It is made when the fawn wants to suckle and snuggle. Does will answer with a soft purr-like blat. It reassures the fawn that all is safe. All the calls of the fawn are good to use early in archery season.

BEST TIMES AND WEATHER CONDITIONS TO RATTLE AND CALL

ON PUBLIC LAND

The best time to rattle and call on land that receives a lot of hunting pressure is between 10 a.m. and 2 p.m. Most hunters leave the woods during these times, and the deer begin to move about more freely. Deer "hung-up" between feeding and bedding areas also tend to move now. Capitalizing on these times increases the odds of rattling or calling a buck to your stand tenfold.

ON PRIVATE LAND

With low amounts of hunting pressure, deer are apt to move any time of the day. When rattling or calling under these circumstances, begin only after good light, around 7 a.m. By rattling or calling earlier you will still attract deer, but they will usually see you before you see them.

with each series of alarm snorts. Finally, after several minutes, the buck made its last move when it stepped out from behind the cedars.

All variations of the snort work as well. You will find, however, the alarm/snort to be the easiest snort to learn and use.

Another effective call is the fawn distress bleat. A fawn that is separated from the group, lost, or one that thinks it is in danger will bleat repeatedly for the doe. When the doe hears the distress call, she will only take minutes to respond. She will often bring the rest of the group with her, and this will frequently include a yearling buck. Occasionally, a mature buck may respond to the call knowing he will locate a doe near the source of the distress call.

The distress bleat must be blown aggressively. It will sound much like a rabbit in distress: "Baa-AAA ... Baa-AAA ... Baa-AAA." The pitch should be higher as you end the call. The more intensely you blow it, the quicker a doe will respond. Blow the call in three successions only every half hour or so; by blowing it more frequently you are likely to attract predators such as coyotes and foxes rather than deer.

All adult and yearling deer make the loud blat. It is the most social call made in the deer woods, and is used to locate, warn, fend off, attract, and generally communicate with each other. It is meant to sound social, and will arouse the curiosity of both bucks and does. This call — "Baa-Baaaaaa . . . Baa-baaaaaa" — should be blown gently. Stretch it out to a whine at the end of the call, and do not blow the call often. Once every 30 to 45 minutes is enough. If you see a deer approaching, stop calling. By eliminating the calling, you will intrigue the deer to intensify its search for the source of the call.

Frank Brzozowski, an avid hunter, knows how well this call works. While using the call in Alabama last year, he attracted and shot an 8-point buck.

"It took the buck only several minutes to respond," said Brzozowski. "I blew the call gently. Remembering I should wait a half-hour between calls, I put it away and began to watch the swamp. Several minutes later, I heard a twig snap and a low blat. I turned and saw the buck. Surprised that he answered me, I almost forgot to shoot. Luckily, I was able to shoot him before he could react to my presence."

A common vocalization that hunters hear in the woods is

the grunt of does and bucks. Grunting occurs throughout the year. Hunters will have optimum success, however, when they imitate the grunt of a buck in rut. The best response to grunting will come between late October and mid-November, and again in mid-December. Grunting reaches its peak when both bucks and does are chasing each other or freshening scrapes during the peak rut. For a grunt call to work most effectively, it should be blown gently. If it is not, you will scare off more bucks than you will attract. Even trophy-sized bucks will sometimes avoid a conflict when hot on the trail of a doe. Smaller bucks are definitely intimidated by deeper guttural grunts. Most hunters describe the grunts they have heard to sounds made by a domestic pig. Others describe it as sounding like a burp. Both are correct. A doe grunt is longer in duration and sounds like, "Aaaaaahhhhhhhhh." The grunt of a buck on the trail of a doe in estrus sounds like a short burp, "Erp-Erp . . . Erp-Erp . . . Erp-Erp." When a hunter hears and sees a buck making this grunt, his best response is to blow two short burp-grunts back. Usually, the buck will lift his head and go straight for what he believes to be another buck on the trail of "his" doe. When you do not see or hear a buck, and want to attract one, extend the length of the call, "Eeeeerrrrp . . . Eeeeeerrrrrp." You will know immediately if you are blowing the call incorrectly if your call sounds like a duck call. Hunters who use the grunt will find it easy to use and one of their most successful calls for attracting bucks to their stands.

Leo Somma, from Long Island, New York, started using a grunt call locally last season. While bowhunting in the first week of December — the late rut — in an area that receives a lot of hunting pressure, Somma began using a grunt call at about 3:15 p.m. He blew two long burps from his tree stand, waited several minutes, and repeated the call. He was going to wait several minutes and blow the call again — when he dropped it!

"I was just about to climb down from my stand to get the call," Somma said, "when I heard a deer approaching. Within moments, a buck stopped 50 yards away. He was on a well-used deer trail, obviously searching for the source of the noise. He began to rub his eyes and forehead on an overhanging branch. He waited several minutes, anxiously glancing around, then

WEATHER CONDITIONS

A cloudy day with a slight breeze can produce excellent calling and rattling results. A light, drizzly, rainy day also produces well. Blue-bird days generally get response early and late. Very cold days (regardless of other weather conditions) are always good times. On very cold days deer move in order to stay warm, and will drift in and out of rattling and calling range. Don't waste your time calling or rattling when the wind is steadily blowing over 20 m.p.h.

FINE POINTS OF RATTLING

TYPE AND SIZE OF ANTLERS

When rattling with natural antlers, always use fresh ones. A small 6- or 8-point rack about 10 to 12 inches wide will work best. You will get about two years of optimum sound from natural antlers before you have to replace them with another fresh pair. Synthetic antlers can serve as a good substitute, though you must be selective. Some manufactures make antlers that are too big, others produce unrealistic tones, and still others are just not durable.

TICKING

Never rattle hard to a deer you can see or a deer closer to you than 50 yards. Ticking or "tickling" antlers will work magic on bucks within that range or that are about to leave the scene. Ticking and tickling are accomplished when the ends of the antlers are gently tapped together a few times.

SCENT

To have a buck respond less cautiously, use a combination of scents. A premium fox scent will mask human odor. Interdigital can be used to roust deer from heavy cover. Tarsal gland scent is excellent to use when rattling, as is a well-made premium estrus scent. Buck urine will craze bucks that are responding to your calling or rattling. Use all scents wisely. Do not overuse them!

CREATE THE ILLUSION

Always create the entire illusion when rattling. Break branches, step on leaves, thump the ground with your feet or antlers, and use calls. Remember, a buck that relates all the smells and sounds of what he thinks are two bucks fighting will respond faster and with his guard down!

went back exactly the way he came. In desperation, I tried to imitate a call by cupping my hand and calling to the buck with my mouth. He didn't hear me and continued off. I have no doubt that I would have attracted the buck much closer than 50 yards had I not dropped my grunt. At the least, I would have been able to rekindle his interest as he left."

Paul Butski, expert wildlife caller, has won several national turkey calling championships and manufactures his own line of game calls. His favorite and most successful deer call is the grunt.

"Before I began using the grunt call, I knew bucks were slipping by me undetected. Now, since I've been using the grunt, bucks are coming in, looking for me," said Butski.

Rattling

To help increase your success when calling, add to the illusion by rattling antlers, which works in almost any part of the deer's range. By combining these two techniques, you will attract bucks not only more quickly but also more willingly.

Husband and wife team Don and Gail Sampson rattle for each other each season in the Northeast. Since they began rattling 10 years ago, the Sampsons have increased their deer sightings and harvests by 15 percent. As Don explained, "Rattling is an important part of our hunting season. My most exciting day of rattling happened last year. We were posted in tree stands about 100 yards apart. Fifteen minutes after I began rattling, Gail saw a big buck pass her, heading toward me. The buck stopped thirty yards from my stand. I ticked the antlers and he trotted directly under my stand, where I arrowed him at five yards! Not wanting to disturb Gail's morning, I waited several minutes before rattling again. Within minutes a second buck trotted by my stand, and I let him pass. Later, after talking about the morning's hunt and the two bucks Gail saw, we discovered four different bucks responded to my rattling!"

All animals that fight with their antlers will respond to rattling. Why shouldn't they? Antler-clashing skirmishes are natural occurrences in the wild. Deer are used to hearing the sounds of clashing and meshing antlers, and they respond to them — just as they respond to the many vocalizations they make to each other year-round. By incorporating these calling and rattling methods and techniques, you will find a more challenging and exciting way to hunt deer. Whether you are hunting whitetails in New York, in the Rockies, in Texas or in Alabama, give calling and rattling a try. You will find both tactics work well. They should: they are natural sounds in nature.

UNMASKING THE THOUGHTS OF WHITETAILS THROUGH BODY LANGUAGE

by Peter Fiducia

Recently, there have been many exciting breakthroughs about the interesting and informative world of body language and the messages communicated to all forms of life. These physical signals unveil what is subconsciously in our minds. Most of us aren't even aware we are sending such strong messages that can be easily interpreted by those who know what to look for.

Every day, we exhibit what we feel through body language. For example, a friend of mine who is fascinated with the study of body language, saved himself from an embarrassing situation at his company. "Even though I had become a bit complacent lately, I felt it was time to ask for a raise," he said. "During a subsequent conversation with my boss, he began to shower me with accolades, telling me I was doing 'a great job,' that my 'motivation was high,' and that I 'contributed a lot to my position.' But all during the conversation, he was shaking his head from side-to-side. I interpreted his body language as a form of subconscious denial of the compliments he was giving me. I immediately decided to change my strategy and, instead of asking for a raise, I asked what I could do to further improve my productivity."

The above scenario is just one example of how body language and being able to read the messages from it, plays a crucial role in our day-to-day lives. Through body language, you telegraph your thoughts by the way you fold your arms, cross your legs, walk, stand, move your eyes, lick your mouth, or touch certain parts of your body. Body language allows all forms of animal life to non-verbally relieve life's everyday tensions. Through body language, animals can demonstrate love, fear, disgust, pleasure, or exhibit threatening postures meant to fend off possible dangers. Without the ability to exhibit body language, these emotions would swell. Soon, the simple matter of walking down a busy street or, in the case of a buck, just meeting up with another buck, would trigger an explosion of reactions.

More important, the ability to quickly read and interpret body language substantially increases your skills to assimilate and react to all types of situations correctly. For deer hunters, being able to read and interpret the body language exhibited by their quarry increases their knowledge of the game they are hunting. This will allow hunters to consistently take not only more deer, but also score on larger racked bucks.

Although deer exhibit a myriad of body language gestures, here are some of the more easily recognizable signals which, when interpreted quickly and correctly, will dramatically change your whitetail hunting strategies.

1. Buck Prancing (a buck walking with its head held high and tail held halfway out): This form of body language is a threatening posture. It indicates the buck may be looking at another buck that a hunter can't see . . . yet. Through his body language, he is announcing to the other buck that he is the more aggressive and dominant animal. He is saying, "Stay where you are, if you know what is good for you." A perceptive hunter makes the immediate decision to either take the buck that is exhibiting the body language, or waits to inspect the surrounding brush that may conceal an even larger buck.

2. A Doe with Her Tail Held Straight Out and Slightly Off to One Side: This is one of the most crucial of deer body language signals during the rut. Hunters who are unable to interpret this signal often decide to shoot the doe or a smaller buck because they did not know how to interpret what they were looking at. A doe exhibiting this type of body language is in full estrus and is accepting bucks. Almost assuredly, she is being followed by a mature buck with subordinate bucks trailing along the fringes. When the doe crosses vulnerable areas, the more mature buck usually hesitates long enough to ensure that the passage is safe, thus allowing the subordinate bucks to catch up with the doe. Hunters who are aware of this fact naturally have the opportunity to take the doe or first buck that is trailing her.

Their second option is to wait and see if a larger buck is about to appear. By being able to read this body language message, you can allow smaller bucks to pass and still remain relatively confident that you will have the opportunity for a shot at a larger buck.

3. A Buck Holding his Head High and Tilted Back with his Upper Lip Curled Exposing the Gums is Exhibiting the Flehman Posture, also Known as Lip Curling: This is an important message. It is made by deer that are trying to find the source of a pleasurable scent — especially estrus. When a hunter sees a buck exhibiting a lip curl, he may be wise to immediately shoot the deer before the scent he is smelling, and following, lures him off in a different direction. If the buck doesn't offer an opportunity for a shot before he is out of range, lay down a commercially-made estrus scent to try and get the buck to return, or to perhaps attract a different buck all together.

4. A Deer Flicking its Tail Side-to-Side: There are several signals a deer sends through different motions of its tail. This is one of the more important signals. If you spot a deer standing still and concentrating on its surroundings, you may be lured into a false complacency that the deer is not alarmed. However, deer often stand still to gather more information before proceeding along a trail. You can be fairly certain that a deer will remain relatively still as long as it does not flick its tail from side-to-side. Once that tail starts flicking, it means that the animal is about to move. If you are thinking about taking that particular animal, do not hesitate.

5. Head Fakes/Head-Bobbing: Many hunters are tricked by deer that display this maneuver. A hunter usually thinks the deer has not spotted him and unconsciously gives himself away to the cagey animal. Deer that suspect something is wrong but cannot identify the problem will extend their heads forward to get a better look. When the hunter doesn't move, the deer tries to trick the perceived danger into giving itself away by pretending it doesn't see or care about what it is looking at. The deer makes believe it is relaxed enough to begin feeding and proceeds to put its head down. At this point, most hunters think it is okay to move. They are surprised to see that the deer never really intended to feed at all — but instead was preparing to instantly lift its head to check out the suspicious object. The hunter is usually caught off-guard when he is not able to interpret this body language maneuver properly. When a deer extends its head and looks at you and then puts its head down, don't move!

6. Foot Stomping: Deer stomp their hooves for a variety of reasons. In most cases, it is meant as a warning or to goad movement from a possible threat. The animal is sending a visual and audio message to deer within seeing and hearing range that it is encountering a problem. Most important, the deer is also leaving a chemical message for other deer that are not close enough to see or hear the warning. The chemical message is left on the ground through a gland between the deer's toes, called the interdigital gland. The scent is meant to warn other whitetails traveling down the trail that another deer encountered danger at this point. Hunters who see deer stomping or who alarm them into repeated stomping should consider relocating their stand. The odds of a deer coming past an area permeated with excess interdigital scent are low, and you will see more deer by changing your location.

7. A Doe with One Ear Cupped Forward and One Ear Cupped Backward: When a hunter sees a doe stop walking down a trail and begin listening for potential danger, he should pay particular attention to the direction in which her ears are pointing. If they are both cupped in one direction, she is probably alone. However, if one ear is forward and the other ear suddenly rotates toward her backtrail, she is listening to what are probably her fawns or yearlings approaching. During the rut, however, the approaching deer could very well be a buck. Your chances of seeing what is coming down the trail will be greatly increased if you do not alarm this doe.

8. Flagging or Tail Waving: One of the most familiar deer body language signs is tail flagging. Deer use it as they run off to warn other deer. Does also use it to let their yearlings and fawns know where they are running. Since does flag much more frequently than bucks, the importance of reading this body language becomes evident. Should a hunter jump some deer, or perhaps have deer driven past him that are on the run with tails held high, he should look for deer running with their tails down or tucked between their legs. A deer running in a group with its tail down is likely to be a buck. Focus your attention on this animal and you will most likely have picked out the only buck in the group.

9. A Buck with his Ears Laying All the Way Back on his Shoulders, his Back Arched, and is Neck Hairs Standing Up: A buck displaying these signs is extremely agitated. He is displaying every form of non-combative aggression he can muster. In most instances, although not always, the deer to which he is displaying is larger than he. By appearing so aggressive and hostile, the buck hopes to fend off his rival with a bluff and avoid actual physical combat. When a hunter sees a buck displaying this type of body language and does not see a second buck, he should use his binoculars to check the surrounding area. Look in the direction the aggressive buck is watching, and chances are you will find yourself looking at another buck.

10. A Buck Pawing a Patch of Ground: Bucks paw the ground for several reasons: to search for acorns and other food, to warn off other deer, and to prepare or freshen scrapes. When a buck is searching for food, his body language will be relaxed. His ears are slightly forward, the tail hangs straight down between his legs, hair lies straight down on his back, and his muscles are relaxed. This deer is content with his surroundings and is unaware of the hunter. A deer pawing the ground in an aggressive manner, however, is on full alert. It may have spotted a hunter or may be fending off another deer. A hunter must read this situation quickly and decide whether to take the animal before it moves off. Finally, a buck that is pawing a round patch of earth and stops repeatedly to scratch, sniff, and urinate on the ground is preparing a scrape. This buck's body language will let you know if you have time to shoot or not. If he is pawing quickly, urinating, and constantly looking in different directions, he is probably freshening the scrape of a more aggressive buck and will not be at the site long. However, if he enters the scrape slowly, paws the earth with purpose, nibbles the overhanging branch, doesn't bother to check his surroundings often, and urinates infrequently, he is probably the buck who originally made the scrape, and will spend considerably more time at the location. This will give you more time to make a decision to either take the buck or let him go.

By learning to absorb, correctly decipher, and then react to the body language signals we receive from people and animals, we will improve our odds of responding properly to any given situation. Reading a deer's body language is one of the most important hunting skills you will ever learn, and it will increase your deer hunting success immensely.

THE EAST

CONNECTICUT, MAINE, MASSACHUSETTS, NEW HAMPSHIRE, NEW JERSEY, NEW YORK, PENNSYLVANIA, RHODE ISLAND, VERMONT

ALTHOUGH A POPULATED PART OF THE COUNTRY with large urban areas, much of the Eastern United States consists of farms, orchards, deep woods, and forests — many within easy driving distance of large cities such as New York and Boston. The Adirondacks, for example, are a mere three-hour drive up the New York State Thruway from the Big Apple — an easy afternoon's journey to quality hunting.

All of the methods used for hunting whitetails are popular here as well — stand hunting, driving, still-hunting, calling, rattling. Opening days can be crowded on public lands, and that's where the lodges listed in this section come into play. They have access to land that others don't, or that others can't reach.

Deer populations are increasing dramatically throughout the region, not only on public lands, but on private tracts, often near urban areas. As such, many northern states (like the southern states) have in general loosened up harvest numbers. In New York (a state where almost 35,000 deer were killed on highways alone in 1999; Pennsylvania had 90,000 road kills), hunters who put in for bow, black powder, doe and rifle tags can, in many parts of the state, take up to six deer during the course of the season.

To get a trophy, look to the lodges in the deep woods of Maine or northern New York in particular. No matter where you go in the Northeast, though, your chances of getting a deer now are better than ever.

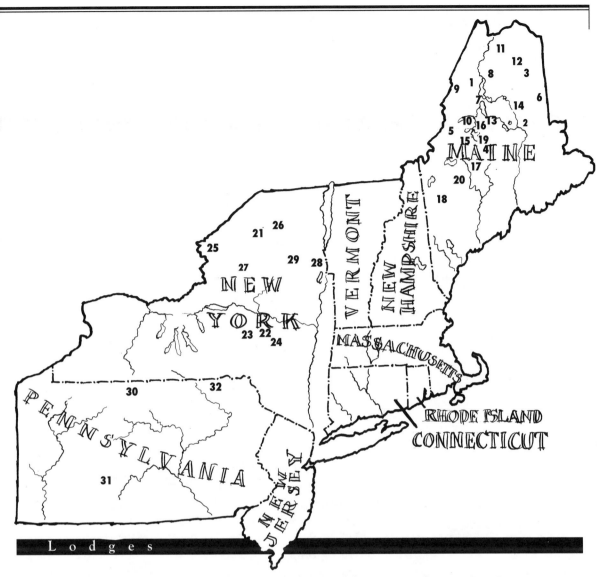

Maine

1 Allagash Guide Service
2 Bowlin Camps
3 Bradford Camps
4 Bucks 'N Bears
5 Cedar Ridge Lodge
6 Conklin's Lodge & Camps
7 Dean's Den
8 Fish River Lodge
9 Foggy Mountain Guide
  Service
10 Gentle Ben's Lodge
11 Homestead Lodge
12 Libby Camps
13 Loon Lodge

14 Matagamon Wilderness
15 Northern Outdoors
16 Northern Pride Lodge
17 Pine Grove Lodge
18 Stony Brook Outfitters
19 Sunset Ridge Lodge &
  Outfitters
20 Western Mountain
  Hunter's Service

New York

21 Cold River Ranch
22 C.P.'s Guiding Service
23 D.C. Outdoor Adventures
24 HWC Guide Service

25 Lucky Star Ranch
26 Middle Earth Expeditions
27 North Country Outdoor
  Adventures
28 Northwoods Wilderness
  Guide Service
29 Outback Outfitters
  Guiding Service

Pennsylvania

30 Big Moore's Run
31 Paradise Outfitters
32 Whitetail Valley

Resources

CONNECTICUT DEPT. OF ENVIRONMENTAL PROTECTION
Wildlife Division
79 Elm St., 6th Fl
Hartford, CT 06106-5127
Ph: 860/424-3011

MAINE DEPT. OF INLAND FISHERIES AND WILDLIFE
284 State St., Station #41
Augusta, ME 04333-0041
Ph: 207/287-8000
Web: www.state.me.us/ifw/homepage.htm

MASSACHUSETTS DIV. OF FISHERIES AND WILDLIFE
100 Cambridge St., Rm. 1902
Boston, MA 02202
Ph: 617/727-3155
Web: www.state.ma.lus/dfwele

NEW HAMPSHIRE FISH AND GAME DEPT.
2 Hazen Dr.
Concord, NH 03301
Ph: 603/271-3422
Fax: 603/271-1438
Web: www.wildlife.state.nh.us

NEW JERSEY DIV. OF FISH, GAME AND WILDLIFE
PO Box 400
Trenton, NJ 08625-0400
Ph: 609/292-2965
Web: www.state.nj.us/dep/fgw

NEW YORK DEPT. OF ENVIRONMENTAL CONSERVATION
50 Wolf Rd.
Albany, NY 12233
Ph: 518/457-3521
Web: www.dec.state.ny.us

PENNSYLVANIA GAME COMMISSION
2001 Elmerton Ave.
Harrisburg, PA 17110-9797
Ph: 717/787-4250
Fax: 717/772-0542
Web: www.pgc.state.pa.us

RHODE ISLAND DIV. OF FISH AND WILDLIFE
Stedman Gov't Center
4808 Tower Hill Rd.
Wakefield, RI 02879-2207
Ph: 401/222-3075
Web: www.state.ri.us/dem

VERMONT DEPT. OF FISH AND WILDLIFE
103 South Main, 10 South
Waterbury, VT 05671-0501
Ph: 802/241-3700
Web: www.state.vt.us/anr

Allagash Guide Service

Allagash, Maine

T HE ALLAGASH GUIDE SERVICE hunts huge country — 2.8 million acres, to be precise — a tract that runs from Baxter State Park west and then north to the confluence with the St. John River. Much of this area is hunted for bear, but you'll also find big deer in these deep woods, where bucks of 6 to 12 points are not uncommon. The habitat here is forest plots in various stages of clear-cut regeneration, which supports about 15 deer per mile. Heavy spruce forests along the innumerable rivers and streams provide cover, but not much food for deer. They travel out of the river bottoms in search of beechnuts, in particular. Oaks bearing acorns don't grow this far north. The last few weeks of the season generally hunt better than the first weeks. Early, deer are beginning the rut, but later they become more concentrated in areas where there's good browse. During years when beechnut mast is abundant, whitetails will work hardwood ridges as long as they can. In other years, you'll find them clipping hardwood browse or working over patches of lichens and mushrooms.

The secret to getting one of Maine's big whitetails? "Do the time," according to Sean Lizotte, owner of Allagash Guide Service. Hunters willing to put in 10 to 12 hour days simply see more deer than their friends who give up after six or seven. Tree stands and ground blinds provide the cover. You keep your eyes open and do the shooting.

Maine's hunts all have a kind of "bargain" ring to them. What kind of hunt could they offer for $900 when a similar whitetail hunt out West costs two or three times the price? Is the hunting really that much better in the Rockies? Yes and no. Sure, the success rate on whitetails is generally double that of most Maine lodges, but the quality of Maine's bucks is hard to pass up. Besides, most folks hunting trophies in the West work hard for a 6x6 or better elk. They have about the same chances of taking a trophy bull as Maine hunters have to nail a heavy 8-point or better buck.

Vital Statistics

THE LODGE:

Modern log lodge has 25 rooms, 35 beds total, all with private baths

SERVICES: Telephone

HUNTS: $550 / 6 days (includes 1-day guided hunt)

PAYMENT: Cash or check

CONFERENCE GROUPS: No

MEAL PLANS: All meals included. The menu is varied. Breakfast consists of French toast, pancakes and eggs on varying days, with toast, bacon, sausage, juice and coffee each day. Lunch consists of sandwiches and desserts packed to go in to the field for the day. Dinner features prime rib, baked ham, pasta, roast turkey, ham-and-cheese-stuffed meatloaf, corn beef-stuffed chicken breast, vegetables, rice, fresh homemade bread, homemade desserts.

NEAREST AIRPORT: Presque Isle, ME

TRANSPORTATION TO LODGE (90 miles): Rental car; van from lodge ($150 round trip)

CONTACT:

Sean Lizotte
Allagash Guide Service
RR 1, Box 131D
Allagash, ME 04774
Ph: 207/398-3418
Email: allaguide@ainop.com
Web: www.allagashguideservice.com

THE HUNT:

SEASON:

- bow: September
- rifle: November
- muzzleloader: December

BEST TIME TO HUNT: Anytime

TERRAIN: The landscape is rolling hills 900 to 1,500 feet above sea level, composed mostly of hardwoods, some mixed woods (hardwoods and softwoods), and several big river valleys and many stream valleys which are full of thick softwoods (spruce, balsam fir, and cedars)

LAND: Approximately one million acres of privately-owned commercial land

DRAW BLOOD POLICY? No

HUNTING METHODS: Stand hunting in ground blinds or tree stands

YEARS IN BUSINESS: 6

STAFF OF GUIDES: 5

HUNTERS SERVED BY EACH GUIDE: 1 - 6

NONHUNTER CHARGE: n/a

LICENSES: Sold over the counter

GAME CARE: Yes

OTHER ACTIVITIES: Black bear hunting, bird hunting, bird watching, canoeing/rafting, fishing, snowmobiling, waterfowling, wildlife photography

BOONE & CROCKETT

"It is very hard to put an average size on the bucks taken in our territory since many are not measured for rack scoring."

Bowlin Camps

P a t t e n ,   M a i n e

ILES OF MARKED TRAILS, old logging roads, hardwood ridges, mixed growth and some old burned areas provide prime deer hunting for guests who venture into this area. Located in the midsection of the state, just east of Baxter State Park in the heart of the Maine wilderness, there are no other camps for miles in any direction, and the area is remarkably void of hunters other than the ones from Bowlin. The fact that the East Branch Penobscot River runs in a north/south direction makes map and compass orientation in these thick woods easy.

Deer hunting in this area can test a hunter to the limit. With cold weather a possibility, hunters must prepare for all conditions, dressing in layers for daytime conditions that can range from 0°F to 70°F, with the average temperature being around the freezing mark for most of the season. Bucks can run large here, with 300-pounders and big racks a real possibility. Just don't expect to see lots of bucks every day; they run few and far between, but the ones you see can indeed be trophies.

The camp is a classic Maine hunting/fishing camp, with a main lodge, dining room, kitchen and living room, where guests usually gather after dinner to coordinate the next day's hunt, or simply swap tales. All meals are served in the dining room. Fresh meats, vegetables from the garden, homemade breads and pastries served family style all await you at the end of the day.

The log cabins, some dating to 1895, are nestled among shade trees and all have a view of the river. Each cabin is heated with a wood stove and has electric and propane lights. They accommodate three to eight people. Some have bathrooms.

Vital Statistics

THE LODGE:

10 log cabins surround the main lodge; 46 beds total, some have private baths

SERVICES: Telephone, TV

HUNTS: From $550 / 6-day unguided hunt to $1,295 / 6-day fully-guided hunt

PAYMENT: Cash, credit card, check (for deposit only)

Meal Plans: All meals included (country home-style cooking)

SPECIAL DIETS: Heart healthy, Kosher, salt/msg free

NEAREST AIRPORT: Bangor, ME

TRANSPORTATION TO LODGE: Rental car, bush flights

BOONE AND CROCKETT

- B&C book bucks taken from property: 2
- Average B&C score: 136
- B&C bucks from this part of state: n/a

CONTACT:

Kenneth Conaser or Michael Stroff
Bowlin Camps
PO Box 251
Patten, ME 04765
Ph: 207/668-4169
Web: www.bowlincamps.com

THE HUNT:

SEASON:
- bow: September 28 - October 27
- rifle: October 30 - November 25
- muzzleloader: November 27 - December 2

BEST TIME TO HUNT: First and fourth weeks of the season

TERRAIN: In the mountainous country of the state; high hills, hardwood cover up high; low-country swamps on rivers and dead waters; cedar and spruce swamps, thickets

LAND: One million acres of timber company land

DRAW BLOOD POLICY? No

HUNTING METHODS: Stand hunting (tripods and metal leaners, custom built), still-hunting, calling

YEARS IN BUSINESS: 8

STAFF OF GUIDES: 6

HUNTERS SERVED BY EACH GUIDE: 2

NONHUNTER CHARGE: Yes

LICENSES: Sold over the counter

GAME CARE: Dressed, packaged, frozen and shipped; shipping costs depend on location

OTHER ACTIVITIES: Other big game hunting (black bear, moose), bird hunting (ruffed grouse), waterfowling, fishing, boating, canoeing, hiking, skiing, swimming, whitewater rafting, wildlife photography, snowmobiling

Bradford Camps

A s h l a n d ,   M a i n e

ONE OF THE BEST OVERALL VALUES in East Coast deer hunting today is provided by the timber company lands north and west of Bangor, Maine. They are vast, rugged, and beautiful. For little more than $100, you can get a permit to hunt and camp in the North Maine woods, and to use the maintained logging roads to gain access to the cedar swamps, clear-cuts, and hardwood ridges that characterize the more than 15,000 square miles of terrain. You might see a monster buck on your first day of hunting, or you might go a week without seeing a whitetail. In this wilderness where Theodore Roosevelt first hunted, some places are so thick that you'll swear you are hunting in a jungle.

If snow is on the ground, one tactic that works is to find a set of large deer tracks and follow them, particularly if you're moving into the wind. At any minute, you might catch up with one of the big-racked, 200-pounders that make this area famous.

Because of its remote location in the center of more than 3 million acres of the North Maine woods, Bradford Camps offers a truly pure hunting experience. The game is wild, unaccustomed to roads, vehicles, houses, farms — or people. And the hunts are classic, where success is more dependent on the hunter's skill, not only with firearm or bow, but with map and compass, tracking game, and anticipation and recognition of game movement. A week of hunting at Bradford Camps on Munsungan Lake, where Teddy Roosevelt liked to stay, costs less than $700, room and board included. With comfortable rooms, a spacious main lodge with all the amenities, and a tradition dating back more than 100 years, Bradford Camps is tough to beat.

A final plus of Bradford Camps is the availability of experienced, knowledgeable hunting guides. Not only are they licensed by the state through a strict testing program, they must also pass muster for Bradford's own requirements. The guides have spent a long time in the woods and waters of the area, and are considered experts in the field. They will be able to bring you to more game than you would find on your own — something definitely worth considering if you've never hunted in this area before. With whitetails, it pays to give yourself any edge you can.

Vital Statistics

THE LODGE:

8 rustic log cabins have 24 beds total, all with private baths

SERVICES: Telephone, ice

HUNTS: $110 / night, $650 / week; meals and lodging included

PAYMENT: Cash, check

MEAL PLANS: All meals included (dinners include full turkey suppers, prime ribs with roasted vegetables, pork loin with fresh vegetables)

SPECIAL DIETS: Heart healthy, vegetarian, salt/msg free

NEAREST AIRPORT: Presque Isle, ME

TRANSPORTATION TO LODGE (100 miles): Rental car; van from lodge; shuttle flight ($120 round trip)

CONTACT:

Igor and Karen Sikorsky
Bradford Camps
PO Box 729
Ashland, ME 04732
Ph: 207/746-7777
Email: Maine@Bradfordcamps.com
Web: www.bradfordcamps.com

THE HUNT:

SEASON:

- bow: October
- rifle: November

BEST TIME TO HUNT: Second and third weeks in November

TERRAIN: Uncut, thick hardwood and softwood forests, hills, mountainous areas; extremely remote

LAND: 500,000 leased private acres

DRAW BLOOD POLICY? No

HUNTING METHODS: Stand hunting (lock-ons and wooden), still-hunting, rattling

YEARS IN BUSINESS: 5

STAFF OF GUIDES: 2

HUNTERS SERVED BY EACH GUIDE: 4 maximum

NONHUNTER CHARGE: No

LICENSES: Sold at the lodge

GAME CARE: Dressed, packaged, frozen and shipped; cost is $200 - $300, depending on shipping

OTHER ACTIVITIES: Other big game hunting (black bear, moose), bird hunting (ruffed grouse), fishing, bird watching, boating, canoeing, hiking, whitewater rafting, wildlife photography, sporting clays

Bucks 'n Bears

Willimantic, Maine

BOB BANDY, OWNER OF BUCKS 'N BEARS outfitting and guide service, hunts the deep woods of northern Maine, near Moosehead and Sebec lakes. With access to more than one million acres of paper company land, Bandy takes hunters deep into the thick woods, moving slowly along logging roads, watching carefully for any sign of movement. Bandy will set up hunters in ground blinds to watch logged-over areas that show evidence of recent deer activity. Cedar swamps are also prime buck hangouts in this country. And, in years of good mast crops, a good whitetail or two can always be found on the beech ridges. It's a question of figuring out what the deer are doing in a certain year, then adapting your strategy accordingly. Snow, of course, makes things a bit easier, as Bandy and his guided hunters will get on the track of a big buck and try to follow it. This can make for exciting hunting, the ultimate still hunt!

To the south, Bandy also takes hunters onto private land and "transition" country, with mixed growth, abandoned farm lands and orchards. Hunters bring climbing stands or hunt out of ground blinds in this territory, and are ever on the lookout for deer moving between bedding and feeding areas.

Bowhunting in October can be especially effective, as hunting takes place before the deer feel pressured from rifle hunters roaming the woods. Rifle season is in November, and muzzleloading in early December. If you hunt later in the season, pack plenty of warm clothing, as temperatures in this part of Maine can really plummet, often getting down near zero. The cold temperatures are actually good for the hunting, though, as the chilled weather keeps whitetails moving throughout the day.

Bandy holds his hunters to standards we can all appreciate. "I believe that quality hunting can be achieved and sustained by maintaining a small operation and providing personalized service," he says. "Your personal safety is my number one priority. A true sportsman is a gentleman, who takes only his part of the woods and leaves the rest for others. Hunting at Bucks 'N Bears lodge commits you to the rules of fair chaise."

At the end of the day, Bandy's hunters head back to his modern, comfortable lodge for some rest, relaxation, and preparation for the next day's hunt.

Vital Statistics

THE LODGE

Lodge has 3 guest rooms, 6 beds total

SERVICES: Telephone, TV

GUN HUNTS: $850 / week

PAYMENT: Cash, check

CONFERENCE GROUPS: No

MEAL PLANS: Guest do their own cooking

NEAREST AIRPORT: Bangor, ME

TRANSPORTATION TO LODGE (55 miles): Van from lodge at no extra charge

CONTACT:

Bob Bandy
Bucks 'n Bears
RFD 2, Box 185
Willimantic, ME 04443
Ph: 207/997-3584; 410/658-6173
Email: bucksnbears@yahoo.com
Web: www.maineguides.org/members/bandy

THE HUNT:

SEASON:

• bow: October

• rifle: November

• muzzleloader: December

BEST TIME TO HUNT:

• gun: second and third week of Nov
• bow: last two weeks of Oct.

TERRAIN: Logging country: clearcuts, cedar swamps, beech ridges; transition country: mixed growth, abandoned farmland/old orchards

LAND: 115 acres owned; hunt paper company land (1 million acres)

DRAW BLOOD POLICY? No

HUNTING METHODS: Stand hunting (ground blinds; hunters welcome to bring their own climbers or lock-ons), still-hunting, snow tracking, calling, rattling

YEARS IN BUSINESS: 13

STAFF OF GUIDES: No

HUNTERS SERVED BY EACH GUIDE: 2 - 4

NONHUNTER CHARGE: Usually 50% of hunt rate

LICENSES: Over the counter before arriving

GAME CARE: Hunter's responsibility

OTHER ACTIVITIES: Other big game hunting (black bear, moose, coyote), bird hunting, waterfowling, golf, wildlife photography

Cedar Ridge Lodge

Jackman, Maine

J ACKMAN, MAINE, is located right in the middle of God's Country. With deep woods, tall mountains, more lakes (they call them ponds) and streams than you can count, it's truly a sportsman's paradise. Known as the snowmobiling capitol of the world, Jackman offers blue-ribbon trout fishing in spring and early summer, canoeing, boating and hiking in summer, and incredibly good black bear and moose hunting in the fall. And, of course, whitetail deer hunting.

At Cedar Ridge Lodge, it is deep woods hunting for bucks that grow big and smart. Owners Hal and Debbie Blood both guide for deer (and moose and bear), and will tell you that hunting these northern whitetails is no cake-walk. On the other hand, when you finally get one, you can be as proud as any successful whitetail hunter can be.

"Bucks here in northern Maine are totally different than those in more southern states, and even those in southern Maine," says Debbie. "You simply can't pattern them. So you have to learn how to read tracks, and that's a skill that comes only with experience. When tracking a buck, you have to be able to tell whether he's getting ready to lie down, if he's feeding, or if he's smelled you. You need to know if he's acting suspiciously, or if he's decided to take off in a straight line for 10 miles without ever stopping. If you can read tracks in our neck of the woods, you can be a successful deer hunter."

© Cedar Ridge Lodge

A hunter at Cedar Ridge takes an 8-pointer.

While you may not have these skills, the Bloods and their guides do, so heading into the woods with them is promised to bring you an exciting, and often educational, experience.

© Cedar Ridge Lodge

The inviting front porch of Cedar Ridge Lodge.

Vital Statistics

THE LODGE:

3 modern cabins have 50 beds total

SERVICES: Telephone, fax, TV

HUNTS: From $325 for an unguided hunt to $1,800 for a one-on-one

PAYMENT: Cash, debit card, check

MEAL PLANS: All meals included (dinners include a turkey, meat loaf, spaghetti and steak, vegetables, potatoes, rice, desserts)

SPECIAL DIETS: Heart healthy, Kosher

NEAREST AIRPORT: Bangor, ME

TRANSPORTATION TO LODGE (2 1/2 hours): Rental car

THE HUNT:

SEASON:

- bow: October
- rifle: November
- muzzleloader: December

BEST TIME TO HUNT: Anytime

TERRAIN: Mountains, dark growth, some wetlands, fir trees, spruce, some hardwoods, old cuts

LAND: More than a million acres of privately-owned property

DRAW BLOOD POLICY? No

HUNTING METHODS: Stand hunting (ground blinds), still-hunting, tracking

YEARS IN BUSINESS: 10

STAFF OF GUIDES: 6

HUNTERS SERVED BY EACH GUIDE: 2

NONHUNTER CHARGE: $325

LICENSES: Over the counter

GAME CARE: Dressed for no charge

OTHER ACTIVITIES: Other big game hunting (black bear, moose), bird hunting, fishing, biking, canoeing, hiking, whitewater rafting, wildlife photography

BOONE AND CROCKETT

- B&C book bucks taken from property: 1
- Average B&C score: 170
- B&C bucks from this part of state: 2 (that they know of)

CONTACT:

Deborah Blood
Cedar Ridge Lodge
PO Box 744
Jackman, ME 04945
Ph: 207/668-4169
Email: Info@CedarRidgeOutfitters.com
Web: www.CedarRidgeOutfitters.com

Conklin's Lodge & Camps

P a t t e n , M a i n e

JUST 100 MILES north of Baxter State Park on the edge of the Allagash country, Conklin's Lodge specializes in big, north-country bucks. While this part of Maine may not have as many deer as areas to the south, the bucks that hunters take can run extremely large — often tipping the scales at over 200 pounds dressed.

At Conklin's, hunters are treated to good, homemade cooking and comfortable lodging — all on the edge of more than 3 million acres of commercial forest land. Hunts are six nights/five days (Sunday to Saturday), and include meals, lodging, pre-placed treestands in areas bucks are known to visit, plus transportation to and from stands. Any type of weapon — bow, rifle, handgun or black powder — can be used. Your guide will be in the area at all times, and will employ a variety of methods to get you your deer. The degree of difficulty in a hunt will be determined by the individual. If you choose to sit in one of the many tree stands, or if you choose to still-hunt, each method will work with the help of your guide.

The success rate at Conklin's for bucks sporting heavy racks and big bodies is one of the highest in the northern part of Maine. In the past few years, about 40 percent of the deer hunters using these camps have taken bucks. Those on guided hunts are successful about 50 percent of the time, while the rate drops to about 30 percent for unguided hunts. Guided hunts here aren't what you'd expect in other parts of the country. In Maine, four hunters share one guide who designs a strategy based on weather, terrain, the movements of the deer, and the abilities of the hunters, including their physical shape. The guide tries his best to put you in a position to cross paths with a buck, be it by still-hunting, stalking, or taking stand in a well-placed tree stand. Typical deer are 4 to 6 points, with dressed weights averaging more than 150 pounds. Older deer are around, but they know the score; taking them requires skill, perseverance in even the toughest of weather conditions, plus a bit of luck.

The schedule at the camps is simple: wake up at 4:00 a.m., depart with lunches to the hunting areas, hunt until 4:15 in the afternoon, then return to camp for dinner at 6:30.

With the deep northern woods at your disposal, and a good chance of seeing a huge buck, what better type of hunting could you hope for?

Vital Statistics

THE LODGE:

6 cabins and one 8-man chalet contain 40 beds total; accommodations are rustic

SERVICES: Telephone, TV

HUNTS:

- $750 / 5-day guided rifle hunt
- $450 / 5-day semi-guided hunt

PAYMENT: Check, traveler's check

MEAL PLANS: All meals included (dinners include baked ham, pot roast, lasagna, roast pork, stuffed Cornish game hen, sirloin steak—with all the fixin's)

SPECIAL DIETS: Heart healthy, Kosher, vegetarian, salt/msg free

NEAREST AIRPORT: Bangor, ME

TRANSPORTATION TO LODGE (110 miles): Rental car; shuttle service ($125)

CONTACT:

Lester Conklin
Conklin's Lodge & Camps
PO Box 21
Patten, ME 04765
Ph: 207/528-2901
Email: guideone@Hotmail.com
Web: Http://www.conklinslodge.com

THE HUNT:

SEASON:

- bow: October
- rifle: November

BEST TIME TO HUNT: Anytime

TERRAIN: Hardwood forests, ridges, swamps

LAND: More than 3 1/2 million acres of paper company land

DRAW BLOOD POLICY? n/a

HUNTING METHODS: Stand hunting (12' ladder stands), still-hunting, by vehicle, calling, rattling

YEARS IN BUSINESS: 13

STAFF OF GUIDES: 5

HUNTERS SERVED BY EACH GUIDE: 6

NONHUNTER CHARGE: Same as semi-guided

LICENSES: Over the counter ($86)

GAME CARE: Dressed, packaged, frozen, shipped

OTHER ACTIVITIES: Other big game hunting (black bear, coyote), bird hunting (grouse, woodcock), rabbit hunting, waterfowling, fishing, biking, boating, canoeing, golf, hiking, skiing, swimming, whitewater rafting, wildlife photography

Dean's Den

E a g l e   L a k e ,   M a i n e

LOCATED ON SPRAWLING EAGLE LAKE in the heart of the Allagash, Dean's Den is in the middle of prime whitetail hunting country. This is big country, more than 4 million acres, and you'll spend your days on your own, hunting hard without seeing other people. The deer you see are quite likely to be trophies traveling their normal patterns, not pressured by hunters. This is deer hunting the way it's supposed to be!

Temperatures can range from balmy to freezing, so be prepared for anything. Most hunters take heavy Polarfleece long underwear, lots of heavy wool socks (with light polypropylene undersocks), plus either wool or fleece over garments. A good hat, wool gloves and insulated boots (1000 mil isn't such a bad idea!) top off your wardrobe. A compass or GPS unit can also come in handy here, as these are thick conifer forests and it's easy to get turned around.

Still-hunting is often the best tactic when hunting the Maine woods. You move slowly through the forest or down one of the many logging trails, taking one slow step at a time, scanning the woods as you go. Look for horizontal lines (which could indicate a deer's back or stomach line), an undefined twitch (which could be the flicking of a deer's ear), or perhaps some glinting sunlight (which might be the sun shining off a buck's rack). Watch where you place your feet, and avoid stepping on branches or twigs that could snap and alert any deer in the area. A good rule when still-hunting is this: If you think you're moving too fast, then you are!

Hunters who prefer tree stands can also use them out of Dean's Den, as owner Dean Paisley has a bunch of them set up at well-known crossings and travel corridors. Most are solid stands made out of pressure-treated wood and set up well before the season opener, so deer get used to seeing them.

After a long day of hunting, guests are taken back to the lodge and camps for some hearty food and good conversation. The main lodge sleeps seven, but most guests stay in one of the five cabins — rustic affairs with all the amenities. With hearty meals that include lasagna, pork chops, baked chicken and steaks, you'll go to bed full — and fueled for the next day afield.

Vital Statistics

THE LODGE:

Lodge sleeps 7; 5 camps each accommodate up to 8 hunters

SERVICES: Telephone, fax, TV

GUN HUNTS:

- $300 / week (unguided)

- $400 / week (guided)

PAYMENT: Cash, check (60 days prior to hunt)

CONFERENCE GROUPS: No

MEAL PLANS: All meals included

NEAREST AIRPORT: Presque Isle, ME

TRANSPORTATION TO LODGE (65 miles): Van from lodge ($40 round-trip)

CONTACT:

L. Dean Paisley
Dean's Den
1075 Sly Brook Road
Eagle Lake, ME 04739

OFF-SEASON:

5806 Pepper Ridge Circle
Wilmington, DE 19808
Ph: 207/444-5379

THE HUNT:

SEASON:

- bow: October

- rifle: November

BEST TIME TO HUNT: Second - fourth week of November

TERRAIN: Hardwood ridges, swamps

LAND: 450,000 acres public land; 4,000,000 acres timber company land

DRAW BLOOD POLICY? No

HUNTING METHODS: Stand hunting (you can bring your own, or use one of Dean's permanent wooden stands), still-hunting, calling, rattling

YEARS IN BUSINESS: n/a

HUNTERS SERVED BY EACH GUIDE: 5

NONHUNTER CHARGE: $200 / week

LICENSES: Over the counter at nearby store

GAME CARE: Dress, package, freeze, ship game for an additional $ .60 to $1.00 / pound

OTHER ACTIVITIES: Bear, moose and coyote hunting; bird hunting, fishing, biking, bird watching, boating, canoeing, hiking, skiing, swimming, whitewater rafting, wildlife photography

BOONE AND CROCKETT

- B&C book bucks taken from property: largest 37 1/4-inch-wide rack

- Average B&C score: 145-165

- B&C bucks from this part of state: n/a

Fish River Lodge

Eagle Lake, Maine

SITUATED IN THE FAR northern tip of Maine, just 18 miles from Canada, Fish River Lodge is smack in the middle of trophy whitetail country. The lodge has access to 26,000 acres of woodland considered to be one of the best hunting grounds in Maine. Whitetail deer, along with moose and bears, reign supreme in this area, with many reaching trophy-class size due to the lack of serious hunting pressure. Each year, some of Maine's largest bucks are taken from this region. With deep woods, few roads, and deer going about their business in a natural, unpressured manner, this is the type of hunting that all whitetail hunters strive to find. Northern Maine will test your hunting skills, sure, but the rewards are truly unforgettable.

Fish River's cabins are located on beautiful Eagle Lake, almost two miles off the main road. American plan guests enjoy the privacy of their own cabins, but eat meals in the rustic dining room in the main lodge. All meals are served family style, and every effort is made to serve hearty meals with homemade breads and desserts. Guests on the housekeeping plan have no worries about groceries or supplies, as two grocery stores are right down the road.

With a spacious lounge that has satellite TV, VCR, bumper pool and darts, guests can choose to socialize at the end of a hard day of hunting, or simply retire to their own cabins to rest up for the next day's hunt.

Vital Statistics

THE LODGE:

8 rustic cabins contain 35 beds total

SERVICES: Telephone, TV, microwave

HUNTS:

• American plan: $375 - $425 / week / person

• housekeeping plan: $400 - $500 / week / cabin (up to 4 in a cabin – additional cost for each person over 4)

PAYMENT: Credit card, check

MEAL PLANS: American plan: all meals included (turkey, pork, chicken, pasta, steak, Shepherd's pie)

SPECIAL DIETS: Heart healthy, salt/msg free

NEAREST AIRPORT: Presque Isle, ME

TRANSPORTATION TO LODGE (1 1/2 hours): Rental car; van from lodge ($25)

CONTACT:

James and Kathleen Lynch
Fish River Lodge
PO Box 202
Eagle Lake, ME 04739
Ph: 207/444-5207
Email: frlodge@ainop.com
Web: Http://www.mainerec.com/frlodge.html

WINTER:

7 Blackstrap Road
Cumberland, ME 04021
Ph: 207/829-6639

THE HUNT:

SEASON:

• bow: September 28 - October 27

• rifle: October 30 - November 25

• muzzleloader: November 27 - December 2

BEST TIME TO HUNT: Anytime (early mornings, dusks are best on a given day)

TERRAIN: Heavily forested, hardwood ridges, logging roads, swamps

LAND: Property abuts 26,000 acres of Maine public land, plus thousands of acres of paper company land

DRAW BLOOD POLICY? No

HUNTING METHODS: Still-hunting, calling, rattling

YEARS IN BUSINESS: 8

STAFF OF GUIDES: n/a

HUNTERS SERVED BY EACH GUIDE: 2

NONHUNTER CHARGE: Food and lodging

LICENSES: Sold at lodge

GAME CARE: Dressed, packaged, frozen, shipped at no charge

OTHER ACTIVITIES: Other big game hunting (black bear, moose), bird hunting (woodcock, grouse), water-fowling (ducks, geese), fishing, bird watching, boating, canoeing, swimming, wildlife photography

Foggy Mountain Guide Service

Dover - Foxcroft, Maine

WITH MORE THAN A million acres of private paper company land or government-owned land at his disposal, master guide Wayne Bosowicz and his crew can take you far and wide in search of a trophy Maine whitetail. And while deer are not as plentiful here as they might be in states to the south, those that are here often run large, topping 200 and even 300 pounds. They need that fat and large bodies to survive the tough, cold winters of Maine. Here, a 200-pound buck is considered a good deer, but not uncommon. About 20 percent of Bosowicz's hunters see bucks, and about 10 percent get one each year. One reason for their relatively high success may lie in the fact that the area Foggy Mountain hunts has had no hunting pressure for a number of years. This area, about 216,000 acres stretching to the Canadian border, is deep, untouched wilderness. Guests stay in housekeeping cabins in the Moosehead/Katahdin area. Either place is worth a stay. Bow season is in October and rifle runs in November. Deer hunts may be guided or unguided.

As Bosowicz puts it, "At Foggy Mountain, our only business is hunting and fishing. We take it seriously. It is not a sideline, it's our livelihood. That means you can have the confidence of knowing we are at work year-round to ensure you a world-class experience."

About the hunting he says, "We will show you a good area. No stress on these deer, as there is little to no hunting pressure on our deer during bow season. Food plots consist of old apple orchards, clover and hayfields along with beechnut ridges and cedar thickets. We may not have many deer, but do have some really big ones."

On rifle or bow hunts, a guide is not needed as Bosowicz or his staff will help you with the layout of the area. Any way you do it, just being in the deep woods of Maine, searching for the trophy buck of a lifetime, is worth a trip to Foggy Mountain.

Vital Statistics

THE LODGE:

Housekeeping plan in rustic accommodations; 15 to 20 beds total

SERVICES: Fax, copying, TV

HUNTS:

- rifle: $350 / 6-day stay, 5-day hunt
- bow: $375 / 6-day stay, 5-day hunt

PAYMENT: Check, cash

MEAL PLANS: Housekeeping

SPECIAL DIETS: n/a

NEAREST AIRPORT: Bangor, ME

TRANSPORTATION TO LODGE (45 miles): Rental car

CONTACT:

Wayne Bosowicz
Foggy Mountain Guide Service
131 Ladd Road
Sebec, ME 04481
Ph: 207/564-3404
Fax: 207/564-8209
Email: foggymtn@kynd.net
Web: www.foggymountain.com

THE HUNT:

SEASON:

- bow: October
- rifle: November

BEST TIME TO HUNT: Anytime

TERRAIN: Hardwood forests, mountains, swamps

LAND: More than a million acres

DRAW BLOOD POLICY? n/a

HUNTING METHODS: Stand hunting (lock-ons, wooden), still-hunting, by vehicle, calling, rattling

YEARS IN BUSINESS: 35

STAFF OF GUIDES: n/a

HUNTERS SERVED BY EACH GUIDE: n/a

NONHUNTER CHARGE: $230 / 6 days

LICENSES: Over the counter

GAME CARE: Dressed, packaged and frozen; no shipping

OTHER ACTIVITIES: Other big game hunting (bear, wolves in Ontario), bird hunting (grouse, woodcock), fishing, boating, canoeing, wildlife photography

Gentle Ben's Lodge

Rockwood, Maine

YOU WON'T FIND MANY OTHER HUNTERS on Gentle Ben's 10,000 acres of hunting land, which is 40 miles north of the main lodge in Rockwood. It's at the end of a gated paper-company road. Beyond the gate are ridges that stem down from the mountains, all in the 2,100-foot range, and a welter of low hills, streams and bogs. Deer here are not as numerous as in states to the south, but they are large. A 10-point buck will generally dress out over 200 pounds, while the rack will normally have a 21-inch spread and score in the 140s. These are good-sized deer, the kind any hunter would be proud to take. In these big, dense woods, deer are unpressured, and tend to move all day. Still-hunting is the most effective way to take them, but sitting over scrapes also produces, as does rattling and calling. Bowhunters hunt from tree stands overlooking active trails. Firearms hunters track deer when there's been snow. Hunting is best in this area during the rut in November.

The main lodge is located on Moosehead Lake and consists of a main dining room and three guest rooms with shared bath. The views of the lake are spectacular, and the food offered by Sherrill Pelletier and her crew are guaranteed to please (and may just add a few pounds to your waistline).

Vital Statistics

THE LODGE:

Main lodge contains 3 guest rooms, 12 beds total, no private baths

SERVICES: Telephone, fax, photocopying, TV (in main lodge)

HUNTS: $695 / 5 1/2-day guided hunt

PAYMENT: Cash, credit card

MEAL PLANS: All meals served family style

SPECIAL DIETS: Can be accommodated with notice

NEAREST AIRPORT: Bangor, ME

TRANSPORTATION TO LODGE (100 miles): Rental car; van from lodge ($100 extra one way)

CONTACT:

Bruce Pelletier
Gentle Ben's Lodge
Box 212
Rockwood, ME 04478
Ph: 207/534-2201; 800/242-3799
Fax: 207/534-2236
Web: www.maineguides.com/Gentle-Bens
Email: gentleben@top.monad.net

THE HUNT:

SEASON:

• bow: October

• rifle: November

• muzzleloader: first week of Dec.

BEST TIME TO HUNT: November

TERRAIN: A mixture of hardwoods and softwoods; rolling hills

LAND: Owns 10,000 acres; lease 2 million acres

DRAW BLOOD POLICY? No

HUNTING METHODS: Stand hunting (ladders and 2-piece climbers), still-hunting, calling, rattling

YEARS IN BUSINESS: 16

STAFF OF GUIDES: 5

HUNTERS SERVED BY EACH GUIDE: 5 (fee is doubled for one-on-one hunts)

NONHUNTER CHARGE: $400 / week

LICENSES: Sold at the lodge

GAME CARE: Dressed, packaged, frozen (.40 / pound) and shipped (cost depends on destination)

OTHER ACTIVITIES: Other big game hunting (black bear, moose), bird hunting, waterfowling, fishing, biking, boating, canoeing, golf, hiking, swimming, whitewater rafting, wildlife photography

BOONE AND CROCKETT

• B&C book bucks taken from property: 2

• Average B&C score: 140

• B&C bucks from this part of state: n/a

Homestead Lodge

Oxbow, Maine

NORTHERN MAINE is known for its endless miles of primeval forest and shadowy bogs, which lure hunters from all over the country in a quest for trophy bucks. Homestead Lodge is located right in the middle of this terrain — perfect for the whitetail hunter who wants to get off on his own. Maine is broken up into Deer Management Districts, and though some districts harvest more deer than Homestead does, they also have many more hunters. If you are looking for a one-on-one experience as well as a trophy, the Homestead Lodge is the place to go.

Having a minimum amount of hunting pressure and heavy cover has allowed area deer to reach maturity with large racks and heavy bodies, with many Homestead deer dressing out at more than 200 pounds. Whether you're looking to hunt on remote land for wild deer, or if you're after a groomed deer run on Homestead's privately-owned property, owner Gloria Nelson and her guides will direct you to active areas and go over maps to ensure you have an understanding of the vast woods.

The lodge combines the classic charm of an old-time farmhouse with modern conveniences. Comfortable rooms, bedding, three home-cooked meals daily, hot showers, pool table, card tables, and more make coming to the Homestead Lodge a wonderful getaway experience.

Vital Statistics

THE LODGE:

Farmhouse has 8 guest rooms, 24 beds total, no private baths

SERVICES: Telephone, TV

GUN HUNTS: Rates are determined by the week and by the animal huntd, or $35 / day / person with breakfast included

PAYMENT: Cash, check

CONFERENCE GROUPS: n/a

MEAL PLANS: All meals included in weekly rates (dinners include roast pork, roast turkey, buffalo stroganoff); breakfast included in daily rate

NEAREST AIRPORT: Presque Isle Airport or Bangor International

TRANSPORTATION TO LODGE (45 miles): Rental car; van from lodge (no additional charge in most cases)

CONTACT:

Gloria Nelson
Homestead Lodge
871 Oxbow Road
Oxbow, ME 04764
Ph: 207/435-6357
Email: adventures@homesteadlodgemaine.com
Web: www.homesteadlodgemaine.com

THE HUNT:

SEASON:
- bow: October
- gun: November
- muzzleloader: December

BEST TIME TO HUNT: Anytime

TERRAIN: Hard and soft wood forests with numerous swampy areas and beechnut ridges; terrain encompasses almost every type a hunter could want

LAND: Owns 350 acres; lease 200,000 acres of paper company land, plus have access to millions of acres of paper company land that is open to the public

DRAW BLOOD POLICY? No

HUNTING METHODS: Stand hunting (portable ladder stands), still-hunting, calling, rattling

YEARS IN BUSINESS: 11

STAFF OF GUIDES: 3

HUNTERS SERVED BY EACH GUIDE: 1 guide / day per party

NON HUNTER CHARGE: Room and board

LICENSES: Over the counter

GAME CARE: Dress and freeze; local butcher is available to package, label, and ship

OTHER ACTIVITIES: Other big game hunting (black bear, moose), bird hunting (grouse, woodcock), waterfowling, fishing, antiquing, biking, bird watching, canoeing, golf, hiking, skiing, snowmobiling, ice fishing

Libby Camps

A s h l a n d ,   M a i n e

ALMOST 150 MILES NORTH OF BANGOR, near the Canadian border, Libby's Sporting Camps are sandwiched between Baxter State Park and the Allagash Wilderness Waterway. The camp has been owned and operated by the Libby family for more than 100 years, with some notable clientele including Teddy Roosevelt and Jack Dempsey.

Back in 1938, some of the cabins were relocated to the current site on the lake shoreline. Today, there are eight guest cabins and a dining lodge. Hunters staying at the cabins are fed well at the main lodge, dining on recipes that have been handed down for generations. There's a huge variety, too, with hearty, home-cooked family-style meals complete with home-baked breads, pies and pastries, garden vegetables and fresh meats. After a filling dinner and a good night's sleep, hunters rise early the next morning to hunt some of Maine's deepest, wildest country. The proximity of the camp to Maine's largest wilderness parks — more than 3 million acres — and most extensive wintering deer populations make Libby's a hunter's paradise. Deer aren't as numerous perhaps as in other parts of the whitetail's range, but the bucks are likely to be big, with large racks and body weights hitting the 300-pound mark on a fairly regular basis.

Hunters venturing into this region should wear warm, layered clothing (as temperatures can be frigid), good sturdy boots capable of negotiating not only deep woods, but ridges and swamps, plus warm hats and gloves. Shots are likely to be anywhere from 50 to 200 yards, depending on whether you're hunting a clear-cut area or deep woods. Calibers should be typical whitetail calibers — from 270 on up. A good pair of binoculars will also come in handy, helping the still-hunter glass ahead, and in scrutinizing heavy brush and cover where a big buck may be bedded.

Vital Statistics

THE LODGE:

8 remote log cabins have 24 beds total

SERVICES: Laundry

HUNTS:

- $725 / week, unguided, double occupancy
- $950 / week, unguided, single occupancy
- $1,200 / week, two-on-one guided hunt, double occupancy
- $1,900 / week, private guide, single occupancy

PAYMENT: Cash, credit card

MEAL PLANS: All meals included (dinners include strip on the grill, grilled salmon fillets, fresh pastas, roast turkey, baked potatoes, vegetables, homemade breads and pastries)

SPECIAL DIETS: Heart healthy, vegetarian, salt/msg free

NEAREST AIRPORT: Presque Isle, ME

TRANSPORTATION TO LODGE (65 miles): Van ($175 round-trip per group); seaplane ($125 round trip per person)

CONTACT:

Matt Libby
Libby Camps
PO Box 810
Ashland, ME 04732
Ph: 207/435-8274
Fax 207/435-3230
Email: matt@libbycamps.com
Web: Http://www.libbycamps.com

THE HUNT:

SEASON:

- bow: October
- rifle: last week of Oct. - last week of Nov.
- muzzleloader: last week of Nov. - first week Dec.

BEST TIME TO HUNT: Anytime

TERRAIN: Mountains, dark growth, some wetlands, fir trees, spruce, some hardwoods, old cuts

LAND: Lease 3 million private acres

DRAW BLOOD POLICY? No

HUNTING METHODS: Stand hunting (portable ladder stands), still-hunting, calling, rattling

YEARS IN BUSINESS: 25 (family in area since 1890)

STAFF OF GUIDES: Up to 14

HUNTERS SERVED BY EACH GUIDE: 1 - 2

NONHUNTER CHARGE: $725 / week

LICENSES: Over the counter

GAME CARE: Dressed/frozen/shipped

OTHER ACTIVITIES: Other big game hunting (black bear, moose), bird hunting, waterfowling, fishing, bird watching, boating, canoeing, hiking, swimming, wildlife photography, seaplane flights

BOONE AND CROCKETT

- B&C book bucks taken from property: Several
- Average B&C score: 130
- B&C bucks from this part of state: Several

Loon Lodge

Millinocket, Maine

DEER HUNTS IN NORTHERN MAINE mean going after big bucks. Hunters don't come to the Allagash to just shoot any deer, they come to hunt for a trophy. Many once-in-a-lifetime bucks have been taken at Loon Lodge. The Allagash consistently produces some of the East Coast's biggest bucks, both in body and rack. Because of the vast forest and lack of hunting pressure, Maine bucks grow to enormous sizes.

© Loon Lodge

This beauty was taken on the public lands hunted by Loon Lodge.

Northern Maine does not have the high number of deer that are found in other areas of the country, but because of the harsh winter and predators, the area produces larger and hardier deer. Bucks that dress out over 200 pounds are taken at the camps every season, and a few always top out over 300 pounds.

Millions of acres of unposted land are available to all Loon Lodge hunters, which is something you seldom experience in this day and age. Whether you like swampy lowland or hardwood ridges, you'll find the type of terrain you like to hunt. Still hunting, stand hunting over scrapes, stalking a buck's tracks, or antler rattling and grunt calling are all tactics that work here.

The camp takes an average of 12 hunters per week for the four-week season. If you're up to a pure north-country challenge, looking for big bucks in big woods, this is one place to go.

© Loon Lodge

The main lodge at Loon Lake, where guests are served up scrumptious, filling meals.

Vital Statistics

THE LODGE:

5 private cabins, 21 beds total, no private baths

SERVICES: Radio contact, shower house

HUNTS:

- $1,400 / 5 days, 1-on-1 guided
- $950 / person / 5 days, 2-on-1 guided
- $795 / person / 5 days, 3-on-1 guided
- $695 / person / 5 days, 4-on-1 guided
- arrive Sunday & leave Saturday

PAYMENT: Cash, checks for deposits, bank or traveler's checks

MEAL PLANS: All meals included (dinners feature roast beef, baked ham, turkey, sirloin steaks, bbq chicken, lasagna, all the fixings)

SPECIAL DIETS: Can accommodate

NEAREST AIRPORT: Bangor, ME

TRANSPORTATION TO LODGE (150 miles): Rental car; can arrange pickup for additional charge

THE HUNT:

SEASONS:

- bow: Oct. 1 - 31
- rifle: Nov. 1 - 30
- muzzleloader: Dec. 1 - 14

BEST TIME TO HUNT: Mid-Nov. - Dec.

TERRAIN: Varies greatly, from cedar swamps to hardwood ridges, all within 5 miles of the main lodge

LAND: Lease and hunt public timber lands covering more than 1 million acres

DRAW BLOOD POLICY? No

HUNTING METHODS: Stand hunting (hunters provide their own), still-hunting, by vehicle, calling, rattling

YEARS IN BUSINESS: 15

STAFF OF GUIDES: 2

HUNTERS SERVED BY EACH GUIDE: 4; other arrangements are available

NONHUNTER CHARGE: $350 / 5 days

LICENSES: Over the counter at lodge

GAME CARE: n/a

OTHER ACTIVITIES: Other big game hunting (bear, moose by permit), bird hunting, waterfowling, fishing, bird watching, boating, canoeing, hiking, swimming, wildlife photography

BOONE AND CROCKETT

- B&C bucks book taken from property: n/a
- Average B&C score: 120s - 130s
- B&C bucks from this part of state: n/a

CONTACT:

Michael and Linda Yencha
Loon Lodge
P.O. Box 404
Millinocket, ME 04462
Ph: 207/745-8168
Email:
relax@loonlodgemaine.com

OFF-SEASON

P.O. Box 2469
Wilkes-Barre, PA 18703
570/287-6915

Matagamon Wilderness

Patten, Maine

MATAGAMON WILDERNESS LODGES are located in the deep Maine woods, as far out in the middle of nowhere as a whitetail hunter needs to be. We're talking deep woods hunting here, where you head out in the early morning, pick up a track, and follow it until you find the deer that made it — which could be a good buck. Either follow that tactic, or still hunt down the many logging trails, moving slowly, scrutinizing the area with every few steps you take, waiting for a buck to walk by. If you stop and start, stop and start, you'll unnerve the deer to the point where he'll get up and bolt. And that's when you've got your chance, when all the hours you put in at the firing range will prove their worth, and when your aim might be true if you can control your racing heart.

Matagamon is in northern Penobscot County, 26 miles west of Patten in excellent deer country. It's a wilderness operation, consisting of four housekeeping cabins and a small general store. The hunting pressure is light due to the vastness of the wilderness. Bucks run large, with many dressing out over 200 pounds, and some as large as 300. Most carry huge racks.

You can hunt on your own here, or hire a registered guide to help you figure out how to navigate the huge northern woods (not a bad idea, certainly for starters). The first three weeks in November have the most hunting pressure; the last week of rifle season and muzzleloading week, on the other hand, see few hunters in the woods. You can expect snow anytime during November, usually by mid-month, and most probably for the last week of the season. Chances for big bucks increase at this time due to the rut, light hunting pressure, and colder weather with tracking snow.

The camps are cozy, warm, and perfect for deer hunting. They are all housekeeping style, with one sleeping nine and the others six. All have propane and wood heat, plus gas cook stoves, lights, and utensils. You bring your own food and beverages, and cook for yourself. Showers are also available.

Vital Statistics

THE LODGE:

4 log cabins contain 26 beds total, no private baths

SERVICES: These are wilderness cabins with no modern services

HUNTS: $140 / week for unguided hunt (4 hunters minimum); add $600 for a guided hunt; $1,200 for a one-on-one trophy hunt

PAYMENT: Cash, check

MEAL PLANS: Bring your own

SPECIAL DIETS: Bring your own

NEAREST AIRPORT: Bangor, ME

TRANSPORTATION TO LODGE (125 miles): Rental car

CONTACT:

Donald Dudley
Matagamon Wilderness
PO Box 220
Patten, ME 04765
Ph: 207/528-2448
Email: matagamoncamps@katahdinoutdoors.com
Web: Http://www.katahdinoutdoors.com/matagamon

THE HUNT:

SEASON:

• bow: October

• rifle: November

• muzzleloader: week after Thanksgiving week

BEST TIME TO HUNT: Anytime

TERRAIN: Hardwood and softwood forests; some is mountainous, some swampy; cutover areas too

LAND: All public land

DRAW BLOOD POLICY? No

HUNTING METHODS: Stand hunting (lock-ons), still-hunting, calling

YEARS IN BUSINESS: 30

STAFF OF GUIDES: 3

HUNTERS SERVED BY EACH GUIDE: 1 - 4

NONHUNTER CHARGE: No (only camp fee)

LICENSES: Over the counter

GAME CARE: No

OTHER ACTIVITIES: Other big game hunting (black bear, moose), bird hunting, fishing, biking, bird watching, boating, canoeing, hiking, skiing, swimming, wildlife photography

Northern Outdoors

The Forks, Maine

ESTABLISHED IN 1975, Northern Outdoors has grown to become one of the most successful trophy whitetail outfitters in the Northeast. Its growth has been founded on one very simple principle: a total commitment to excellence. To fulfill that promise, owner Wayne Hockmeyer has assembled a staff of topnotch guides, boasting more than 100 years of combined hunting experience in Maine. Northern Outdoors is their career, and their dedication is one of the biggest reasons the outfitter is so successful. As a group, the guides are true professionals who display pride in their reputation. As individuals, they are humble; when they have a bad week, they suffer the defeat along with the hunters. They never stop learning, and every year make changes to improve their clients' chances of success.

According to Hockmeyer, " Our philosophy has created a unique atmosphere and resulted in many different people from different states coming back year after year . . . A hunting camp is supposed to be fun, one of friendship and camaraderies. We do not want anyone to feel he has to prove himself, only that he is a good sport and enjoys himself . . .Hunting is a hard, mentally punishing sport where a person is faced with defeat day after day, and sometimes season after season. There are expert hunters and novice hunters, but lady luck can shine on the worst and shut out the best, and sometimes she will do it for what seems an unreasonable amount of time."

Hockmeyer is realistic about a hunter's chance of success. "We do not have a large population of deer per square mile in northern Maine," he says. "Hunters shouldn't come up here with expectations of seeing lots of deer during the course of their hunt. What we do have is some of the most extraordinary trophy whitetail hunting in the U.S. There are probably very few areas in the world that contain more 200-pound-plus bucks per square mile than the northwoods of Maine.

"The main reason the deer get so big in our area has to do with genetic selection, otherwise known as survival of the fittest," he concludes. "Maine lies at the northernmost edge of the whitetail deer's range, and the winters are so severe that only the big-bodied deer can survive. The larger body size allows the deer to accumulate greater amount of fat reserves, thus allowing them to live through the lean time of winter when the nutritious food sources aren't so available."

Another reason the deer get so big in this area is that there is little hunting pressure, plus the area is so immense. Many deer have rarely even seen a hunter, much less been shot at.

With the exception of the occasional hunter who is physically able and skillful enough to track a big buck (usually when there is snow on the ground), most hunters at Northern Outdoors hunt from tree stands. All three of the Northern Outdoors camps — Mountain Camp, Pond Camp (100 miles northwest of Baxter State Park), and the lodge itself — rely heavily on stands. The theory is simple: find an area that deer prefer and wait for them to show up. Sooner or later they will! Northern Outdoors' guides locate prime areas for stands and then place hunters in prime areas who then wait for a trophy to come by. Sound easy? It isn't. Hunting from a stand can be difficult. It requires incredible concentration, perseverance and confidence. A person needs to remain very still and quiet, while also staying warm and comfortable.

"Keeping warm is key," says Hockmeyer. "Hunters should dress lightly for the initial hike to the stand, and pack in heavier clothes to put on once they have arrived. Perspiration is a hunter's worst enemy." Not only will it increase your body odor, but it will make you cold once you have settled in on your stand and are not moving. Many hunters quit their stands around 11 a.m. and head back to camp for lunch and a nap (those who sit all day are usually the ones who get big deer, however).

From his resort in The Forks where the Dead River joins the Kennebec, Hockmeyer hunts a 150-square-mile area of private paper company land. Guests are accommodated in the lodge with its rustic yet modern bedrooms, each with private baths, bar and restaurant. Before dawn, guides load hunters into 4WDs for the drive to their stands. Hunters are picked up midmorning, if they wish, or they can stay all day. Hunter success at all three camps is about twice the state average, with many hunters passing on a lot of spikes and forkhorns.

Vital Statistics

THE LODGE:

Lodge and cabins at The Forks Resort Center contain 50 guest rooms (total for all three camps), 100 beds total, all with private baths; wall tents with stoves are at the 2 out-camps

SERVICES: Telephone, fax, copying, TV, laundry

GUN HUNTS:

• Remote camps: $725 / week if you use Northern Outdoors vehicles, $695 / week if you use your own

• The Forks Lodge and cabins: prices vary, depending on whether you stay in the lodge or one of the cabins, but average about $650 / week for guided hunts, $475 / week for unguided hunts

PAYMENT: Cash or credit cards

CONFERENCE GROUPS: Yes

MEAL PLANS: All meals included (dinners are sumptuous, and include such hearty fare as steak, chicken, and fish)

NEAREST AIRPORT: Bangor, ME

TRANSPORTATION TO LODGE (100 miles): Rental car; van from lodge ($1 per mile)

CONTACT:

Jim Yearwood
Northern Outdoors
Route 201, PO Box 100
The Forks, ME 04985
Ph: 800/765-7238
Fax: 207/663-2244
Email: info@northernoutdoors.com
Web: www.mainedeerhunting.com

THE HUNT:

SEASON:

• rifle: November 1 - 30

• muzzleloader: December 1 - 7

BEST TIME TO HUNT: Anytime

TERRAIN: Hills/mountains to 2,500 feet, hardwood ridges, spruce/fir stands, clear-cuts, dense woods, swamps

LAND: 150 square miles of paper company land

DRAW BLOOD POLICY? No

HUNTING METHODS: Stand hunting (most are portable API climbers), still-hunting, calling, rattling

YEARS IN BUSINESS: 26

STAFF OF GUIDES: 10

HUNTERS SERVED BY EACH GUIDE: Up to 6

NONHUNTER CHARGE: Yes

LICENSES: Over the counter; purchase before arriving

GAME CARE: No

OTHER ACTIVITIES: Fishing, canoeing, golf, hiking, skiing, swimming, tennis, whitewater rafting, wildlife photography, sea kayaking, rock climbing, snowmobiling

BOONE AND CROCKETT

• B&C book bucks taken from property: 3

• Average B&C score: n/a

• B&C bucks from this part of state: n/a

Northern Pride Lodge

Kokadjo, Maine

TUCKED AWAY IN MAINE'S DEEP WOODS off the Golden Road in the tiny village of Kokajo in the Moosehead Lake region, Northern Pride Lodge has access to some of the state's finest hunting. The lodge is surrounded by hundreds of thousands of acres owned by large paper companies, all open to public hunting. The terrain varies from large cedar and spruce swamps to high, open hardwood ridges; open clear-cuts are scattered throughout most of the area.

The deer here grow large because of the abundance of feed associated with the large cutting operations and beechnut ridges. In addition, the hunting pressure is low, resulting in mature bucks often being taken. The local tagging station in town tags 130 to 150 deer a year, with almost 50 percent of them dressing over 200 pounds! Some deer over 250 pounds are brought in each year, while 8- to 10-pointers are common. Common Boone and Crockett racks range from the 130- to 140-class, with occasional 150 - to 170-class bucks being taken.

The lodge is a haven of luxury and comfort. Built in 1896 and nestled on five acres, it sits next to 550 feet of beautiful shoreline frontage. The lodge is uniquely furnished in Victorian antiques, coupled with northwoods' outdoor decor. The guest rooms are spacious, and can accommodate singles, families or groups. Hunters who find themselves at the lodge during daylight hours enjoy beautiful views of the grounds and lakefront. Barbara's excellent first-class meals are an additional bonus. Room rates include a hearty Maine breakfast, while the full-meal package adds great dinners (filet mignon, duck) and box lunches to take with you while out for a day of hunting.

© Northern Pride Lodge

*Richard Anette, a guide at Northern Pride Lodge, took this
240-pound 8-pointer on paper company lands.*

Vital Statistics

THE LODGE:

Modern main lodge has 5 guest rooms, 12 beds total, no private baths

SERVICES: Telephone, TV, laundry

HUNTS:

- $560 / week unguided hunt
- $1,250 / week guided hunt
- $905 / week 2-to-1 guided hunt
- $790 / week 3-to-1 guided hunt

PAYMENT: Cash, credits cards, checks

Meal Plans: All meals included (full Down East breakfast, box lunch with beverage, dinners of filet mignon, roast duck, fish, pasta)

Special Diets: Hearty healthy, vegetarian, salt/msg free

Nearest Airport: Bangor, ME

Transportation to Lodge (1 1/2 hours): Rental car; can arrange pickup/drop off for additional $100

BOONE AND CROCKETT

- B&C bucks book taken from property: n/a
- Average B&C score: 130 - 140 class is common
- B&C bucks from this part of state: n/a

CONTACT:

Wayne and Barbara Plummer
Northern Pride Lodge
HC 76, Box 588
Kokadjo, ME 04441
Ph: 207/695-2890

THE HUNT:

SEASONS:

- bow: October 1 - 31
- rifle: November 1 - 30
- muzzleloader: first week of Dec.

BEST TIME TO HUNT: Second and third week of November at the peak of the rut (there is usually tracking snow at this time too)

TERRAIN: Thousands of acres of paper company land that is open to public hunting; the land contains hundreds of miles of logging roads that provide easy access; the terrain ranges from large swamps, clear-cuts, hardwood ridges and mature growth, mixed hardwood and softwood forest

LAND: Hundreds of thousands of acres of paper company land

DRAW BLOOD POLICY? No

HUNTING METHODS: Stand hunting (14' ladder stands with 2' x 2' platforms), still-hunting, by vehicle, calling, rattling, tracking

YEARS IN BUSINESS: 3

STAFF OF GUIDES: Lodge owners are all registered guides; additional guides are available as needed

HUNTERS SERVED BY EACH GUIDE: 2 - 3

NONHUNTER CHARGE: $560 / week (food and lodging)

LICENSES: Over the counter

GAME CARE: Northern Pride dresses all game; all processing is done by a local butcher; price varies

OTHER ACTIVITIES: Moose hunting, bird hunting (grouse, woodcock), fishing, biking, bird watching, boating, canoeing, hiking, swimming, wildlife photography

Pine Grove Lodge

Bingham, Maine

PINE GROVE LODGE is located in the mountainous region of west-central Maine, one mile from Wyman Lake and just three miles from the Kennebec River. Run by Bob Howe, a Maine guide for 26 years, Pine Grove is in the middle of some prime deer hunting country.

"We have thousands of acres of public and private land to hunt on," says Howe. "These lands offer perfect locations for close- or long-range shooting, and are good for the bowhunter, muzzleloader hunter and rifle hunter. We also have top deer-hunting guides who can assist you whether you like to hunt in a stand, still-hunt, or track trophy deer. Our guides also use maps made by GPS and Toposcout computer programs, which can be printed off and handed to each hunter." This is a nice feature, as each hunter knows exactly where he or she is, and doesn't have to worry about getting lost. These maps also come in handy when planning hunting tactics.

"We now also offer new river float trips, one-on-one and two-on-one hunts," Howe continues. "Deer hunting is one of our specialties, and we want to make your stay with us one of your most memorable hunts."

Hunts at Pine Grove generally run five days, with Sunday arrival after lunch and departure the following Saturday. Prices include food, lodging, and guide, while the license is extra.

Those visiting Pine Grove can stay either in the main house in antique-style bedrooms, in one of two cabins on the property, or in the bunkhouse. The bunkhouse is ideal for large families or groups. It is divided into two rooms, dormitory style, with three bunk beds in one, and two bunk beds in the other. Each room has a complete bathroom. There is a living room between the two bedrooms, with two couches, a television, refrigerator, and extra bed. A complete breakfast is included in the B&B rates, while all meals are included in the weekly hunting rate.

Two Pine Grove Lodge hunters show off a good-sized 8-pointer.

© Pine Grove Lodge

Vital Statistics

THE LODGE:

9 guest rooms (5 in main lodge, 2 in bunkhouse, 1 in each cabin), 34 beds total; 4 rooms have private baths

SERVICES: Telephone, fax, TV, internet access, hot tub

HUNTS: $650 / week, all-inclusive

PAYMENT: Cash, check, credit cards

CONFERENCE GROUPS: Yes

MEAL PLANS: All meals included (for breakfast, you'll find eggs, meats, even baked beans; lunches of soups and pheasant stew; dinners of roasts and fowl, homemade desserts)

SPECIAL DIETS: Can accommodate

NEAREST AIRPORT: Bangor International, Bangor, ME

TRANSPORTATION TO LODGE (1 1/2 hours): Rental car; van from lodge ($75)

THE HUNT:

SEASON:

• bow: October
• rifle: November
• muzzleloader: first 2 weeks of Dec.

BEST TIME TO HUNT: Anytime

TERRAIN: Mixed hard and soft woods with some regrown clearcuts; some fields and power lines, logging roads; some farmland as well

LAND: Mostly public land, which includes thousands of acres of paper company land; also hunt private land

DRAW BLOOD POLICY? No

HUNTING METHODS: Stand hunting (wooden and steel ladder stands), still-hunting, calling, rattling

YEARS IN BUSINESS: 27

STAFF OF GUIDES: 4 - 5

HUNTERS SERVED BY EACH GUIDE: Up to 5

NONHUNTER CHARGE: $400 / week

LICENSES: Sold at lodge

GAME CARE: No

OTHER ACTIVITIES: Other big game hunting (black bear, moose), small game (coyote, bobcat, snowshoe hare), bird hunting (grouse, woodcock), waterfowl, fishing (salmon, trout, perch, splake, bass, northern pike), antiquing, biking, bird watching, boating, canoeing, golf, hiking, whitewater rafting, wildlife photography, kayaking, ice fishing, cross-country skiing, snowmobiling. In the summer, the lodge has a flyfishing school, an archery school, and a whitetail hunting school.

CONTACT:

Robert Howe
Pine Grove Lodge
HC 65, Box 76
Bingham, ME 04920
Ph: 207/672-4011
Fax: 207/672-9350
Email: info@pinegrovelodge.com
Web: www.pinegrovelodge.com

Stony Brook Outfitters

Wilton, Maine

STONY BROOK HUNTS OVER 1,000 SQUARE MILES of paper company land throughout Maine's northwestern corner, about an hour west of Bangor and an hour south of Jackman near the Quebec border. Oak and beech ridges and swampy drainages hold good-sized deer. A typical trophy carries eight points and weighs about 180 pounds. Normally, hunting is done in the early morning and late afternoons from stands that overlook rubs, scrapes and trails. During midday, still-hunting occasionally pays off. About one in four hunters at Stony Brook takes a trophy-class buck here.

This can be tough hunting. Plan to bring a good pair of boots as you may do a bit of hiking if nothing comes by your stand. Pack some warm clothing, too, as late November can be chilly in this part of Maine. Parker and his guides know where a lot of the big bucks live in this area, and if you've got the gumption, they'll take you where you can still-hunt all day long. If you see a buck, chances are it'll be a good one. Know how to shoot your rifle well, as you normally only get one shot at these bucks before they're gone into the thick stuff.

Bear and deer are Stony Brook's staples, but they also run hunts for bobcat and moose (if you're lucky enough to draw a moose permit). Hunters stay in the lodge in Weld, a functional affair with seven bunkrooms varying in size to accommodate parties from two to eight. Baths are shared and meals are the kind that keep lumberjacks going. Cook Phil Rafter's bean soup draws raves and requests for the recipe.

Vital Statistics

THE LODGE:

Modern, main lodge has 7 rooms (4 handicapped accessible), 17 beds total

SERVICES: Telephone, VCR

HUNTS: $600 / 5-day hunt

PAYMENT: Cash, check

MEAL PLANS: All meals included (dinners feature pot roast, ham, fried chicken, turkey, spaghetti, steaks, vegetables, breads, desserts)

NEAREST AIRPORT: Bangor or Portland, ME

TRANSPORTATION TO LODGE (70 miles): Rental car

CONTACT:

Bob Parker
Stony Brook Outfitters
55 Morrison Hill Road
Wilton, ME 04294
Ph: 800/322-2327
Email: stonybrooklodge@hotmail.com

THE HUNT:

SEASON:

• bow: October (Stony Brook only takes a few bowhunters per year)

• rifle: November

BEST TIME TO HUNT: November

Terrain: Oak and beach ridges, cedar swamps, lakes shores, creek drainages, low ridges with numerous knobs and draws

LAND: More than 1,000 square miles of paper company land

DRAW BLOOD POLICY? No

HUNTING METHODS: Stand hunting (ladder stands or bring your own), still-hunting

YEARS IN BUSINESS: 20

STAFF OF GUIDES: 5 - 6

HUNTERS SERVED BY EACH GUIDE: 1 - 2

NONHUNTER CHARGE: Yes

LICENSES: Over the counter

GAME CARE: Dressed, quartered, and frozen free of charge; local butcher can cut venison into steaks, roasts, etc, for a fee

OTHER ACTIVITIES: Other big game hunting (black bear, spring black bear in Quebec, moose, bobcat), bird hunting (grouse), fishing, wildlife photography

Sunset Ridge Lodge & Outfitters

S e b e c ,   M a i n e

ACCORDING TO OWNER BEN PINKHAM, "We hunt some of the best whitetail country in the East. If you're going to hunt Maine for trophy bucks, you might as well do it right the first time . . . Our lodging and meals are second to none, and we take you hunting, not sight-seeing. My guides and I are the best in the business. We are in excellent shape, and we hunt hard. Our tree stands are on private land, so you have no outside interference. That is important if you are going to be successful."

Pinkham likes to speak his mind — he tells it like it is, plain and simple. He'll tell you outright that if you're a smoker, you'd better stop smoking before deer season. Either that, or don't show up at his lodge. It's smoke free, and chances are, if you smoke, you don't have the wind to keep up on this hunts anyway. This can be a demanding hunt, taking you though deep woods, up low ridges, over streams, through pine groves — in short, when you're in the deep Maine woods, you're on the move, traipsing through cedar swamps, up knobs, and through thick brush. It's also prime deer country. Do it right, have your gun ready, and you'll have a chance at a buck. If you don't keep up, or get tired and down, your hunt might as well be over for the day.

Pinkham hunts some fine whitetail country. A look at his brochure or photo album at the lodge will have you convinced about the huge whitetails that inhabit this part of Maine. The deep woods here contain a well-balanced whitetail herd. The bucks often go large, over 200 pounds, and carry racks of 8- to 10-points. Then it's a matter of intercepting them — no small task, although staying at a top-notch lodge such as Pinkham's can sure give you an edge.

At Sunset Ridge, Pinkham and his crew try to create a comfortable atmosphere for clients who stay in the lodge or in the rustic log cabins on the lake. The lodge offers a game room to relax, electric heat, hot showers and the best in home-cooked meals. And as already mentioned, the lodge and the hunts are smoke-free.

Vital Statistics

THE LODGE:

3 guest rooms, 12 beds total

SERVICES: Telephone, fax, copying, TV

GUN HUNTS: $850 / 6-day hunt

PAYMENT: Cash, credit cards

CONFERENCE GROUPS: Yes

MEAL PLANS: All meals included

NEAREST AIRPORT: Bangor, ME

TRANSPORTATION TO LODGE (40 miles): Rental car; van from lodge at no additional cost

CONTACT:

Ben or Starr Pinkham
Sunset Ridge Lodge & Outfitters
158 Sunset Drive
Sebec, ME 04481
Ph: 207/564-3559
Fax: 207/564-3643
Email:info@sunsetridgeoutfitters.com
Web: www.sunsetridgeoutfitters.com

THE HUNT:

SEASON:

• bow: October

• rifle: November

• muzzleloader: December

BEST TIME TO HUNT: Anytime

TERRAIN: Mountains, swamps, fields, hardwood and softwood forests

LAND: Own and lease a total of 8,000 acres

DRAW BLOOD POLICY? Yes; depends on hit

HUNTING METHODS: Stand hunting (lock-ons, wooden), still-hunting, calling, rattling, ATV

YEARS IN BUSINESS: 30

STAFF OF GUIDES: 2

HUNTERS SERVED BY EACH GUIDE: 4

NONHUNTER CHARGE: Half the price of guided hunt

LICENSES: Over the counter (available 2 miles from lodge)

GAME CARE: Dress, package, freeze and ship for approximately $125

OTHER ACTIVITIES: Other big game hunting (bear, bob-cat, moose), bird hunting (ruffed grouse), water-fowling, fishing, boating, canoeing, golf, hiking, swimming, whitewater rafting, wildlife photography

Western Mountain Hunter's Service

Temple, Maine

WESTERN MOUNTAIN Hunter's Service, located in west-central Maine, sits in some of the finest deer country in the Northeast. The surrounding area has a good mix of deep woods and overgrown farmland. Unlike areas of northern Maine that have primarily spruce and fir forests, the west-central region abounds in hardwoods such as oak and beech, food staples of deer.

For the past several years, the Maine Department of Fisheries and Wildlife has maintained a bucks-only law in an effort to improve the quality of the deer herd. Doe hunting is allowed by lottery permit only. During this period, Western Mountain Hunter's Service has accepted deer hunters on a very limited basis. As a result, the deer herd in the area has made a strong comeback. The mountains around Western Mountain's camp now hold many heavy-bodied bucks with trophy-sized racks. Bucks, many in excess of 200 pounds field-dressed, are not uncommon.

New this year is an outpost camp. Its remote location and close proximity to the hunting areas make an ideal setup for do-it-yourselfers. Accommodations are warm and dry with comfortable beds, wood heat, gaslights and hot shower.

Hunters planning to hunt Western Mountain should pack for a variety of weather conditions, as November temperatures can range from unusual hot spells that can sometimes soar into the 80s, down to below 0°F. Items to bring include a warm sleeping bag, rifle and gun case (don't forget your bullets: 30-06, 270 and 7mm are especially popular), appropriate clothing (pack layers so you can add if it's cold, shed if it's warm; good thermal long johns are a must), gloves and warm hat, rain gear, a reliable flashlight with extra batteries, binoculars in the 7x24 or 8x30 range, comfortable worn-in boots, and a hunting license from your state of residence (don't forget!).

Vital Statistics

THE LODGE:

Lodge contains 3 guest rooms, 20 beds total, no private baths; outpost camp is also available

GUN HUNTS: $600 / week

PAYMENT: Cash, check

CONFERENCE GROUPS: Yes

MEAL PLANS: All meals included

NEAREST AIRPORT: Bangor, ME

TRANSPORTATION TO LODGE (90 miles): Rental car

CONTACT:

Ron Rackliff
Western Mountain Hunter's Service
245 Temple Road
Temple, ME 04984
Ph: 207/778-3987
Fax: 207/778-0211

THE HUNT:

SEASON:

- rifle: November

- muzzleloader: October

BEST TIME TO HUNT: Anytime is good, though the rut occurs in mid-November

TERRAIN: Woods and farmland

LAND: 30,000 acres (owned, leased and public land)

DRAW BLOOD POLICY? No

HUNTING METHODS: Stand hunting (lock-ons and wooden stands), still-hunting, rattling; ATVs are sometimes used to access stands or hunting areas

YEARS IN BUSINESS: 32

STAFF OF GUIDES: 2

HUNTERS SERVED BY EACH GUIDE: Depends on group size, preferences

NONHUNTER CHARGE: $300

LICENSES: Over the counter before arriving

GAME CARE: Dress, package and freeze game for no additional charge

OTHER ACTIVITIES: Other big game hunting (bear over bait or with hounds, moose), bird hunting (grouse, woodcock), waterfowl hunting, fishing (trout), wildlife photography

Cold River Ranch

Tupper Lake, New York

Whitetail hunting in the Adirondack Mountains of New York State is bound to evoke images of still-hunting deep in the big woods from a spike camp each day, a compass and topo map your only guides. There's nothing wrong with that definition of eastern adventure, but now there's something new and quite different: packtrain hunting!

This decidedly western twist on northeastern hunting has you riding through some of the most rugged, wildest country this side of the Front Range. Hunters set out from the Cold River Ranch in Tupper Lake (in the northern reaches of six-million-acre Adirondack Park) for a 14-mile ride into a camp consisting of a dining tent, a 16- by 25-foot guest tent, and a geodesic supply tent. The area holds not only big-bodied Adirondack deer that have rarely seen humans, but a large black bear population as well. It's an isolated outdoor experience that's tough to find in this part of the country.

Run by veteran guide John Fontana, who has more than 30 years experience guiding hunters through the region, the horseback hunt is one that every serious deer hunter should try. Just make sure you pack for a variety of conditions, as cold weather and snow can come early to this part of the world. If it does, you can always opt to stay at the ranch itself, hunt on foot each day on the millions of acres of public land at Fontana's doorstep, then head back to the lodge for a comfortable bed.

Riding horses out to Cold River Ranch's outpost camp is sure to be a hunting experience not soon forgotten.

Vital Statistics

THE LODGE:

Lodge has 12 guest rooms that share a common bath; camp has 6 beds

SERVICES: Telephone, fax, copying, TV, laundry

GUN HUNTS:

• lodge: $41 / day, no dinner

• camp: $160 / day, full service

PAYMENT: Credit cards, check

CONFERENCE GROUPS: No

MEAL PLANS: Breakfast and lunch at the lodge, three meals a day at the camp

NEAREST AIRPORT: Lake Clear, NY

TRANSPORTATION TO LODGE (16 miles): Van from lodge, no additional charge

CONTACT:

John Fontana
Cold River Ranch
Rt. 3 Coreys
Tupper Lake, NY 12986
Phone: 518/359-7559
Fax: 518/359-9761

THE HUNT:

SEASON:

• bow: Sept. 27 - Oct. 20

• rifle: Oct. 21 - Dec. 3

• muzzleloader: Oct. 14 - 20

BEST TIME TO HUNT: Anytime

TERRAIN: Mixed hardwoods, mountains, swamps

LAND: More than half a million acres of public land

DRAW BLOOD POLICY? No

HUNTING METHODS: Stand hunting, still-hunting, rattling

YEARS IN BUSINESS: 30

STAFF OF GUIDES: 2

HUNTERS SERVED BY EACH GUIDE: Varies

NONHUNTER CHARGE: Same as hunter

LICENSES: Over the counter

GAME CARE: No

OTHER ACTIVITIES: Bird hunting, waterfowling, fishing, biking, boating, canoeing, hiking, skiing, wildlife photography, horseback riding

C.P.'s Guiding Service

Richfield Springs, New York

C.P.'S REMOTE WILDERNESS whitetail deer hunts take place in the Adirondack Mountains in northern New York. The walled-tent camp is approximately a five-hour drive from New York City. It's located in Hamilton County, the heart of the Adirondacks, which has a long history of producing some of the finest whitetail deer trophies in the state. Some of the bucks taken annually in this area weigh 300 pounds live weight, with trophy racks to match. The camp is located several miles by air from the nearest road and is accessible by boat only (a six-mile ride from the launching ramp). For a hunter looking for a true wilderness hunt, going one-on-one with big woods whitetails, this is the place! Add this to the fact that the area's whitetail deer population has been growing due to mild winters and limited hunting pressure, and this is a win-win situation for anyone willing to rough it a bit.

For bowhunters, C.P.'s offers one bowhunt out of a southern zone camp that is timed for the peak of the rut. Hunters stay at the Chyle Country Inn, just 20 minutes from historic Cooperstown, New York, home of the baseball hall of fame. A beautiful Greek Gothic revival built in the mid-1800s and recently remodeled, the Inn has private suites with two spacious bedrooms, living room with French doors and hardwood floors, an elegant dining room, full kitchen, private baths, and private entrances — a perfect place to relax after a hard day afield. The hunt takes place on privately-owned and managed land. The southern deer herd is also in excellent condition due to the mild winters and abundance of corn, alfalfa and clover grown in the area.

Hunters planning to take a trip to upstate New York should pack a variety of clothing, as weather is totally unpredictable. One year it will be in the high 70s during deer season; the next, it will be down to 0°F. Good raingear is a must, as are boots that are at least 800 mil thickness. Gloves, warm hats, and layered clothing should complete your clothing lineup.

Vital Statistics

THE LODGE:

2 guest rooms, 8 beds total

SERVICES: TV, laundry

GUN HUNTS: $450 / 3-day hunt

PAYMENT: Cash only

CONFERENCE GROUPS: No

MEAL PLANS: All meals included (breakfasts include eggs, sausages, muffins, tea, coffee and juice; lunches consist of hamburgers, cold cuts and salads; dinners feature roast beef, chicken, pork, salads, home baked desserts)

NEAREST AIRPORT: Albany, NY

TRANSPORTATION TO LODGE (one hour): Rental car

CONTACT:

Chris Palumbo
C.P.'s Guiding Service
574 County Highway 29
Richfield Springs, NY 13439
Ph: 315/858-2958
Web:
www.biggamehuntingny.com/deer_hunting.htm

THE HUNT:

SEASON:

• bow: Sept. - Nov.

• gun: Oct. 21 - Dec. 2

• muzzleloader: Dec.

BEST TIME TO HUNT: Mid-November is the peak of the rut

TERRAIN: Mix of rolling hills, ridges and hard woods

LAND: Own and lease 3,000 acres

DRAW BLOOD POLICY? No

HUNTING METHODS: Stand hunting (tripods and lock-ons with full swivel seats), still-hunting, calling, rattling

YEARS IN BUSINESS: 11

STAFF OF GUIDES: 2

HUNTERS SERVED BY EACH GUIDE: 4

NONHUNTER CHARGE: Full charge

LICENSES: Over the counter or by mail before arrival

GAME CARE: Field-dressing; taxidermy can be arranged

OTHER ACTIVITIES: Other big game hunting (bear, coyotes), bird hunting, fishing

D.C. Outdoor Adventures

Farmingville, New York

ENNIS CARACCIOLO is sort of an outdoors-man jack of all trades — and a good one at that. Depending upon the time of year, he can take you just about anywhere in New York State and show you excellent fishing or hunting. You want trout or bass in fresh water? He'll take you upstate or to some secret ponds he has lined up on Long Island. How about salt water? He'll get his charterboat ready, and take you out on the Atlantic for tuna, striped bass, bluefish or sharks. Small game? He knows where to find pheasants, rabbits and grouse. Turkey? In spring or fall, he'll take you to spots in the mountains that are loaded with birds. And for whitetails, he can take you bow or rifle hunting to the Finger Lakes region (Otsego County) or the Adirondacks (Hamilton County) for big bucks, or for shotgun and archery hunts on Long Island. Whatever your preference, Caracciolo can make it happen.

Accommodations depend, of course, on where you are. The lodging for the Otsego hunt consists of two trailers situated one mile up a hardwood-covered mountain; it's a remote setting where you bring your own food and water. Clients who don't like camping can stay at local motels down the road. The Adirondack hunts are in remote areas where Caracciolo and his guides set up camp using tents or lean-tos. The Long Island hunts are based out of local motels (with good restaurants nearby).

Success rates have been running 50 percent for bucks and 90 percent for does. (The state average is 12 percent for bucks and 25 percent for does.) D.C. Outdoor Adventures takes no more than 10 hunters per given day. They hunt prime private property on Long Island and in Otsego County, and state wilderness areas in the Adirondacks. Hunters staying at the Otsego camp enjoy delicious home-cooked meals. At D.C.'s, it all depends on what you want to do.

Vital Statistics

THE LODGE (UPSTATE):

Accommodations are in lodge, rustic cabins, trailer, tent or motel; main lodge has 10 beds total, no private baths

SERVICES: TV at lodge

HUNTS:

• $400 / 3-day rifle hunt, lodging included

• $240 / 3-day hunt without lodging (clients stay at a motel)

PAYMENT: Cash, money orders

MEAL PLANS: All meals included (breakfasts include pancakes, scrambled eggs, sausage, bacon; lunch is cold cuts, hot soup and sandwiches; dinners feature steaks, chicken cutlets, salads, rice and noodles)

Special Diets: Heart healthy, salt/msg free

Nearest Airports: McArthur, Kennedy, LaGuardia, NY

Transportation to Lodge (250 miles): Rental car; van from lodge ($80)

CONTACT:

Capt. Dennis Caracciolo
D.C. Outdoor Adventures
PO Box 682
Farmingville, NY 11738
Ph: 631/451-1941
Email: dcooutdooradvent@webtv.net
Web: www.huntfishny.com

THE HUNT:

SEASONS:

• bow: October 15 - November 19

• rifle: November 20 - December 14

• muzzleloader: December 15 - 20

BEST TIME TO HUNT: November 20 - 29

TERRAIN: Hardwood forests, flat hilltops with thick cover; treestands overlook active trails, travel routes and escape routes

LAND: Own 150 acres, access to more than 1,000 acres

DRAW BLOOD POLICY? No

HUNTING METHODS: Stand hunting (ground blinds, permanent wooden stands, climbing stands), drives, calling, rattling

YEARS IN BUSINESS: 6

STAFF OF GUIDES: Owner

HUNTERS SERVED BY EACH GUIDE: Up to 3

NONHUNTER CHARGE: One-half of regular rate

LICENSES: Over the counter or by mail

GAME CARE: Dress, package, freeze and ship game, no extra charge

Other Activities: Turkey hunting, bird hunting (woodcock, grouse), waterfowling, fishing, bird watching, boating, canoeing, hiking

BOONE AND CROCKETT

• B&C book bucks taken from property: 0

• Average B&C score: 175

• B*C bucks from this part of state: 5

HWC Guide Service

Stamford, New York

I F YOU WANT TO KNOW about HWC Guide Service, you have to go straight to the source: owner/operator/guide Hank Cioccari.

"I concentrate on the average bowhunter," Cioccari says, talking about his hunting operation. "Our rates are relatively low compared to other higher priced plantation type hunts. Our policy at HWC Guide Service is strictly fair chase."

While Cioccari doesn't lodge hunters, he does arrange for them to stay at comfortable, clean and affordable motels and hotels in the area. You will be guided to a predetermined location in the early morning hours by Cioccari, who does extensive scouting in the area before the season begins. Most hunts take place on state forest lands, which consist of mixed hardwoods, rolling hills and ridges, and on the fringes of local farmlands.

"Every deer taken with a bow is a trophy," he concludes. "That's what I strive for. We do have monster bucks in this region, but they are few and far between. But there are many, many deer . . ." and hunters have a good chance of getting one during their hunt with Cioccari.

HWC is based about three hours northwest of New York City, in the northwestern part of the Catskill Mountains. Cioccari hunts land in Schoharie, Delaware, Chenango and Otsego counties, plus has access to some prime tracts close to New York City, in bowhunting-only Westchester County. Cioccari advises bow hunters to book early for these hunts, as they are very limited. Prices include lodging and guide service.

"I just want to add that if you're an average type of hunter who has not had much luck hunting deer with a bow or gun, call me!" says Cioccari. "We are catering to you! We do not guarantee the weather or the hunt, but we do guarantee a good time." And a solid effort.

Vital Statistics

THE LODGE:

No accommodations on the properties; guests stay at local motels and hotels

SERVICES: Telephone, fax, copying, TV

GUN HUNTS: $450 / person / 2-day hunt (includes lodging)

PAYMENT: Cash or check

CONFERENCE GROUPS: Yes

MEAL PLANS: Breakfast and lunch only; guests eat dinner at local restaurants

NEAREST AIRPORT: Albany, NY

TRANSPORTATION TO LODGE (depends on which area hunted; usually about an hour): Rental car, or Cioccari will pick you up at no additional charge

CONTACT:

Hank Cioccari
HWC Guide Service
25 Roosevelt Ave.
Stamford, NY 12167
Ph: 607/652-8049
Email: cioccari58@aol.com
Web: www.homestead.com/HWCGUIDE/index.html

THE HUNT:

SEASON:

• bow: Sept. 27 - Dec. 31 (varies depending on area)

• rifle: Nov. 15 - Dec. 12

• muzzleloader: Oct. 13 - 20, Dec. 12 - 18

BEST TIME TO HUNT: Mornings and evenings, especially during the rut

TERRAIN: Mostly old farmlands and state forest lands (mixed hardwoods)

LAND: Approximately 2,000 acres in 5 different counties

DRAW BLOOD POLICY? No

HUNTING METHODS: Stand hunting (lock-ons, wooden platforms, semi-enclosed blinds), drives, still-hunting, calling, rattling

YEARS IN BUSINESS: 4

STAFF OF GUIDES: None

HUNTERS SERVED BY EACH GUIDE: 2

NONHUNTER CHARGE: No

LICENSES: Over the counter

GAME CARE: Dress, package, freeze and ship game (extra charge)

OTHER ACTIVITIES: Turkey hunting

Lucky Star Ranch

Chaumont, New York

O RIGINALLY GAINING FAME AS a sprawling exotic hunting preserve featuring fallow deer, red stag, mouflon sheep and Russian wild boar, Lucky Star Ranch has been moving more and more toward white-tailed deer hunting. Today, it offers hunting for whitetails on both a preserve and a free-ranging area. The enclosure itself is 2,700 acres, while the area surrounding the preserve is almost 2,000 acres. Thanks to an intense management program featuring controlled genetics and superior nutrition, many prime whitetail bucks are taken each year from both sectors, with many weighing more than 200 pounds. The area outside the preserve produced two New York State big buck records, in the 1976 and 1988 seasons. Both bucks scored high enough to make the prestigious Boon and Crockett record book, the 1976 buck scoring 173 and the 1988 buck scoring 176.

This is classic whitetail hunting, with most of it done from comfortable, heated, European-style shooting houses that overlook deer trails leading into and out of bedding areas and social areas. The terrain is typical upstate New York/New England, with mixed hardwood forests, open fields, swamps, and rolling terrain. Shots can be anywhere from 25 to 250 yards.

The lodge itself is unique, decorated with antique European furniture brought over when Baron Josef Kerckerinck bought the sprawling ranch 23 years ago. Add the engaging atmosphere to the first-rate cuisine, and you've got a very special hunting establishment.

© Peter Fiduccia

Markus Wilhelm proudly displays the magnificent 10-pointer he took while visitng Lucky Star Ranch.

Vital Statistics

THE LODGE:

Main lodge and separate hunting lodge contain10 beds total, some private baths

SERVICES: Telephone, fax, copying, TV, laundry, Internet

HUNTS: Outside of fence: $250 / person / day. No trophy fees — only a $300 charge for transporting animal to cooler. Inside of fence: $3,750 for 3-day hunt, including meals and rooms, for bucks up to 149 points; $5,750 for bucks 150 and up.

PAYMENT: Cash, credit cards, checks

MEAL PLANS: All meals included (dinners feature pheasant, steaks, chicken)

SPECIAL DIETS: Heart healthy, vegetarian, salt/msg free

NEAREST AIRPORT: Syracuse, NY

TRANSPORTATION TO LODGE (80 miles): Rental car; can arrange pickup for $20 round-trip

CONTACT:

Josef Kerckerinck
Lucky Star Ranch
13240 Lucky Star Road
Chaumont, NY 13622
Ph: 315/649-5519
Fax: 315/649-3097
Email: lucky@luckystarranch.com
Web: www.luckystarranch.com

THE HUNT:

SEASONS:

• rifle/bow/muzzleloader seasons outside the fence concur with regular New York deer seasons

• inside fence season runs Sept.1 - Dec. 31

BEST TIME TO HUNT: Anytime

TERRAIN: Forest, open fields, swamps, mostly flat terrain

LAND: 4,500 private acres

DRAW BLOOD POLICY? No

HUNTING METHODS: Stand hunting (some seats approximately 8' off the ground, some ground blinds), still-hunting, rattling

YEARS IN BUSINESS: 5

STAFF OF GUIDES: 3

HUNTERS SERVED BY EACH GUIDE: 1

NONHUNTER CHARGE: Yes, room and meals

LICENSES: Over the counter (if required)

GAME CARE: Field dressing is $50 - $100 for caping and quartering; shipping extra

OTHER ACTIVITIES: Other big game hunting (exotics, turkeys), bird hunting, waterfowling, fishing, antiquing, bird watching, boating, golf, hiking, skiing, swimming, tennis, whitewater rafting, wildlife photography

BOONE AND CROCKETT

• B&C book bucks taken from property: 2

• Average B&C score: 125 - 150

• B&C bucks from this part of state: n/a

Middle Earth Expeditions

Lake Placid, New York

ALTHOUGH NEW YORK CITY is only a four hour-drive down the New York State Thruway, many urban residents have no idea what sprawling Adirondack Park has to offer. All the better for those who do know. With more than 6 million acres of public land (the largest public park in the lower 48 states), the Park is home to black bears, bobcats, moose, coyotes, and some legendary whitetails.

Budget hunters can go it on their own by staying at one of many state campgrounds throughout the park. Be warned, however — this is big country, and it's easy to get turned around. If your woods skills are a bit rough, or if you just don't have time to get into the woods and do the type of pre-season scouting you should, play it safe and call Wayne Failing of Middle Earth Expeditions. Failing has been guiding bow and rifle hunters in the Lake Placid area for more than 15 years, and his reputation for putting hunters onto good-sized bucks is legendary. For $150 per day or less, he'll lead deer hunters into prime buck country in the mornings, and then put them up at one of his eight rustic cabins at night.

© Middle Earth Expeditions

Wayne Failing (left) with a successful hunter.

His lodge — the Mt. Hoevenberg Bed & Breakfast (the bobsled run was on Mt. Hoevenberg in the 1980 Winter Olympics) — can handle up to 28 sportsmen a day, which is not many when you consider the huge territory being hunted. Black bear season starts the third Saturday in September and runs into December, while the whitetail season starts on the third Saturday in October, and goes into early December. For a chance at a big buck, Wayne Failing will give you as good a shot as you're likely to get.

*Mt. Van Hoevenberg Bed & Breakfast is where you'll stay
when visiting Middle Earth Expeditions.*

Vital Statistics

THE LODGE:

8 rustic cabins and the main farmhouse lodge contain 21 beds total

SERVICES: Telephone, TV, sauna

HUNTS: Range from $75 / day for 4-on-1 guided hunt to $250 / day for 1-on-1; lodging is extra

PAYMENT: Cash, credit cards, check

CONFERENCE GROUPS: Yes

MEAL PLANS: Breakfast in farm house (includes pancakes and sausage, bacon and eggs, omelets, French toast, juice, coffee, fruit); guests cook other meals in cabins

NEAREST AIRPORT: Lake Clear, NY (15 miles) or Burlington, VT (75 miles)

TRANSPORTATION TO LODGE: Rental car

THE HUNT:

SEASON:

- bow: third Saturday in Sept. to second Friday in Oct.

- muzzleloader: second Saturday in Oct. to third Friday in Oct.

- rifle: third Saturday in Oct. to first Sunday in Dec.

BEST TIME TO HUNT: Mid-November

TERRAIN: Hardwood forests, high mountains, and swamps

LAND: Approximately 2.5 million acres of public land — very little hunting pressure

DRAW BLOOD POLICY? No

HUNTING METHODS: Stand hunting (metal ladder stands or fixed wooden stands or blinds), drives, still-hunting, calling, rattling

YEARS IN BUSINESS: 22

STAFF OF GUIDES: Failing guides everyone

HUNTERS SERVED BY EACH GUIDE: 1 - 4; Failing takes out each party, who

determine the size

NONHUNTER CHARGE: Same as hunter

LICENSES: Over the counter

GAME CARE: Facilities are available for hunters to do it on their own, or a local butcher will butcher and package deer for a fee

OTHER ACTIVITIES: Other big game hunting (black bear, coyotes), fishing, antiquing, biking, bird watching, canoeing, golf, hiking, skiing, whitewater rafting, wildlife photography

CONTACT:

Wayne Failing
Middle Earth Expeditions
Rt. 73, HCR 01, Box 37
Lake Placid, NY 12946
Ph: 518/523-7172
Email: Wayne2@northnet.org
Web: www.adkhunting.com

North Country Outdoor Adventures

Carthage, New York

NORTH COUNTRY Outdoor Adventures is a small operation, with one hunting cabin located in the Adirondack foothills in Lewis County, approximately 15 miles from the village of Croghan. The cabin has two bedrooms, living room and a kitchen, and can accommodate four clients at a time. There is no electricity, so the cabin operates on propane appliances and lights, along with woodstove heat. All meals are provided in camp by the guide, and clients are asked when booking what they prefer to eat.

Hunting conditions in this area vary during whitetail season. In October you will usually encounter warm days with cool nights. In November, you should expect to hunt in snow at any time. Tracking conditions can never be guaranteed, but it's an unusual season if you don't have snow by November 15. Snow depths can get to a couple of feet by mid-December.

North Country hunts both private and public land. Being located on the deer-rich foothills of the Adirondacks, they have access to approximately 75,000 acres of public hunting lands within just a short distance from camp. The terrain is mostly rolling hills of mixed hardwoods with numerous old logging roads and ridges. Elevations vary from 400 to 3,000 feet, depending on the area hunted. Guests also hunt on several farms along the Black River Valley in the Lowville area where you'll find a mixture of agricultural fields, hardwood forests and swamps. The terrain is relatively flat, with occasional rolling hills.

For hunters who would like to try a different type of hunt, North Country also offers a fly-in to a wilderness camp set up with an outfitters tent. This is more for the hunter who likes to be isolated and rough it. North Country owner Alan Queary works with Adirondack pilots who will fly to certain lakes, drop off hunters and gear, then come and pick them up at the end of their stay. Trips last from three to seven days, with prices varying according to length of stay.

And the bucks? There are big one is these hills, and finding them is mostly a matter of patterning their movements, then setting up a stand at the right place. November is usually very productive, although with light hunting pressure, your chances of success are equally good throughout any week of the season. If you are looking for bigger racks, head to the more remote sections for your best chances. The lower rate of buck harvest results in an overall older age of bucks living in remote regions, which means more trophy antlers. Hunting tactics include stand hunting, still-hunting and deer drives, all of which are very productive.

Vital Statistics

THE LODGE:

Cabin has 2 guest rooms, 4 beds total, no private baths

SERVICES: Telephone, TV

HUNTS:

- $125 / day / person
- $325 / 3-day hunts
- $500 / 5-day hunts
- fly-in hung: add cost of meals and airplane

PAYMENT: Cash, checks

MEAL PLANS: All meals included (breakfast includes omelets, hash browns, pancakes, scrambled eggs, cereal; lunch consists of sandwiches, soups, chili, macaroni and cheese; dinner means huge helpings of lasagna, beef stew, turkey, fettuccine, spaghetti and beef stroganoff, vegetables and desserts)

SPECIAL DIETS: Call in advance

NEAREST AIRPORT: Syracuse, NY

TRANSPORTATION TO LODGE (100 miles): Rental car, van from lodge ($25)

CONTACT:

Alan Queary
North Country Outdoor Adventures
9 Madison Street
Carthage, NY 13619
Ph: 315/346-6763

THE HUNT:

SEASONS:

- bow: Oct 1 - first day of rifle season (though you can also use a bow during rifle season)
- rifle: next to last Sat. in Oct. - first Sun. in Dec.
- muzzleloader: 7 days before and 7 days after regular rifle season

BEST TIME TO HUNT: Anytime, as the bucks are unpressured

TERRAIN: A mixture of rolling hills, hardwood forests, farmlands and swamps

LAND: Lease approximately 1,000 acres; also hunt public lands (75,000 acres)

DRAW BLOOD POLICY? No

HUNTING METHODS: Stand hunting (portable lock-on stands, wooden stands), drives, still-hunting, calling, rattling

YEARS IN BUSINESS: 3

STAFF OF GUIDES: Lodge owner is a registered guide

HUNTERS SERVED BY EACH GUIDE: 1 - 2

NONHUNTER CHARGE: Cost of food and lodging

LICENSES: Over the counter

GAME CARE: Dress, package, freeze and ship game for clients

OTHER ACTIVITIES: Other big game hunting (black bear, turkey), bird hunting (grouse, woodcock), fishing (trout, bass, pike, walleyes), boating, canoeing, hiking, wildlife photography

Northwoods Wilderness Guide Service

Schroon Lake, New York

I MAGINE YOU ARE ALONE in the dark on a clear, frosty morning in late fall. Your guide has just left you on stand for the morning hunt. Gradually, the sky begins to lighten in the East and the woods start to come alive with the sounds of a new day. Distant forms begin to take shape as the sun rises. The forest floor is frosty and leaves crunch beneath your boots; you dare not move. Shortly after sunrise, a twig snaps to your right. As if by magic, three does appear at a stream crossing. You watch intently. Two does cross the stream, but the third pauses to watch her backtrack. Suddenly, out of nowhere, there he is, in all his woodland glory! Your eyes cannot believe the antlers, with bases as thick as your wrists. With his neck swelled from lust, his nose to the ground, he steps clear of the brush to cross the stream. Without realizing it, the gun is to your shoulder and he is in your sights, as you squeeze the trigger on the dream of a lifetime. This is Adirondack deer hunting!

Come to the East's most magnificent wilderness area — the Adirondack Mountains — for the supreme whitetail hunting challenge. You can hunt with the firearm of your choice — muzzleloader, long gun, bow or handgun. The Adirondacks contain some of the largest whitetails in the East, with a good number of big bucks in the 200-plus-pound class. Most of these deer are rarely hunted; much less have ever seen a human being. Chances for a good rack and a record-book deer are excellent. All Northwoods hunts are in wilderness areas, in the true Adirondack tradition.

The Adirondack hunting experience is not for the faint of heart. The hunt here is rugged, with numerous hardwood ridges, thick cedar swamps, and brushy streams to tramp through. The weather can be warm and sunny, or change quickly to below freezing with heavy snow. This is remote deer hunting.

The area hunted by Northwoods Wilderness is the 36,000-acre Hoffman Notch Wilderness area, just outside the village of Schroon Lake. Hoffman Notch has elevations from 1,200 to almost 4,000 feet. The terrain is rugged and dense, containing an excellent variety of deer habitat. Virtually trailless, there is an excellent whitetail population in this rugged region. Of all the Adirondack counties, Essex County has the highest trophy buck take in the state. Lodging is at the Northwoods camp in Schroon Lake.

Vital Statistics

THE LODGE:

2 guest rooms, 4 beds total, no private baths

SERVICES: Telephone, TV, laundry

GUN HUNTS:

- $400 / 3-day hunt
- $500 / 4-day hunt
- $600 / 5-day hunt (per person)

PAYMENT: Cash, personal/company check

MEAL PLANS: All meals included (dinner entrees usually consist of but are not limited to beef, pork, chicken, venison, pasta, veggies, potatoes, breads, pies, cakes)

SPECIAL DIETS: Heart healthy; salt/msg free; can accommodate hunter requests

NEAREST AIRPORT: Albany, NY

TRANSPORTATION TO LODGE (100 miles): Van from lodge (no additional cost); rental car

CONTACT:

John Huston
Northwoods Wilderness Guide Service
Box 805
Schroon Lake, NY 12870
Ph: 518/899-6880

THE HUNT:

SEASON:

- bow: Sept. 27 - Friday before rifle season
- rifle: third Saturday in Oct. - first Sunday in Dec.
- muzzleloader: one week before rifle season

BEST TIME TO HUNT: Usually from Election Day to the end of December

TERRAIN: Cedar swamps at 1,000 feet or high mountain ridges at 4,000 feet

LAND: Owned and state land

DRAW BLOOD POLICY: n/a

HUNTING METHODS: Stand hunting (natural ground blinds), drives, still-hunting, calling, rattling

YEARS IN BUSINESS: 16

STAFF OF GUIDES: No

HUNTERS SERVED BY EACH GUIDE: 1 - 3

NONHUNTER CHARGE: Yes; food and lodging

LICENSES: Over the counter before arriving at the lodge

GAME CARE: n/a

OTHER ACTIVITIES: Other hunting (spring turkey, rabbits, grouse); brook, brown and rainbow trout fishing (canoe and floatplane trips); nature and photography day-hikes

BOONE AND CROCKETT

- B&C book bucks taken from property: Unknown
- Average B&C score: Unknown
- B&C bucks from this part of state: 18

Outback Outfitter Guiding Service

C o c h e c t o n ,   N e w   Y o r k

ROBERT SAUER-JONES hunts the sprawling, extremely remote 108,500-acre Siamese Ponds Wilderness Area, located in the Adirondack towns of Johnsburg, Thurman, Wells, Lake Pleasant and Indian Lake in Hamilton and Warren counties. The topography is generally low rolling hills with a few mountain summits reaching the 3,000- to 4000-foot elevation level. It is estimated that there are seven to 12 deer per square mile in the Siamese Pond Wilderness Area. The region offers a unique hunting experience: hunters who are willing (and able) to walk deep into the terrain are unlikely to see another hunter and may get an opportunity to harvest a deep-woods trophy buck. Bucks of nine points or better are commonly taken in this part of the Adirondacks. Such bucks usually don't see people all year, and are generally going about their natural, unpressured routines when hunting season opens. This is fun, classic hunting, where you have to figure out where the deer are going, and what they are doing, in order to be successful. As opposed to having to figure out what pressured deer are going to do (where they will head to escape other hunters), this wilderness hunting demands that you know a lot about the deer, and that you are able to recognize signs and interpret them.

The area has a good supply of beechnuts and acorns, which offer ample food for the deer and for the growing black bear population. Hunters should check heavy mast areas for best chances of success. Mountaintops in particular are good spots to still-hunt, especially in the warm early season as the cooler altitude makes them attractive to deer. When the rut is on, big bucks can be almost anywhere as they intensify their search for does throughout the open woods. Find the does and chances are you won't have to wait too long before you find a buck as well.

If you like deep-woods wilderness hunting, and if you like to rough it a bit, then this hunt is for you. You leave your tent camp early in the morning, and head to areas where whitetails are known to frequent. Moving through hardwood forests or climbing slowly up the sides of ridges, you have to creep along, still-hunting ever so slowly. With each step, you pause and carefully scan your surroundings. A glint of an antler, a horizontal line in the woods (denoting a deer's back), perhaps a quick movement from a flicking ear — it's the alert hunter who knows what to look for, and who will be ready when the moment arrives.

If you get a buck, your season isn't over in the Adirondacks. The region has excellent grouse hunting, and fishing in the Siamese Wilderness is spectacular.

*Remote camping and hunting in the
Siamese Pond Wilderness Area are Outback Outfitter's specialties.*

Vital Statistics

THE LODGE:

CAMP 1: 6 to 8 hunters can be accommodated in two 15' x 18' wall tents on Thirteenth Lake

CAMP 2: 2-bedroom house located at the base of Harvey Mt. can accomodate 6 people

GUN HUNTS:

• Guided and semi-guided hunts are available; meals and lodging included in the price

• call for price specifics

PAYMENT: Cash, credit cards

CONFERENCE GROUPS: No

MEAL PLANS: All meals included (home-cooked steaks, veggies, chicken, potatoes, desserts)

NEAREST AIRPORT: Albany, NY

TRANSPORTATION TO LODGE (100 miles): Rental car; van from lodge ($50)

THE HUNT:

SEASON:

• bow: Starts Sept. 9
• rifle: Oct. 23 - Dec. 3
• muzzleloader: Oct. 14 - 22

BEST TIME TO HUNT: Late Nov. - early Dec.

TERRAIN: Mountains up to 4,000 feet, down to flat country with swamps and mixed hardwoods

LAND: 108,503 acres in the Siamese Ponds Wilderness Area

DRAW BLOOD POLICY? No

HUNTING METHODS: Stand hunting (limited; there are lock-ons for those who want to use stands), still-hunting, calling, rattling

YEARS IN BUSINESS: 3

STAFF OF GUIDES: 3

HUNTERS SERVED BY EACH GUIDE: 2

NONHUNTER CHARGE: Hunter rate

LICENSES: Must be purchased by client before arrival

GAME CARE:
Dressing, packaging, shipping can be arranged for an additional charge

OTHER ACTIVITIES: Black bear hunting, grouse hunting, waterfowling, fishing

BOONE AND CROCKETT

• B&C book bucks taken from property: n/a

• Average B&C score: 150

• B&C bucks from this part of state: n/a

CONTACT:

Robert Sauer-Jones
Outback Outfitters Guiding Service
Adirondack Siamese Ponds
Wilderness Trips
387 New Turnpike Road
Cochecton, NY 12726
Ph: 845/932-8598
Email: outbackguide@catskill.net
Web: www.outbackoutfitter.com

Big Moore's Run Lodge Ltd

Coudersport, Pennsylvania

HAVING MORE THAN ONE MILLION WHITETAIL HUNTERS, more than one and a quarter million whitetails, and an annual kill of 350,000 deer, Pennsylvania is clearly one of the best deer hunting states in the country. And Potter County, hard by the New York border in the heart of the Alleghenies, is the state's best-known deer hunting county. With broad ridges, steep slopes, and elevations rising to more than 2500 feet, Potter is ideal whitetail habitat. Mixed hardwood forests cover most of the county.

Potter County offers hunters easy access to the many state forests and game lands in the area. This is big buck country, offering classic Pennsylvania whitetail hunting. And in the heart of it all, in sprawling Susquehannock State Forest, is Big Moore's Run, a classy, well-run lodge. Bill and Barb Haldaman have been operating the lodge for 15 years, catering to whitetail hunters in fall, turkey hunters in spring and fall, and fishermen throughout the year. In October, bowhunters are placed in tree stands not only in the state forest, but on game-rich land owned by the lodge. Once rifle season starts in late November, firearms hunters get their chances from tree stands on the first day of the hunt, and then participate in organized drives.

"These aren't really drives," stresses Haldaman. "When we push, we post our hunters in places that overlook natural escape routes. Our guides then move slowly through the woods, along game trails and through bedding areas, gently moving deer in the direction of our standers. The trick is to not alarm the deer into flight."

Big Moore books only a limited number of hunters each year, as the focus here is on quality hunting, not quantity. Last year, 65 percent of the hunters had shooting opportunities.

Clients may also shoot sporting clays, or attend the wingshooting school at Big Moore's Run; or they may choose to grab a book and relax in the lodge's comfortable living room. The log lodge is on the side of a wooded hill with a deck overlooking the lawn, lake, and Susquehannock State Forest. Guests stay in comfortable rooms with private baths. Family-style dinners include gamebirds, trout, and New York strip steaks. Big Moore's Run Lodge is Orvis endorsed.

Vital Statistics

THE LODGE:

Modern lodge has 6 rooms, 10 beds total, all with private baths

SERVICES: Telephone, fax, TV

HUNTS: $650 / 3-day hunt

PAYMENT: Cash, check, credit cards

CONFERENCE GROUPS: Yes

MEAL PLANS: All meals included, family style (includes eggs, home fries, French toast and pancakes for breakfast; bag lunches; and ham, roast beef, chicken, with vegetables and all the fixin's for dinner)

NEAREST AIRPORT: Bradford, PA

TRANSPORTATION TO LODGE (70 miles): Rental car; van from lodge ($100 round-trip)

CONTACT:

Bill or Bob Haldaman
Big Moore's Run Lodge Ltd
RD #3, BOX 204A
Coudersport, PA 16915
Ph: 866/5659-3474 (toll-free) 814/647-5300
Email: bigmoors@penn.cm
Fax: 814/647-9928
Web: www.bigmoores.com

THE HUNT:

SEASON:

• bow: early Oct. - mid-Nov.

• rifle: late Nov. - mid-Dec.

BEST TIME TO HUNT: Anytime

TERRAIN: Hardwoods and fields, ridges

LAND: Private land with easy access to 220,000-acre state forest

DRAW BLOOD POLICY? No (yes for exotic hunts on 1,500-acre preserve)

HUNTING METHODS: Stand hunting, still-hunting, drives

YEARS IN BUSINESS: 15

STAFF OF GUIDES: 4

HUNTERS SERVED BY EACH GUIDE: 4 maximum

NONHUNTER CHARGE: $148.40 (meals and lodging)

LICENSES: Over the counter

GAME CARE: Field dress only

OTHER ACTIVITIES: Other big game hunting, turkey hunting, bird watching, flyfishing, golf, hiking, nature tours, sporting clays, wildlife photography, flyfishing and wingshooting schools. The lodge recently added exotic game hunting on a 1,500-acre preserve that is available year-round with any weapon.

Paradise Outfitters

Bellwood, Pennsylvania

OVER THE PAST FIVE YEARS Paradise Outfitters has assembled a family of sporting lodges, over 10,000 acres of prime habitat, and more than six miles of private spring creeks and rivers. In this setting, guests can choose from a wide array of outdoor adventures, including whitetail deer hunting.

At Paradise, deer hunters have access to more than 2,000 acres of prime land, all surrounded by 11 miles of game-proof fencing. Yes, this is a high-fence operation, and as good a one as you'll find anywhere. Paradise operates under special permit from the state of Pennsylvania to manage its own whitetail herds. In the past three seasons, more than 30 bucks have been taken that scored more than 170 B&C. Intensive management of genetics, age, nutrition and habitat allow Paradise to grow monster bucks, and to hunt them on challenging terrain.

The whitetail habitat is in Centre and Somerset counties. An aerial view of the properties reveals a huge patchwork of a variety of habitats. Whitetails thrive in an environment of diverse habitat and terrain types, and Paradise manages its properties to provide this diversity.

About 50 percent of the property is maintained in clear-cut growth from one to 12 years. This thick, tangled terrain makes hunting extremely challenging, but that's where the biggest bucks hide. Perhaps 20 percent of the property is in small, 10- to 30-acre plots of mature hardwoods (mostly oak mixed with beech, maple and hickory). In years of abundant acorns, these hardwood stands are hotbeds of feeding activity. Ten percent of the property is open food plots — and like the mature timber stands, most of these plots are one to 20 acres and scattered around in small chunks.

The balance of the property is transition habitat of fields to clear cuts to mature plots. As you know, whitetails love to work the edges, so more than 20 miles of transition edges are maintained for optimum whitetail viewing.

The terrain itself is steep and rugged, with scores of hollows, knobs, draws and saddles. The Highlands property, in particular, is covered with boulders, cut tree-tops and thick mountain laurel.

Hunting methods vary at Paradise — it's all up to the client. Depending on your preference, you can spot and stalk, still-hunt, grunt and rattle, sit on a stump, climb into a treestand (they've got permanents and portables), watch a food plot from an elevated stand or box blind, or hunt from a ground level blind strategically placed along game trails or near a food plot. Sometimes, when the bucks refuse to move, drives are also employed.

At the end of a long day of hunting, guests retire to one of Paradise's two lodges. The first, Paradise Lodge, is built on a ridge overlooking the Bald Eagle Valley. A beautiful 12,000-square-foot cedar-sided lodge, Paradise offers sportsmen luxurious accommodations and superb cuisine. It has eight huge bedrooms, each with is own Jacuzzi and each decorated with designer touches that reflect a different part of the country. The other lodge is the Highland Lodge. Nestled in the Laurel Mountains of Somerset County, this 4,000-square-foot lodge offers all the comforts of home in a rustic retreat setting. Highlands offers a more camplike environment than Paradise. Its large 30' x 50' Gathering Room with a 24-foot-long walnut bar, huge oak estate table and massive fireplace, is the hub of activity. There are four separate bunkrooms, each with its own private bath.

With first-class accommodations, first-class dining, and first-class hunting, Paradise is truly a hunter's paradise.

Vital Statistics

THE LODGE:

8 guest rooms, 18 beds total, all with private baths

SERVICES: Telephone, fax, copying, TV, laundry

GUN HUNTS: From $2,495 - $9,900

BOW HUNTS: From $3,295 - $9,900

PAYMENT: Cash, credit cards, check

CONFERENCE GROUPS: Yes

MEAL PLANS: All meals included; hearty country style

NEAREST AIRPORT: State College, PA

TRANSPORTATION TO LODGE (15-20 minutes): Rental car; van from lodge at no additional cost

BOONE AND CROCKETT

• B&C book bucks taken from property: Many
• Average B&C score: 150
• B&C bucks from this area: n/a

THE HUNT:

SEASON:

• bow/rifle/centerfire: Sept. - mid-December

BEST TIME TO HUNT: Oct. - Nov.

TERRAIN: Mountain laurel, thick brush, woods, fields, clover

LAND: Two 1,000-acre parcels, 100% fenced

DRAW BLOOD POLICY: Yes, draw blood is a kill

HUNTING METHODS: Stand hunting, drives, still-hunting, calling, rattling

YEARS IN BUSINESS: 34

STAFF OF GUIDES: 7 - 10

HUNTERS SERVED BY EACH GUIDE: 1 - 2

NONHUNTER CHARGE: Yes; the cost of meals and lodging

LICENSES: None required

GAME CARE: Client's responsibility

OTHER ACTIVITIES: Other big game hunting, bird hunting, waterfowling, fishing, biking, bird watching, golf, hiking, skiing, wildlife photography

CONTACT:

Mike Harpster
Paradise Outfitters
P.O. Box 97
Bellwood, PA 16617
Ph: 800-282-5486
Fax: 814-742-3298
Email:
paradiseinfo@toparadise.com
Web: www.toparadise.com

Whitetail Valley

Rome, Pennsylvania

WHITETAIL VALLEY IS A MANAGED game ranch that offers trophy hunting for whitetails, elk and wild boar. This is a 400-acre high-fenced reserve that's absolutely packed with trophy-class animals. You pay for what you shoot here, with prices beginning at $2,500 for 120-to 125-class bucks, and ranging up to $15,900 for bucks over 196 B&C (yes, they're here). Ninety percent of the area is wooded. While reserve hunting is not for every hunter, the owners of Whitetail Valley pride themselves on quality animals and quality hunts. With rustic lodging available on the premise, they're confident any dream hunt can come true here.

Vital Statistics

THE LODGE:

Main lodge contains 2 guest rooms, 4 beds total, no private baths

SERVICES: n/a

HUNTS: Start at $2,500 and go up, depending on rack size

PAYMENT: Cash, credit cards, checks

MEAL PLANS: All meals included

SPECIAL DIETS: n/a

NEAREST AIRPORTS: Binghamton, NY

TRANSPORTATION TO LODGE (40 miles): Rental car; van from lodge (no extra charge)

BOONE AND CROCKETT

• B&C bucks taken from property: 6

• Average B&C score: 140

• B&C bucks from this part of state: n/a

THE HUNT:

SEASONS:

• rifle/bow/muzzleloader: September - December

BEST TIME TO HUNT: Oct. - Nov.

TERRAIN: Hardwood hills, soft woods in bottoms

LAND: 400 private acres, 90% fenced

DRAW BLOOD POLICY? Yes

HUNTING METHODS: Stand hunting (lock-ons, wooden), drives, still-hunting, calling, rattling

YEARS IN BUSINESS: 7

STAFF OF GUIDES: Owner

HUNTERS SERVED BY EACH GUIDE: 1 - 2

NONHUNTER CHARGE: No

LICENSES: No license required inside of fence

GAME CARE: Field dressing, package, freeze, ship ($.29/pound)

OTHER ACTIVITIES: Other big game hunting (elk, boar, red stag), bird hunting (chukars, pheasants), hiking, wildlife photography

CONTACT:

Mark Kuhlman
Whitetail Valley
RD2, Box 2071
Rome, PA 18837
Ph: 570/395-3667
Fax: 570/395-4196
Web: www.huntguide.com

Co-author Jay Cassell with a nice buck.

SOUTH

ALABAMA, DELAWARE, FLORIDA, GEORGIA, KENTUCKY, LOUISIANA, MISSISSIPPI, NORTH CAROLINA, SOUTH CAROLINA, TEXAS, VIRGINIA, WEST VIRGINIA

STRETCHING FROM Texas to Maryland and south to Florida, the South as defined in this book contains deer hunting of all kinds — from sprawling Texas ranches where big-racked bucks are abundant and you need to study a rack carefully before deciding to pull the trigger, to the famed Black Belt of Mississippi and Alabama where smart bucks grow big thanks to good genes and better nutrition, and north to Virginia and Maryland where hunting traditions have been in place for hundreds of years.

Where to go? It depends on the type of hunting you like. Do you prefer to stay in the lap of luxury on an old plantation in Georgia or Virginia? Or would you prefer to be on a working ranch where you really get the flavor of the area's lifestyle, as in Texas? No matter — you'll find that the South has innumerable places to choose from for different size wallets. One bonus is that many states in this region have long seasons, often stretching into January. If you're a northerner and all your hunting seasons close in December, what better way to finish your deer hunting season than by booking a mid-January hunt in Mississippi or Alabama?

Lodges

Alabama

1 BLACK WARRIOR HUNTING SERVICE
2 HAMILTON HILLS PLANTATION
3 LAKEWOOD HUNTING LODGE
4 MASTER RACK LODGE
5 PAINT ROCK VALLEY LODGE & RETREAT
6 POPE-LOCKE HUNTING PRESERVE
7 RIVER BOTTOM HUNTING LODGE
8 SOUTHERN SPORTSMAN HUNTING LODGE
9 WATER VALLEY LODGE
10 WESTERVELT LODGE
11 WHITE OAK PLANTATION

Florida

12 DIXIE WILDLIFE SAFARIS

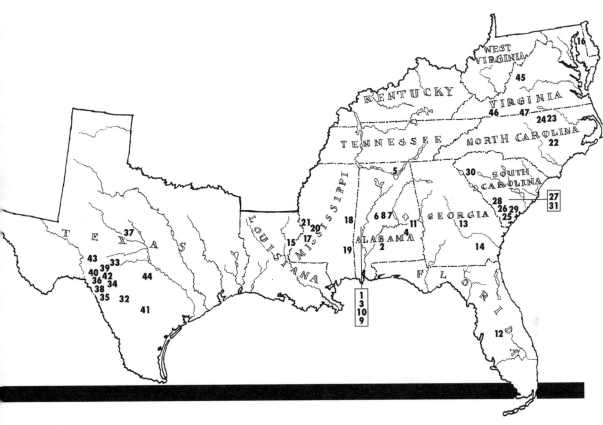

Georgia
13 BROUGHTON PLANTATION
14 GOPHER PLANTATION

Louisiana
15 GILES ISLAND HUNT CLUB

Maryland
16 SCHRADER'S HUNTING

Mississippi
17 CANEMOUNT PLANTATION
18 CIRCLE M PLANTATION
19 MCKENNA RANCH OUTFITTERS
20 ROSE HILL PLANTATION
21 TARA WILDLIFE, INC.

North Carolina
22 BUFFALO CREEK GUIDE SERVICE
23 OCCONEECHEE LODGE
24 ROANOKE TAR GUIDE SERVICE

South Carolina
25 BOSTICK PLANTATION
26 CEDAR KNOLL HUNTING LODGE
27 PARADISE VALLEY HUNTING CLUB
28 COWDEN PLANTATION
29 DEERFIELD PLANTATION
30 LITTLE RIVER PLANTATION
31 SNAKE RIVER HUNTING LODGE

Texas
32 777 RANCH INC.
33 ADOBE LODGE
34 COMMANCHE SPRING RANCH
35 DOUBLE C RANCH
36 J-BAR-C RANCH OUTFITTERS
37 TEXAS BEST OUTFITTERS
38 MORNING STAR RANCH
39 OAK KNOLL RANCH
40 RAFTER W RANCHES
41 RESERVE RANCH
42 ROBBY ROBINSON RANCHES
43 ROCKIN' J OUTFITTERS
44 Y.O. RANCH

Virginia
45 FALKLAND FARMS
46 FORT LEWIS LODGE
47 PRIMLAND RESORT

Resources

ALABAMA DEPT. OF CONSERVATION
AND NATURAL RESOURCES
Div. of Game and Fish
64 N. Union St.
Montgomery, AL 36130-1456
Ph: 334/242-3465
Fax: 334/242-3489
Web. www.dcnr.state.al.us/agfd

DELAWARE DIV. OF FISH AND
WILDLIFE
89 Kings Hwy., Box 1401
Dover, DE 19901
Ph: 302/739-5297
Web. www.dnrec.state.de.us

FLORIDA FISH AND WILDLIFE
CONSERVATION COMMISSION
620 S. Meridian St.
Tallahassee, FL 32399-1600
Ph: 850/487-3796
Web. www.state.fl.us/fwc/

GEORGIA WILDLIFE RESOURCES
DIV.
2070 U.S. Hwy 278 SE
Social Circle, GA 30025
Ph: 770/918-6400
Web. www.dnr.state.ga.us/

KENTUCKY DEPT. OF FISH
AND WILDLIFE RESOURCES
#1 Game Farm Rd.
Frankfort, KY 40601
Ph: 800/858-1549, Fax: 502/564-6508
Web. www.state.ky.us/agencies/fw/kdfwr.htm

LOUISIANA DEPT. OF WILDLIFE
AND FISHERIES
Box 98000
Baton Rouge, LA 70898-9000
Ph: 225/765-2800
Web. www.wlf.state.la.us

MARYLAND DEPT
OF NATURAL RESOURCES
Wildlife and Natural Heritage Div.
Tawes State Office Bldg.
Annapolis, MD 21401
Ph: 410/260-8582
Web. www.dnr.state.md.us

MISSISSIPPI DEPT. OF WILDLIFE,
FISHERIES AND PARKS
Box 451, Jackson, MS 39205
Ph: 601/362-9212
Web. www.mdwfp.com

NORTH CAROLINA WILDLIFE
RESOURCES COMMISSION
1701 Mail Service Center
Raleigh, NC 27699-1701
Ph: 919/733-3391
Fax: 919/733-7083
Web. www.state.nc.us/wildlife/management

SOUTH CAROLINA DEPT. OF
NATURAL RESOURCES
Div. of Wildlife and Freshwater Fisheries
Rembert C. Dennis Bldg.
Box 167
Columbia, SC 29202
Ph: 803/734-3889
Web. www.dnr.state.sc.us

TENNESSEE WILDLIFE
RESOURCES AGENCY
Box 40747
Ellington Agricultural Center
Nashville, TN 37204
Ph: 615/781-6500
Web. www.state.tn.us/twra

TEXAS PARKS AND WILDLIFE
DEPT.
4200 Smith School Rd.
Austin, TX 78744
Ph: 512/389-4800222222
Web. http://www.tpwd.state.tx.us

VIRGINIA DEPT. OF GAME
AND INLAND FISHERIES
4010 W. Broad St., Box 11104
Richmond, VA 23230-1104
Ph: 804/367-1000
Email: dgifweb@dgif.state.va.us
Web. www.dgif.state.va.us

WEST VIRGINIA DIV. OF NATURAL
RESOURCES
Building 3, Room 819
1900 Kanawha Blvd. E.
Charleston, WV 25305
Ph: 304/558-2754
Fax: 304/558-3147
Web. www.dnr.state.wv.us

Black Warrior Hunting Service

Fosters, Alabama

BLACK WARRIOR HUNTING SERVICE (BWHS) is located 20 miles south of Tuscaloosa in the rich bottom-lands of the Black Warrior River. Hardwood timber, cotton, corn, and soybeans are grown here. There is also a huge whitetail herd. The BWHS carefully manages the herd in its hunting territory — the basic principle is to kill an acceptable number of does and some bigger spikes, but to let the 4-, 6- and 8-pointers go, and to shoot only mature bucks that are 8 points and up, measuring 16 inches and wider. With this type of strict management, hunters are assured of quality deer hunts.

The BWHS has 4,000 acres of huntable property, including corn, wheat, and clover fields as well as oak flats in the hardwood timber stands. They offer very exclusive hunting to both the bowhunter and well as the rifle hunter. They also don't hunt more than eight hunters at a time, so guests don't have to worry about contending with large groups.

Two kinds of hunts are available — the bow hunt and the trophy rifle hunt. The trophy rifle hunt is for the serious deer hunter who may take one doe and one trophy buck (a trophy being 8 points or better, with a minimum measurement of 16 inches outside the ears). If you shoot anything smaller, be prepared for a fine!

BWHS also offers some of the finest bowhunting in the South. Many deer in the area would qualify for Pope and Young records. The bow season opens on October 15 and runs all the way through January, giving you the option of hunting during the pre-rut, rut, or post-rut. If you can't hunt in January in your home state, this is an excellent way of extending your hunting season.

Hunters can stay in the lodge, a hotel in town, or if they wish, they can bring motor homes and hook up near the hunting areas — whatever suits you best. The point is to get here, because the bucks run large, the hunting territory is sprawling and spacious, and if you come, you'll be guaranteed of having a quality hunt.

Vital Statistics

THE LODGE

4 guest rooms, all have private baths, 12 beds total

Services: Telephone, TV

Hunts:

- $1,480 / 4-day rifle hunt
- $850 / 3-day bowhunt

Payment: Check, cash

Meal Plans: All meals included (dinners include grilled steaks and Caesar salads, homemade French bread, pork chops, collard greens, sweet potatoes, corn bread, fried flounder or catfish, cole slaw, french fries)

Special Diets: Heart healthy, salt/msg free

Nearest Airport: Birmingham, AL

Transportation to Lodge (60 miles): Rental car

THE HUNT:

Season:

- bow: October 14 - January
- rifle: November - January

Best Time to Hunt: When the weather is clear and cold

Terrain: River bottom, hardwood forest, swamps and open farmland

Land: 4,000 acres (half owned, half rented)

Draw Blood Policy? Yes

Hunting Methods: Stand hunting (tripods and metal ladder stands)

Years in Business: 18

Staff of Guides: 1

Hunters served by each guide: 2 - 4

Nonhunter Charge: $50 / day

Licenses: Over the counter

Game Care: No

Other Activities: Turkey hunting in spring, wildlife photography

CONTACT:

Clay Wiggins
Black Warrior Hunting Service
P.O. Box 40
Fosters, AL 35463
Ph: 205/349-4889

BOONE AND CROCKETT

- B&C book bucks taken from property: 1
- Average B&C score: n/a
- B&C bucks from this part of state: 20 - 25

Hamilton Hills Plantation

M i n t e r ,   A l a b a m a

LOCATED IN THE WORLD-FAMOUS Black Belt region of Alabama (home of some of the finest whitetail hunting available in the South), Hamilton Hills Plantation is a family-owned and operated hunting plantation. Lyle and Doug Smith, the two principal guides, were both born and raised in these hills. They have hunted it all of their lives, and know it about as well as one can. Hunters who come to Hamilton Hills will find many different types of terrain to hunt, including food plots, green fields, woodland trails, scrape lines, hardwood bottoms, clearcuts, and pasture lands.

Vital Statistics

THE LODGE:

2 guest rooms, 7 beds total, no private baths

SERVICES: Telephone, TV, laundry

GUN HUNTS: $400 / day

PAYMENT: Bank check

MEAL PLANS: 3 meals a day (southern fried chicken, roast beef, pork chops)

SPECIAL DIETS: n/a

NEAREST AIRPORT: Montgomery, AL

TRANSPORTATION TO LODGE (60 miles): Rental car; lodge van

BOONE AND CROCKETT

• B&C book bucks taken from property: 1
• Average B&C score: n/a
• B&C bucks from this part of state: 20 - 25

CONTACT:

Doug and Lyle Smith
Hamilton Hills Plantation
P.O. Box 56
Minter, AL 36761
Ph: 334/875-5704
Email: LSmith9157@aol.com
Web: http://hometown.aol.com/hamhplant/

THE HUNT:

SEASON:

• rifle: November 18 - January 31

BEST TIME TO HUNT: Anytime

TERRAIN: Food plots, fields, woodland trails, scrape lines, hardwood bottoms, clearcuts, pasturelands, swamps; flat creek bottoms to fairly steep ridges

LAND: 3,850 private acres

DRAW BLOOD POLICY? Yes

HUNTING METHODS: Stand hunting (14' ladder stands, 12' enclosed stands)

YEARS IN BUSINESS: 14

STAFF OF GUIDES: 3

HUNTERS SERVED BY EACH GUIDE: 2

NONHUNTER CHARGE: n/a

LICENSES: Over the counter; $77 / 7-day non-resident license

GAME CARE: Dressed and packaged for no extra charge.

OTHER ACTIVITIES: Coyote and bobcat hunting

Lakewood Hunting Lodge

DAVID COLLINS and his crew opened Lakewood Hunting Lodge in 1986 with several specific goals in mind: to provide clients with the best deer, turkey, and dove hunting in west-central Alabama. To accomplish this, they constantly work to improve their hunting areas. They also wanted their hunting trips to be something the average person could afford. They know that clients expect and deserve friendly, personalized service, along with comfortable facilities. Collins and his group are dedicated to providing this type of hunting environment.

For deer hunters, Lakewood hunts almost 3,500 acres of prime riverbottom swampland. There are 34 food plots on that territory, consisting of winter wheat, oats, and crimson clover. Also planted are soybeans, corn, and peas. The food plots provide plenty of nourishment for the deer herd, which is healthy and growing.

As a visiting hunter, all you have to do is put yourself in the hands of one of Lakewood's experienced guides. He'll take you to areas on the property that he has scouted ahead of time for those big southern bucks. Most times, you'll be hunting out of an enclosed ladder stand, waiting for a buck to come out to a food plot just as dusk is beginning to settle over the land. If your nerves are steady, that buck you've been dreaming of will be yours. For excellent southern deer hunting, this is a great place to visit.

© Lakewood Hunting Lodge

Wild turkey hunting is another activity offered at Lakewood Hunting Lodge.

Vital Statistics

THE LODGE:

Modern, rustic main lodge has 2 guest rooms, 10 beds total, with private baths

SERVICES: Telephone, TV, laundry

HUNTS:

- bow: $175 / day
- firearms: $215 / day
- muzzleloader: $185 / day

PAYMENT: Cash, checks

CONFERENCE GROUPS: Yes

MEAL PLANS: Breakfast and supper (dinners include steaks, catfish, quail and duck as main courses)

NEAREST AIRPORT: Meridian, MS

TRANSPORTATION TO LODGE (50 miles): Van from lodge, no additional charge

CONTACT:

David Collins
Lakewood Hunting Lodge
PO Box 208
Livingston, AL 35470
Ph: 205/652-7524
Lodge ph: 205/455-2748
Fax: 205/652-7661
Email: Lakewood_Lodge@Yahoo.com

THE HUNT:

SEASON:

- bow: mid-October – late January
- rifle: early November – late January
- muzzleloader: January 15 - 31

BEST TIME TO HUNT: Anytime in January

TERRAIN: There are 6 different tracts of land: one planted pine plantation, three tracts of hardwood creek bottoms, one river swamp, and one tract a mixture of hardwood and pine located along the river

LAND: 3,500 private acres; no public areas hunted

DRAW BLOOD POLICY? No

HUNTING METHODS: Stand hunting (enclosed metal ladders), still-hunting, calling, rattling

YEARS IN BUSINESS: 14

STAFF OF GUIDES: 9

HUNTERS SERVED BY EACH GUIDE: 4 maximum

NONHUNTER CHARGE: Only charge is for lodging

LICENSES: Sold at the lodge

GAME CARE: Dress game, no charge

OTHER ACTIVITIES: Wild turkey hunting, dove hunting, fishing, wildlife photography

BOONE AND CROCKETT

- B&C book bucks taken from property: 2
- Average B&C score: best buck scored 178
- B&C bucks from this part of state: n/a

Master Rack Lodge

Union Springs, Alabama

L OCATED 10 MILES SOUTH OF UNION SPRINGS near the headwaters of the Conecuh River, Master Rack Lodge offers hunting on some 8,000 acres of mixed woodland and fields. Swampy riverbottoms thick with tangled vines offer heavy cover for whitetails here. Mornings and evenings find the deer coming out of the woods to feed in the corn, pea, and bean fields. More than 70 shooting houses and 60 portable shooting stands give hunters a bird's-eye view of surrounding terrain. The shooting houses are roofed and weatherproof.

The property is divided into two main sections. On the 3,500-acre trophy land, hunters are allowed one buck with at least an 8-point rack, 15-inch minimum spread per day. The remaining acreage has a 4-point minimum spread requirement. Hunter success on the trophy area runs to a bit more than 50 percent and rises to 75 percent in the four-point area.

According to Jay Pipkins of Master Rack, "Our desire is to provide an action-packed, challenging hunt by day and a relaxing resort atmosphere by night. At Master Rack Lodge, the sportsmen and women have a chance to experience quality hunting with personal attention to their varied needs. Accommodations are spacious and comfortable, and the local people have that good old southern hospitality."

Vital Statistics

THE LODGE:

10 guest rooms, 22 beds total, all have private baths

Services: Telephone, fax, copying, TV, laundry

HUNTS:

• rifle: $1,295 / 3-day hunt

• bow: $995 / 3-day hunt

PAYMENT: Check, cash

MEAL PLANS: 3 meals a day (dinners include pork chops, steak, fish, ribs and two vegetables per meal)

SPECIAL DIETS: Heart healthy, Kosher, vegetarian, salt/msg free, other

NEAREST AIRPORT: Montgomery, AL

TRANSPORTATION TO LODGE (45 miles): Rental car; lodge van

CONTACT:

Steve Maxwell
Master Rack Lodge
13096 CR14
Union Springs, AL 36089
Ph: 334/474-3600
Fax: 334/474-3400
Email: stevemax@ustconline.net
Web: www.masterracklodge.com

THE HUNT:

SEASON:

• bow: Oct. - Jan.

• rifle/muzzleloader: Nov - Jan.

BEST TIME TO HUNT: Anytime

TERRAIN: Prime woodlands, open fields, tended food plots of corn, peas, wheat and natural vegetation

LAND: 7,500 acres

DRAW BLOOD POLICY? n/a

HUNTING METHODS: Stand hunting (shooting houses, ladder stands), calling, rattling

YEARS IN BUSINESS: n/a

STAFF OF GUIDES: n/a

HUNTERS SERVED BY EACH GUIDE: 4

NONHUNTER CHARGE: 50%

LICENSES: Sold at the lodge

GAME CARE: Dressed and packaged; no shipping

OTHER ACTIVITIES: Fishing, antiquing, biking, bird watching, golf, hiking

Paint Rock Valley Lodge & Retreat

Estill Fork, Alabama

ALABAMA IS WELL-KNOWN for its fine whitetail hunting, long seasons, and liberal bag limits (generally one buck and one doe per day). If you want to get in on some of the spectacular hunting, look no further than Paint Rock Valley Lodge and Retreat. Bret and Edley Prince have a well-kept, modern lodge that's located smack in the middle of 4,000 acres of some of the finest whitetail habitat in the south. You can hunt the property a number of different ways, but most hunters prefer to sit in one of the many stands. Your guide (if you want one) will take you to the stand early in the morning, well before daylight, where you'll sit quietly, overlooking either a food plot or a deer trail. If you're using a bow, you'll have to wait, patiently, for an animal to come within range — about 40 yards maximum. If you're using a muzzleloader, your range should be about 75 yards (no scopes are allowed). And if a rifle is your weapon of choice, shots could be up to 300 yards across a field or food plot; although, most hunters try to wait for the buck of their dreams to get in closer.

No matter which weapon you prefer, chances are you'll get an opportunity to use it on a whitetail at Paint Rock. The best time to hunt? Anytime you can, of course, although hunters who come during the rut, which extends from mid-November well into December, usually have the best chance at a good-sized buck.

The lodge itself is special — the perfect place to relax after a long day afield. Paint Rock has 18 bedrooms with two double beds in each room. The spacious living room with a rock fireplace and the large television room are comfortable and inviting, great places to swap hunting stories at the end of the day. The front porch of the lodge is filled with oversized rocking chairs for those who wish to watch the sun go down. Or you can take a dip in the indoor pool, relax in the hot tub, or play a friendly game of pool in the game room. Good hunting, comfortable lodging, excellent food — what are you waiting for?

Vital Statistics

THE LODGE:

Main lodge has 18 guest rooms, 35 beds total, no private baths

SERVICES: Telephone, fax, copying, TV, laundry, other

HUNTS:

• gun: $495 / 2 days

• bow: $395 / 2 days

PAYMENT: Credit cards, checks

Conference Groups: Yes

MEAL PLANS: All meals included (buffets with vegetables, salad bar, desserts, drinks)

NEAREST AIRPORT: Huntsville, AL

TRANSPORTATION TO LODGE (50 miles): Rental car; van from lodge ($30 one way)

CONTACT:

Edley R. Prince
Paint Rock Valley Lodge & Retreat
County Road 9
Estill Fork, AK 35745
Ph: 256/776-2253
Fax: 256/776-4576

THE HUNT:

SEASON:

• bow: Oct. 15 - Jan. 31

• rifle: Nov. 18 - Jan. 31

• muzzleloader: Jan 15 - 31

BEST TIME TO HUNT: Anytime

TERRAIN: Mountainous with hardwood forests

LAND: Own 3,200 acres, lease 1,000 acres

DRAW BLOOD POLICY? No

HUNTING METHODS: Stand hunting (tripods, shooting houses, blinds), still-hunting, calling, rattling

YEARS IN BUSINESS: 6

STAFF OF GUIDES: 8

HUNTERS SERVED BY EACH GUIDE: 2 - 4

NONHUNTER CHARGE: None

LICENSES: Over the counter

GAME CARE: Dress, package, freeze and ship for $40 - $50

OTHER ACTIVITIES: Turkey hunting, quail hunting, fishing (bass, redeyes), waterfowling, biking, bird watching, canoeing, hiking, skiing, swimming, sightseeing (there are numerous caves in this area, and the Jack Daniel's Distillery is only 45 miles away), horseback riding, four wheeling

Pope-Locke Hunting Preserve

Marion Junction, Alabama

P OPE-LOCKE HUNTING PRESERVE is located in Dallas County, Alabama, approximately 60 miles west of Montgomery in prime white-tailed deer country. The property is set on the backwaters of the Alabama River, which protects three sides of the land. Pope-Locke has a beautiful new lodge that accomodates groups of up to 10 hunters.

All hunts include home-cooked meals, experienced guides, and friendly service. The lodge has a year-round game-management plan that includes extensive habitat management and harvest strategies developed by the state of Alabama's Wildlife Management Program. This program is designed to promote maximum body growth and antler development in the deer herd.

Hunting is done from shooting houses located on wildlife plots, clear cuts, and power line right-of-ways, as well as from ladder stands located along trails leading to and from bedding and feeding areas. The rut occurs in mid to late January. Each hunter is allowed to take one mature buck and two or three does while permits are available. Additional bucks may be taken for a $700 fee. Spikes and immature bucks may not be harvested, and carry a $500 fee.

It's a good idea to bring raingear and waterproof boots at this time of year, along with warm clothing that can be layered.

Vital Statistics

THE LODGE:

Modern lodge, 12 beds total

SERVICES: Telephone, TV, laundry

HUNTS:

- bow: $300 / day
- rifle: $425 / day
- muzzleloader: $425 / day

PAYMENT: Cash or check

CONFERENCE GROUPS: Yes

MEAL PLANS: All meals included (typical southern cooking)

Nearest Airport: Montgomery, AL

Transportation to Lodge (60 miles): Rental car; van from lodge ($100)

CONTACT:

Floyd Plummer, Jr.
Pope-Locke Hunting Preserve
4160 Moors Ferry Road
Marion Junction, AL 36759
Ph: 334/996-3223, 334/875-8667
Fax: 334/872-0180
Email: plumcattim@fortunehitech.net
Web: www.popelocke.com

THE HUNT:

SEASON:

- bow: mid-Oct. - Nov. 30
- rifle/muzzleloader: mid. Nov. - Jan. 31

BEST TIME TO HUNT: Late December and January

TERRAIN: Food plots (oats, wheat, ryegrass, crimson clover), hardwood bottoms, pine plantations, some clear-cuts

LAND: 9,000 private acres

DRAW BLOOD POLICY? No

HUNTING METHODS: Stands (box stands)

YEARS IN BUSINESS: 10

STAFF OF GUIDES: 2

HUNTERS SERVED BY EACH GUIDE: Up to 3

NONHUNTER CHARGE: $100 / day

LICENSES: Most clients purchase at Bass Pro

GAME CARE: Dress, package and freeze; clients must handle their own shipping arrangements

Other Activities: Wild turkey hunting

BOONE AND CROCKETT

- B&C book bucks taken from property: 1
- Average B&C score: n/a
- B&C bucks from this part of state: n/a

River Bottom Hunting Lodge

Selma, Alabama

RIVER BOTTOM HUNTING LODGE is located near Statesville in Autauga County, Alabama, smack in the middle of the state's finest hunting region. The property covers more than 7,000 acres, and has been family-owned for more than 50 years. River Bottom, under new management, has strictly managed the property in order to produce superior quality whitetail deer (not to mention an abundant population of eastern wild turkeys). The lodge's land is made up of various tracts of woodland systems including stands of pines, hardwood ridges and bottoms, swamps, planted greenfields, and the renowned river bottoms. The goal at River Bottom Hunting Lodge is to share the rich heritage of the area, and offer Southern hospitality and superior hunting.

If you visit, you will stay in a newly-built, 5,600-square-foot lodge. Comfortable as well as modern, the lodge features gracious sleeping quarters and classic porches with wonderful views of the lawn and the Alabama River. You will be served three full meals a day featuring Southern home-style food.

With an estimated population of 1.5 million white-tailed deer, the state of Alabama has a generous hunting season and a variety of different bag limits, depending upon where you hunt in the state. Alabama is a good place to hunt throughout the fall and, if you come from the North, you can extend your season by heading south after the first of the year for some fine January hunting.

Vital Statistics

THE LODGE:

Modern main lodge has 8 guest rooms, 4 with private baths, 19 beds total

SERVICES: Telephone, fax, copying, TV, laundry

Gun Hunts:

- $1650 / 3-day hunt / person
- $1250 / 2-day hunt / person

PAYMENT: Credit cards, checks

CONFERENCE GROUPS: Yes

MEAL PLANS: All meals included (Southern home-style foods; buffet)

NEAREST AIRPORT: Montgomery, AL

TRANSPORTATION TO LODGE (40 miles): Rental car; van from lodge (no additional charge)

CONTACT:

River Bottom Hunting Lodge
800 Co. Rd. 1 South
Selma, AL 36703
Ph/fax: 334/418-4707
Web: www.riverbottomlodge.com

THE HUNT:

SEASON:

- bow: October 15 - January 31
- rifle/muzzleloader: Nov. 20 - Jan. 31

BEST TIME TO HUNT: Nov. 20 - Dec. 15, or January

TERRAIN: Hardwood forests, swamps, planted green field, river bottoms

LAND: 7,340 private acres

DRAW BLOOD POLICY? No

HUNTING METHODS: Standing hunting (permanent stands, tripods, box stands and lock-ons with safety rails)

YEARS IN BUSINESS: 5

STAFF OF GUIDES: 4

HUNTERS SERVED BY EACH GUIDE: 2 - 3

NONHUNTER CHARGE: $100 / day

LICENSES: Over the counter

GAME CARE: Dress, package, freeze and ship game for $45

OTHER ACTIVITIES: Wild turkey hunting, fishing, antiquing, biking, boating, golf, hiking, wildlife photography

BOONE AND CROCKETT

- B&C book bucks taken from property: 51
- Average B&C score: 120 - 150 (largest - 167)
- B&C bucks from this part of state: Numerous

Southern Sportsman Hunting Lodge

Hayneville, Alabama

I F YOU'RE A SERIOUS HUNTER, you have to learn more about Southern Sportsman Hunting Lodge. Located in the heart of Alabama's Trophy Black Belt region, Southern Sportsman offers some of the best hunting in the U.S. The lodge has attracted hunters such as Jackie Bushman, Ben Rogers Lee, Pete Sheply, Dick Kirby, Bill Macoy, and Paul Butski, and hosts the Buckmaster Classics annually. Southern Sportsman is also the film location for many hunting videos on the market today.

When you consider that the kill success ratios for deer hunts here are between 70 and 85 percent, you know this place is hot. Combine this with fine southern-style cooking, excellent lodge facilities, practice ranges, experienced guides, and plenty of southern hospitality, and you have a place every serious hunter should consider visiting.

A typical day at the lodge begins at 4:30 a.m. with a hearty breakfast and lots of coffee. At 5:15, your guide takes you to your stand. You will hunt either from 4' x 4' gun houses located on soybean, corn, and green field food plots, or from ladder stands located on trails, scrape lines, ridges, and bottoms. Shooting distances range from 20 to 300 yards. You'll be picked up from your stand around 10:30 a.m. and taken back for an energy-reviving lunch, then returned to your stand around 2, where you'll hunt until dark.

If you get a deer (6 points or better, please), it will be cleaned and hung in one of the walk-in coolers, while you wash up and wind down before being served a satisfying hot dinner. Hunters are also allowed to take one doe apiece.

Vital Statistics

THE LODGE:

Log lodge has 11 guest rooms, 28 beds total, no private baths

SERVICES: Telephone, fax, TV, laundry

HUNTS: $400 / day

PAYMENT: Cash or check

CONFERENCE GROUPS: Yes

MEAL PLANS: All meals included (breakfasts of bacon, sausage, toast, eggs, grits, hash browns and pancakes; lunches of cold cuts, rolls or corn bread, vegetables; suppers of steaks, catfish, fowl, spaghetti, barbecue)

NEAREST AIRPORT: Montgomery, AL

TRANSPORTATION TO LODGE (30 miles): Rental car; van from lodge ($30 round trip)

CONTACTS:

Dave Lyon, Jim Mason
Southern Sportsman Hunting Lodge
7715 County Rd. 17
Hayneville, AL 36040
Ph: Phone: 334/872-9740
Fax: 334/872-9529
Web: www.southernhunting.com

THE HUNT:

SEASON:

• bow: Oct. 15 - Jan. 31

• rifle/muzzleloader: mid-Nov. - Jan.

BEST TIME TO HUNT: Dec. - Jan.

TERRAIN: Hardwood forests, pine plantations, cutovers, farmland, more than 300 food plots (wheat, clover)

LAND: 15,000 private acres

DRAW BLOOD POLICY? No (6-point rule or better; $200 fine for shooting smaller deer)

HUNTING METHODS: Stand hunting (ladder stands up to 12'; box shooting houses are 6' off the ground)

YEARS IN BUSINESS: Since 1982

STAFF OF GUIDES: Yes, 8

HUNTERS SERVED BY EACH GUIDE: 4 at most

NONHUNTER CHARGE: $50 / day (includes meals)

LICENSES: Call for more information

GAME CARE: Field dress, butcher, quarter, prepare for shipping (no extra charge)

OTHER ACTIVITIES: Turkey hunting, bird hunting (quail, dove), horseback riding if you bring your own horse, sporting clays, wildlife photography

Water Valley Lodge

Gilbertown, Alabama

FOUND IN SOUTHWESTERN Alabama's legendary Black Belt, Water Valley Lodge is in the heart of trophy whitetail deer country. And with a rigorous wildlife management program, this lodge can assure visiting hunters of quality hunting experiences.

Morning hunts are from 5:15 to 10:30, while afternoon hunts run from 2:30 until dark. The lodge controls more than 12,000 acres of hardwood and pine plantations, clear cuts, swamplands, riverbottoms, hills and flat land — the kind of terrain that any hunter would be pleased to cover. Much of the land has been owned by the Utsey family since 1849. Most of the hunting is done either from ground or elevated stands that overlook well-used game trails and food plots.

The lodge itself is more than 12,000 square feet, and contains guest rooms with private baths, satellite television, a huge fireplace, porches with rocking chairs, a large steam sauna and classic spa to relax in at the end of a long day afield. Small cabins are also available if you want to hunt alone on designated land, and prepare your own meals. Either lodging is a good choice. Excellent food, a courteous staff, and knowledgeable hunting guides round out the offerings of Water Valley Lodge, a place that will pamper you, and put you onto some mighty fine southern deer.

Vital Statistics

THE LODGE:

12 guest rooms, 8 rooms have private baths, 40 beds total (although the Utseys don't like to take that many hunters at a time)

SERVICES: TELEPHONE, fax, TV, laundry, sauna, hot tub

HUNTS:

• bow: $900 - $1,250 / 3- to 5-day hunts

• rifle : $1,200 - $1,800 / 3- to 5-day hunts

PAYMENT: Check (for deposit), cash or bank check for balance

MEAL PLANS: 3 meals a day (steak, fried catfish, chicken, hamburgers, pork barbecue, pork chops, pork loin — there is no shortage of good food!)

SPECIAL DIETS: Can accommodate any diet with advance notice

NEAREST AIRPORT: Meridian, MS

TRANSPORTATION TO LODGE (60 miles): Free pick up and drop off; the Lodge encourages guests to rent a car if they fly into Mobile, AL (2 hours); Birmingham, AL (3 hours) or Jackson, MS (3 hours)

CONTACT:

Treobye B. Utsey
Water Valley Lodge
2742 Melvin Rd.
Gilbertown, AL 36908
Ph: 205/459-3799, 3690. Fax: 205/459-4479
Email: hunting@water-valley.com
Web: www.water-valley.com

REPRESENTED BY AGENT:

Andy Dyess, 205/459-3799

THE HUNT:

SEASON:

• bow: October 15 - January 31

• rifle: November 20 - January 31

BEST TIME TO HUNT: Anytime, but especially the pre-rut in November and the frenzy rut in January

TERRAIN: Hardwood plantations, pine plantations, clear cuts, swampland, riverbottoms, hills and flat land

LAND: 12,000-plus private acres, unfenced

DRAW BLOOD POLICY: Yes

HUNTING METHODS: Stand hunting (tripods, lock-ons, boxes, buddy stands), still-hunting, stalking, by vehicle (ATV), calling, rattling

YEARS IN BUSINESS: 4

STAFF OF GUIDES: 3 - 6

HUNTERS SERVED BY EACH GUIDE: 2 - 3

NONHUNTER CHARGE: $100 / day

LICENSES: Sold at the lodge

GAME CARE: Dress, package, and pack in ice for travel (complimentary)

Other Activities: Other big game hunting (wild boar, turkey), waterfowling, antiquing, biking, bird watching, golf, hiking, swimming, tennis, wildlife photograpy, historic tours

Westervelt Lodge

Tuscaloosa, Alabama

WESTERVELT LODGE HAS LONG been associated with quality deer hunting in the South. In business for more than 25 years, Westervelt has helped to lead the way not only in trophy deer management, but in treating clientele with first rate, down-home southern hospitality.

Westervelt's deer hunting customers bought in on a deer herd improvement partnership several years ago, and are realizing excellent dividends today. The year-round intensive habitat management, scientific harvest prescriptions, and the willingness of hunters to pass up younger bucks have produced terrific results. The 8-point-or-better rule for bucks, and the diligent harvest of does, has allowed the remaining bucks to reach greater maturity. The herd has a more balanced sex ratio, and there's plenty of nutritious forage. All the indicators of herd condition — weights, antler measurements, breeding dates, browse surveys — show continued progress. Additionally, the true measure of a program such as this — customer satisfaction — continues to get even better. Long-tined, heavy-beamed 8- and 10-pointers are typical fare for hunters who visit Westervelt — much to their delight!

Westervelt bucks are as smart as whitetails anywhere, however, and hunting them is no piece of cake. After all, they don't reach maturity by being dumb! Westervelt's knowledgeable guides can help tip the odds in your favor though. Year after year, the hunters who follow the briefing tips from their guides — to sit still and stay quiet in the right places — connect with good deer. Morning hunts generally take place in the woods, with hunters watching likely trails and crossings from ladder stands. Afternoons see hunters climbing into covered shooting houses and watching wheat, oats, and clover food plots. Guests can also bring their own climbing stands if they desire.

Having quality gear is highly recommended. Be ready for anything from hot (sometimes up to 80°F) to cold temperatures in the 20s, and you'll be comfortable on your stand, and a more efficient hunter because of it. Familiarity with your bow or firearm is also critical for success.

Aside from the excellent deer hunting, Westervelt also offers quality quail and spring turkey hunting. The lodge prides itself on its ability to handle corporate retreats. It has just the right mix of quality food and comfortable accommodations to make a variety of people feel welcomed and relaxed. The lodge is set up with a fireplace on each end of a great room. There are big screen TVs on each end attached to satellite dishes, ensuring guests a wide variety of stations. The great room joins the dining area, and the guest rooms are on wings off each end of the lodge. There is also a separate house, away from the main lodge, that sleeps three to four guests.

Vital Statistics

THE LODGE:

Main lodge has 10 guest rooms, all with private baths, 20 beds total

SERVICES: Telephone, fax, copying, TV, laundry

HUNTS:

• gun: $650 / day

PAYMENT: Cash, credit cards, checks

CONFERENCE GROUPS: Yes

MEAL PLANS: All meals included (dinners of ribeye steaks, bbq pork ribs, cornish game hens, catfish, and all the fixin's)

NEAREST AIRPORT: Birmingham, AL

TRANSPORTATION TO LODGE (2 hours): Rental car

CONTACT:

Charles Bedwell and Jay Steen
Westervelt Lodge
PO Box 2362, Tuscaloosa, AL 35403
Ph: 205/373-8212. Fax: 205/373-2654
Email: westervelt@pickens.net
Web: www.westervelt.com

THE HUNT:

SEASON:

• rifle: November 20 - January 1

BEST TIME TO HUNT: Anytime; the rut is usually between Christmas and the end of January, with deer activity highly dependent on the weather

TERRAIN: Bottomlands, hardwoods interspersed with pine ridges in the Tombigbee River bottoms

LAND: 10,000 private acres

DRAW BLOOD POLICY? n/a

HUNTING METHODS: Stand hunting (shooting houses overlook food plots, ladder stands in the woods)

YEARS IN BUSINESS: 25

STAFF OF GUIDES: 2

HUNTERS SERVED BY EACH GUIDE: 6 (guides take you to your stand, pick you up, give you hints on how to hunt each area)

NONHUNTER CHARGE: $100 / day

LICENSES: Over the counter

GAME CARE: Dress, package, freeze, and ship game

OTHER ACTIVITIES: Wild turkey hunting, quail hunting, fishing, wildlife photography, bowhunting and turkey hunting schools

White Oak Plantation

T u s k e g e e ,   A l a b a m a

I IMAGINE 15,000 ACRES IN Alabama's prime Black Belt country — every last inch of it managed for wildlife — deer and turkey, mostly, but also quail and ducks. Then consider a well-researched, long-term program designed to produce, not necessarily the most game, but the absolute best game that improved habitat can sustain. Hunting this land doesn't require you to take out a home equity loan, either. The result is Bo Pitman's White Oak Plantation, quite simply a hunter's paradise.

Deer grow big in this region where the dark, fertile soil is rich in minerals and other nutrients. They are plentiful, too, so much so that you can take two a day — two does, or one doe and one buck — throughout a season that starts in October and runs into January.

Hunting in a variety of terrain from swamps to hardwood forests to planted fields, hunters head out in the morning after a sumptuous breakfast to shooting houses that overlook trails and green fields that deer frequent. Stands are drawn at the beginning of each hunting session to give every hunter in camp an equal opportunity, and sectors are rotated daily to minimize disturbance. About half of the available 500 tree and tower stands and camo houses overlook planted fields of wheat, rye and clover. The other half are positioned along well-used trails that meander through connecting blocks of hardwoods, pines and swamps.

It doesn't matter where you hunt, though, as you will see bucks in this country — each and every day, weather, of course, permitting. It's really a matter of deciding what you want to shoot, and when. The hunting is that good.

At the end of each day, hunters return to the main lodge, a classic southern plantation with a sitting room complete with a small library and mounted deer heads on the walls. The lodge overlooks a 13-acre bass lake that's full of trophies. Throw in a huge porch with rocking chairs, country barbecues when it's warm, enough food to keep you from losing any weight, and you've found a perfect place to hunt in the South.

White Oak Plantation has it all — excellent food, comfortable accommodations, terrific scenery, and a huge whitetail herd.

Vital Statistics

THE LODGE:

13 guest rooms, 30 beds total, all rooms have private baths

SERVICES: Telephone, fax, copying, TV, laundry

HUNTS:

- $1,425 / 3-day early gun hunt
- $1,650 / 3-day late gun hunt
- $900 / 3-day bowhunt
- more for 4-day hunts

PAYMENT: Cash, credit cards, check

MEAL PLANS: 3 meals a day (huge southern-style breakfasts, lunches and dinners of hearty southern fare — fried catfish, bbq chicken, baked ham, quail, turkey, fried chicken)

SPECIAL DIETS: Anyhing requested

NEAREST AIRPORT: Montgomery, AL (1 hour) and Atlanta, GA (1 hour, 45 minutes)

TRANSPORTATION TO LODGE: Rental car, van from lodge

THE HUNT:

SEASON:

- bow: Oct. - mid-Nov.
- rifle/muzzleloader: Nov. - Jan.

BEST TIME TO HUNT: Anytime

TERRAIN: Creek/swamp, pine/hardwood forest, planted fields

LAND: More than 15,000 private acres

DRAW BLOOD POLICY? No

HUNTING METHODS: Stand hunting (shooting houses, ladder stands), calling, rattling

YEARS IN BUSINESS: 18

STAFF OF GUIDES : 6 - 10

HUNTERS SERVED BY EACH GUIDE: Depends

NONHUNTER CHARGE: $125 / day

LICENSES: Sold at the lodge

GAME CARE: Dressed, packaged (quartered in plastic bags)

OTHER ACTIVITIES: Bird hunting, waterfowling, fishing, antiquing, bird watching, wildlife photography

BOONE AND CROCKETT

- B&C book bucks taken from property: None
- Average B&C score: n/a
- B&C bucks from this part of state: 20

CONTACT:

Robert Pitman
White Oak Plantation
5215 County Road 10
Tuskegee, AL 36083
Ph: 334/727-9258
Fax: 334/727-3411
Web:
www.whiteoakplantation.com

Dixie Wildlife Safaris

Lake Wales, Florida

ACCORDING TO OUTDOOR writer Chris Christian, Mike Acreman is one of the best deer hunters on the planet. Acreman has been stomping around the Florida swamps and palmetto country for more than 20 years, and if anyone can pry a wary Florida whitetail out of the thick stuff, it's Acreman. According to Christian, you could plunk Acreman down in the middle of the woods anywhere on the continent, and he'd be able to find where the big bucks live in less than a day. The guy knows whitetails!

Acreman's outfit, Dixie Wildlife Safaris, hunts exotics on a 1,000-acre fenced area in the middle of a total 5,000 acres. Outside of the fence, you'll find whitetails, plus wild boars and occasional Eastern turkeys. Bowhunters, rifle hunters, muzzleloaders, and handgunners are all welcome. Just try to team up with Mike, as he's the one who can show you where to go and what trails to watch for a big ol' southern buck.

Accommodations are at Mike's farmhouse — a comfortable country place where guests from all over the U.S. come to wind down after a day of hunting. Gain a few pounds on the fine southern cuisine served from the kitchen, kick up your feet, and relax a bit after dinner. Then it's off to bed, with visions of monster bucks walking under your treestand the next morning.

Vital Statistics

THE LODGE:

Farmhouse has 3 guest rooms, 2 with private baths, 10 beds total

SERVICES: Telephone, TV

HUNTS: $750 minimum / 1 1/2-day hunt

PAYMENT: Cash or credit cards

CONFERENCE GROUPS: n/a

MEAL PLANS: All meals included (dinners include fried chicken, potatoes, biscuits, vegetables, ham, black beans and rice, bbq, beans, cole slaw)

NEAREST AIRPORT: Orlando, FL

TRANSPORTATION TO LODGE (5 miles): Rental car

BOONE AND CROCKETT

• B&C book bucks taken from property: n/a

• Average B&C score: 95 to 105

• B&C bucks from this part of state: 1

CONTACT:

Mike Acreman
Dixie Wildlife Safaris
4431 Walk 'n Water Rd.
Lake Wales, FL 33853
Ph: 863/696-3300

THE HUNT:

SEASON:

• bow: starts October 26

• rifle: starts November 4

• muzzleloader: starts October 30 (call for details/hunts run past January 1)

BEST TIME TO HUNT: Anytime

TERRAIN: Swamps, palmetto flats, piney woods, oak hammocks

LAND: Lease 5,000 acres

DRAW BLOOD POLICY? Yes

HUNTING METHODS: Stand hunting (ground blinds), drives, still-hunting, by vehicle, calling, rattling

YEARS IN BUSINESS: 20

STAFF OF GUIDES: Acreman guides everyone

HUNTERS SERVED BY EACH GUIDE: 1

NONHUNTER CHARGE: $100 / day

LICENSES: Over the counter

GAME CARE: Dress deer only

OTHER ACTIVITIES: Other big game hunting (exotics such as axis, fallow and sitka deer, red stag, Pere David deer, black buck antelope, nilgai, oryx, more; also wild boar and wild turkeys), quail hunting

Broughton Plantation

Newborn, Georgia

WHEN IT COMES TO DEER HUNTING in Georgia, much of the best hunting is on private land. Yes, good public hunting is available in the mountains in the northern part of the state and in the swampy areas to the south, but unless you're willing to spend the time and the energy to get back into the thick stuff, away from the roads and the access points, chances are you're going to encounter other deer hunters wherever you go.

Your choices for finding a whitetail deer hunt are two: join a private hunt club, which a lot of residents do, or book a hunt at a private lodge, which is the best option for nonresident hunters.

You can do both at Broughton Plantation. An old dairy farm on the outskirts of Newborn, Broughton is just one hour east of Atlanta on Route 20. The country rolls beneath second-growth forests of pine and scrub oak interspersed with bean and cornfields and acreage that lies fallow. Broughton runs hunts on four parcels of land, totaling 2,000 acres. Hunters sit in stands at dawn and dusk, watching and waiting for bucks to come out of feeding or bedding areas. Book a day's hunt, or sign up for three, four or five days of hunting — it's almost like you're in a private hunting club.

Broughton also offers quail hunting, and can accommodate off-season parties, meetings, and weddings.

Warren and Ken Howard, owners, live on the property, and are friendly, hospitable, and willing to go the extra mile to help you get a shot at a deer. Bucks and does are legal, though the Plantation rule is 8 points or better for bucks.

Some hunters come for one day, heading back to Atlanta after dark. Others stay in the rustic lodge, dining on home-style southern cuisine, then waddling off to one of the four private rooms with baths. Come morning, it'll be off to the stand for another day of watching, waiting, and, oftentimes, getting a shot at a deer.

Vital Statistics

THE LODGE:

Rustic lodge has 4 guestrooms, all with private baths, 10 beds total

SERVICES: Telephone, fax, copying, TV, laundry

GUN HUNTS:

• $700 / 2 person/1-day bowhunt (includes one buck or doe for each hunter, plus lunch, transportation and guide)

• $900 / 2 person/1-day firearms hunt (includes one buck or doe for each hunter, lunch, transportation, and guide)

• $1,450 / 1 person/3-day firearms hunt (includes one buck and two does, lodging, meals, transportation and guides)

PAYMENT: Cash, credit cards, checks

CONFERENCE GROUPS: Yes

MEAL PLANS: Lunch included with day hunts; lunch and dinner included with overnight hunts; Southern cuisine

NEAREST AIRPORT: Atlanta/Hartsfield, GA

TRANSPORTATION TO LODGE (50 minutes): Rental car; van from lodge $50 additional

CONTACT:

Warren or Ken Howard
Broughton Plantation
3580 Broughton Road.
Newborn, GA 30056-0172
Ph: 706/342-2281
Fax: 706/342-9810
Web: www.findoutfitters/Broughton

THE HUNT:

SEASON:

• bow: mid-September - January 1

• rifle: October 23 - January 1

• muzzleloader: mid-October - January 1

BEST TIME TO HUNT:

• bow: early October

• rifle : opening week, and first week in Nov

• muzzleloader: opening week

TERRAIN: Hunts are conducted from stands overlooking food plots or hardwood bottoms, swamps, and near agricultural fields

LAND: Own approximately 2,000 acres

DRAW BLOOD POLICY? No

HUNTING METHODS: Stand hunting (quads, pods, ladders, lock-ons), calling, rattling

YEARS IN BUSINESS: 4

STAFF OF GUIDES: 2

HUNTERS SERVED BY EACH GUIDE: Guide does not sit with hunter

NONHUNTER CHARGE: None

LICENSES: Over the counter

GAME CARE: Dress, package and freeze for $65; extra for shipping

OTHER ACTIVITIES: Bird hunting (quail, pheasant, chukar)

Gopher Plantation

Douglas, Georgia

I F YOU WANT TO EXPERIENCE southern deer hunting at its finest, then the place to go is Gopher Plantation. Owned and managed by Bennie Overstreet, Gopher Plantation (named after the endangered Gopher Tortoise, which is found on the property) is comprised of 4,100 acres of cypress ponds, beaver ponds, numerous streams, and the Satilla River meandering through hardwood bottoms. Arnold Bay, consisting of some 200 acres, is located in the middle of the property and provides habitat and refuge for wildlife.

Hunters are directed to strategically-located permanent deer stands at the beginning of each day — this, after a 4:30 wakeup call and a quick cup of coffee and continental breakfast (the full-blown southern breakfast comes in the late morning, after deer activity has subsided). These aren't just any deer stands, either, having sides and tops, and swiveling easy chairs. Some stands easily accommodate three chairs, and are ideal for parent-child hunts. All you have to do is decide which stand you want to hunt. You can choose the river swamp, Carolina bays, oak thickets, or upland pine plantations. Overstreet and his guides will fill you in on deer activity in a given area, as they are constantly in the woods scouting, patterning deer, and looking for a great buck for your wall.

The plantation complex is a museum of a typical Georgia farm from around the turn of the century. Outbuildings include a log corncrib, log smokehouse, syrup boiler, mule drawn cane mill, and hog-scalding boiler. Old-time farming equipment can also be found throughout the property.

The 5,800-square-foot log lodge has a huge wrap-around porch, a monster fireplace with granite mantelpiece nestled in the 1,000-square-foot great room, and a spacious old-fashioned kitchen (with modern appliances). Some bedrooms have king-size canopy beds, pot-bellied stoves for extra warmth on those chilly mornings, plus an adjoining bathroom with a claw-foot bathtub, antler towel racks and armadillo light shades. One of the adjoining cabins features two bedrooms and a bath, and was originally built in 1870. It offers a special charm for those who stay there.

At the end of a day of hunting for the big bucks that roam this area (average trophy deer go 8 points and better, with 16- to 17-inch spreads, 165 pounds live weight) hunters enjoy sitting down for a hearty meal. The evening feast consists of southern farmland-type food with a touch of the wild. Unusual game dishes are part of the Gopher Plantation experience. Afterwards, you'll finish your peach cobbler and ice cream dessert, push back your chair, and meander out to the porch where you can spend the evening relaxing in a swing or rocking chair, reliving the day's events with other hunters, all the while listening to the chatter of frogs, barn owls, and whippoorwills, with the moon shining through the Georgia pines.

Vital Statistics

THE LODGE:

11 guestrooms, (5 are in the main log lodge, which was originally built in 1870; 6 are in cabins), 4 have private baths, 21 beds total

SERVICES: Telephone, TV

HUNTS: $295 / day

PAYMENT: Cash or check

CONFERENCE GROUPS: Yes

MEAL PLANS: All meals included (dinners include charcoal-broiled pork chops, fried rabbit, green beans, broccoli casserole, creamed corn, homemade biscuits with homemade jellies and jams, cane syrup, peach cobbler with ice cream)

NEAREST AIRPORT: Jacksonville, FL

TRANSPORTATION TO LODGE (90 miles): Rental car

BOONE AND CROCKETT

• B&C book bucks taken from property: At least 6

• Average B&C score: 140

• B&C bucks from this part of state: n/a

CONTACT:

A.B. Overstreet
Gopher Plantation
2150 Industrial Blvd.
Douglas, GA 31533-8140
Ph: 912/384-3238
Fax: 912/384-8237

THE HUNT:

SEASON:

• bow: mid-September - first week of January

• rifle: last week of October - first week of January

• muzzleloader: late October 21

BEST TIMES TO HUNT: October 1 - 27; all of November; December 23 - January 7

TERRAIN: Upland pine plantations, Carolina bays, hardwood bottoms, upland oak ridges, hardwood bottoms along river flood plains

LAND: Own 4,100 acres

DRAW BLOOD POLICY? No (8-point-or-better rule)

HUNTING METHODS: Stand hunting (tripods and boxes that all have tops and sides with cushioned swivel chairs), still-hunting, calling

YEARS IN BUSINESS: 15 (4 commercial)

STAFF OF GUIDES: 2

HUNTERS SERVED BY EACH GUIDE: 6

NONHUNTER CHARGE: $75 / day

LICENSES: Must apply for licenses; Plantation will purchase them ahead of time if arrangements are made

GAME CARE: Dress, package, freeze and ship game ($95)

OTHER ACTIVITIES: Turkey hunting, quail hunting, waterfowling, fishing, antiquing, biking, bird watching, canoeing, hiking, sporting clays

Giles Island Hunting Club

Ferriday, Louisiana

THOUGH ACCESSIBLE FROM a river levee road west of Ferriday, Louisiana, Giles Island Hunting Lodge technically lies in Adams County, Mississippi, and is therefore subject to the hunting regulations of the Magnolia State. Mississippi has an extremely liberal hunting season, with plenty of time for hunting opportunities. As far as Giles Island is concerned, however, we're talking trophy whitetail bucks, not bag limits. And Giles Island has its share of trophies.

Jim Bowie, the legendary knife fighter from Louisiana who fought and died at the Alamo, established his reputation on the grounds of what is now Giles Island. The deer hunting here is as legendary as Bowie. In fact, at the end of each season, lodge manager Jimmy Riley videotapes the remaining bucks to see what will be available the next year. When you see all the 140-plus-class bucks still roaming the property, you won't believe your eyes! A large part of the reason for this is that owner Speed Bancroft and managers, Chad Pugh and Jimmy Riley, carefully manage the deer herd on the property, making sure only a certian percentage of the bucks are taken each year, that the buck-to-doe ratio is kept within reason, and that all of the deer have plenty of nutritious greenfields to feed on.

Privately owned by Speed Bancroft of Bancroft Paper Company, the island retreat was established as a members-only hunting club. After several years, however, Mr. Bancroft decided to market Giles Island as a commercial hunting operation. To say that move has been a success would be an understatement.

The room and board at Giles is as top-notch as the hunting. Juice, coffee, and a sweet roll before the morning hunt holds guests over until the midmorning brunch, which consists of a full southern breakfast including a hot bowl of cheese grits. Dinners in the evenings are all southern cuisine specialties: pork chops, fried chicken, a wide variety of vegetables, salads, and desserts. You don't go away hungry at Giles Island.

Accommodations are well appointed, with plenty of closet and floor space. A reading chair with a good table lamp and a stack of hunting magazines in each bedroom is a nice touch. And when we last spoke with the people at Giles, there were plans for a new, larger main lodge to offer even more client comfort (which would be hard to imagine).

If you're searching for a first-class whitetail deer hunt, with a true chance at a trophy, call Giles Island without delay. Bow and gun hunters are both welcome.

Vital Statistics

THE LODGE:

6 log cabins have 6 guest rooms, 18 beds total

SERVICES: Telephone, fax, copying, TV, laundry

HUNTS:

- $1,200 / 3-day bowhunt in Oct.-Nov.
- $1,500 / 3-day bowhunt in Dec.-late Jan.
- $3,000 / 3-day gun hunt after Christmas

PAYMENT: Cash, credit card, check

CONFERENCE GROUPS: Yes

MEAL PLANS: All meals included (dinners include beef tips, prime rib, bbq chicken, chicken tetrazzini, prime ribs, baked country hams, veggies, salads, homemade breads, and desserts such as butter pecan cake, chocolate chip pound cake, banana pudding, earthquake cake, Italian cream cheese cake, and strawberry cake-brownies). Don't plan on losing weight here!

NEAREST AIRPORT: Jackson, MS, or Baton Rouge, LA

TRANSPORTATION TO LODGE: Rental car; "We will pick up at no charge if clients fly to one of the local airports, such as the Natchez airport."

CONTACT:

Jimmy Riley
Giles Island Hunting Club
449 Old River Boat Camp Road
Ferriday, LA 71334
Ph: 877/944-5374
Fax: 866/944-5374
Email: jimmy@gilesisland.com
Web: gilesisland.com

THE HUNT:

SEASON:

- bow: Oct.-Christmas, Jan. 15-31
- rifle: Dec. 26-Jan. 15

TERRAIN: Mississippi River bottoms, hardwood forests

LAND: 9,400 private acres

DRAW BLOOD POLICY? Yes

HUNTING METHODS: Stand hunting (box stands and ladders for rifle hunters; ladders and climbers for bowhunters), still-hunting, calling, rattling

YEARS IN BUSINESS: 2

STAFF OF GUIDES: 10

HUNTERS SERVED BY EACH GUIDE: 1 - 4

NONHUNTER CHARGE: $450 / 3 days

LICENSES: Over the counter

GAME CARE: Dress, package, freeze and ship game for $150 / deer

OTHER ACTIVITIES: Wild turkey hunting, waterfowling, fishing, bird watching, boating, hiking

BOONE AND CROCKETT

- B&C bucks taken from property: 1
- Average B&C score: 130-140
- B&C bucks from this part of state: Many

Schrader's Hunting

Millington, Maryland

FOR THE SERIOUS BOW or gun hunter, Schrader's offers a wide variety of terrain to choose from, including swampland, deep woods, marshes, and open fields. All four areas are heavily populated with herds of whitetails.

Archery hunts are conducted from portable stands that have been carefully placed in areas previously scouted by Schrader's guides. These areas generally have everything a deer needs: feed, cover, water, and the security of light hunting pressure. Deer are generally going about their normal routines, giving hunters a chance to take an unpressured buck in a natural setting.

Gun hunts take place in the same type of terrain, although hunters may hunt from sturdy wooden ladder stands or from portables. The stands are safe, and at varying heights, depending on the area, to give a gunner the clearest shot possible. Guides also scout the areas before each hunt, and make changes or adjustments to the stands as needed.

Hunters may also wish to hunt one of the Managed Trophy Areas. A buck taken from one of these areas must have a minimum antler spread of 16 inches, roughly the width of the ears. These areas are closely managed in order to produce big bucks, the type any hunter would be proud to take.

In addition to the regulated feeding stations, deer also have the opportunity to feed on standing corn, soybeans, and a wide variety of clover and grasses. With more than 20,000 acres available and no more than 25 hunters in camp at a time, each hunter at Schrader's is guaranteed a quality hunt in a pristine, natural environment.

© Schrader's Hunting

A hunter at Schrader's Hunting shows off his beautiful 8-pointer.

Vital Statistics

THE LODGE:

Two Victorian housse have 12 guest rooms each, 30 beds total, all with private baths (Schrader's prefers to accommodate only 25 hunters at a time)

SERVICES: Telephone, fax, copying, TV, laundry

HUNTS:

• bow: $200 / person / day

• shotgun/muzzleloading: $200 - $300 / person / day, depending on time of year

PAYMENT: Cash, credit card, personal/company check

MEAL PLANS: All meals included (a variety of home-cooked meals)

SPECIAL DIETS: Available with advance notice

Nearest Airport: Baltimore/Washington International (1 1/2 hours)

TRANSPORTATION TO LODGE: Rental car or van pickup (additional charge)

CONTACT:

Ken Schrader
Schrader's Hunting
900 Red Lion Branch Road
Millington, MD 21651
Ph: 410/778-1895
Email: letsgohunting@schradershunting.com
Web: Http://www.schradershunting.com

THE HUNT:

SEASON:

• bow: Sept. 15 - Jan. 31

• shotgun: Nov. - Dec.

• muzzleloader: mid-Oct. (3 days), Dec. - Jan.

BEST TIME TO HUNT: The entire season can be good

TERRAIN: Hardwoods, pines, river edges, marshes, deer feed from agricultural fields such as soybeans, corn, clover, alfalfa, and wheat

LAND: Owns/leases more than 20,000 acres

DRAW BLOOD POLICY? No

HUNTING METHODS: Stand hunting (lock-on stand with centipede bendable ladders), calling, rattling

YEARS IN BUSINESS: 20

STAFF OF GUIDES: 20

HUNTERS SERVED BY EACH GUIDE: 2

NONHUNTER CHARGE: No

LICENSES: Over the counter

GAME CARE: Dressed, packaged, frozen, and shipped for $50 and up

OTHER ACTIVITIES: Spring turkey hunting, dove hunting, waterfowling, small game hunting (rabbits, squirrels), fishing, antiquing, golf, wildlife photography

BOONE AND CROCKETT

• B&C book bucks taken from property: 2

• Average B&C score: 170 - 180

• B&C bucks from this part of state: 10

Canemount Plantation

Lorman, Mississippi

C ANEMOUNT PLANTATION is a 10,000-acre plantation in southwestern Mississippi. Located in one of the most beautiful and historic areas of the state, it has a healthy and growing whitetail deer herd, plus an abundance of Russian boar and turkeys.

The plantation house was built in 1855, and is considered the finest example of Italianate Revival Architecture in Claiborne County, Mississippi. It's nestled in a beautiful park-like setting, and is now the home of Ray and Rachel Forrest. Canemount has been selected as one of the top 20 Inns in the South by *National Geographic Traveler*. It has also been featured in *Southern Living* and *Victorian Homes* magazines, and on the television program, *Woods & Wetlands*.

According to Forrest, "We now offer archery hunts for whitetail deer. They are very exclusive hunts, and accommodations are in the inn. Canemount has been on a deer management program with the Mississippi Department of Wildlife, Fisheries & Parks for the past 17 years. We have also worked closely with Mississippi State University and Dr. Harry Jacobsen in his buck mortality survey. All has been done in an effort to improve and upgrade our deer herd. A great deal of hard work and research has gone into the projects, resulting in the development of one of the finest deer herds in the state. All of our hunts are guided, with a very limited number of hunters."

Archery hunts run for four days, beginning with arrival on Sunday at noon and ending with the morning hunt on Thursday. The hunts include all meals and accommodations, and are limited to six hunters at one time so that each guest is able to enjoy the beauty of Canemount without being crowded. Archery hunts are semi-guided, and the bag limit is one trophy buck per hunt. You may also take one doe per day and a Russian boar when one is available

Every hunt begins early in the morning with a full Southern plantation breakfast prepared by Wilma Green. After loading up on biscuits and gravy and Wilma's blueberry pancakes (which are famous in these parts), hunters head out to their stands. Most hunters opt to come back to the big house for lunch, and then head back to their stands for the afternoon. Dinners, needless to say, are a specialty, with stuffed quail, prime rib, and grilled fish just some of the many main courses you're likely to be served. Cocktails and dinner take place at "The Persnickety Pig," an old dairy barn that has been transformed into an elegantly casual dining room where the evening meal is created by Chef Georgia Jackson.

Vital Statistics

THE LODGE:

Plantation house has 6 guest rooms, all with private baths

SERVICES: Telephone, fax, copying

HUNTS: $1,780 / 4 days

PAYMENT: Cash, check, credit card

CONFERENCE GROUPS: Yes

MEAL PLANS: All meals included (dinners of stuffed quail, prime rib, grilled fish, vegetables, homemade breads, and enough desserts to keep you loosening your belt)

NEAREST AIRPORT: Jackson, MS

TRANSPORTATION TO LODGE (60 miles): Rental car

CONTACT:

Ray Forrest
Canemount Plantation
4003 Hwy. 552 West
Lorman, MS 39096
Ph: 601/877-3784
Email: cmount@vicksburg.com
Fax: 601/877-2010
Web: canemount.com

THE HUNT:

SEASON:

• bow: October 1 - January 21

BEST TIME TO HUNT: Anytime

TERRAIN: Some hilly and some swamplands

LAND: Own 10,000 acres

DRAW BLOOD POLICY? No

HUNTING METHODS: Stand hunting (open tree stands)

YEARS IN BUSINESS: 5

STAFF OF GUIDES: 3

HUNTERS SERVED BY EACH GUIDE: 2

NONHUNTER CHARGE: $50 / day

LICENSES: Over the counter (lodge obtains customer licenses)

GAME CARE: Dress, package, freeze and ship game

OTHER ACTIVITIES: Big game hunting (wild turkeys, Russian boar), bird watching, wildlife photography

Circle M Plantation

Macon, Mississippi

THE FIRST SPORTSMAN to own the Circle M was the governor of Oklahoma, who bought the place in the 1920s. Later, the presidents of Archer-Daniels, General Mills, and Weyerhaeuser pooled their resources and bought the plantation for its bird hunting.

Quail is the Circle M's mainstay, but from October through January, host Lanier Long and his guides serve about 125 whitetail hunters. From stands and blinds overlooking feed plots, rub and scrape lines, swamp and river bottoms, and trails through piney woods, hunters wait for whitetails that average 8 points with 15-inch or better spreads. Hunters get up around 5 a.m., are fed a light breakfast, and driven to their stands long before daylight. The morning hunts wrap up around 10. Back at the lodge, there's a light snack waiting. Then there's the choice of bird hunting, five-stand, or bass fishing one of the plantations four ponds. After lunch and a nap, hunters return to their stands around 3:30, where they stay until dark.

Circle M offers hunters private lodges that accommodate up to five hunters. Each contains four bedrooms that have private baths. The lodges are tastefully furnished in a blend of traditional country and modern styles. Dinners of such Old South favorites as fried quail and venison are served in the wide-pineboard-floored dining room where, if there's a chill, a fire will warm the hearth. Catering not only to individuals, Circle M hosts many corporate groups.

Vital Statistics

THE LODGE:

Modern/rustic lodges have 12 guestrooms, 9 with private baths, 24 beds total

SERVICES: Telephone, fax, copying, TV, laundry

HUNTS:

- $700 / 2-day rifle hunt

- $600 / 2-day bow or muzzleloader hunt

PAYMENT: Credit cards, checks

MEAL PLANS: 3 meals a day (dinners include venison, quail, pork, chicken, catfish, vegetables, desserts and beverages)

SPECIAL DIETS: n/a

NEAREST AIRPORT: Golden Triangle, Columbus, MS

TRANSPORTATION TO LODGE (45 miles): Rental car; van ($25)

CONTACT:

Lanier Long
Circle M Plantation
Rt. 3, Box 710
Macon, MS 39341
Ph: 662/726-5791
Fax: 662/726-9300

THE HUNT:

SEASON:

- bow: Oct. 1 - Nov. 20, Jan. 21 - 31

- rifle: Nov. 20 - Dec. 1, Dec. 16 - Jan. 20

- muzzleloader: Dec. 1 - 15

BEST TIME TO HUNT: Dec. 20 - Jan. 15

TERRAIN: Hardwood bottoms and green fields

LAND: Own 3,500 acres, lease 2,500 acres

DRAW BLOOD POLICY? No

HUNTING METHODS: Stand hunting (wooden, tripods, boxes), still-hunting

YEARS IN BUSINESS: 6

STAFF OF GUIDES: 5

HUNTERS SERVED BY EACH GUIDE: 3

NONHUNTER CHARGE: No

LICENSES: Over the counter

GAME CARE: Quarter and provide ice

OTHER ACTIVITIES: Bird hunting, fishing, bird watching, hiking, wildlife photography, wagon rides

BOONE AND CROCKETT

- B&C book bucks taken from property: 0

- Average B&C score: 180

- B&C bucks from this part of state: 5

McKenna Ranch Outfitters

Pachuta, Mississippi

THE MCKENNA RANCH HAS A FAMILY ATMOSPHERE and is ideally suited for those looking for a great hunt at a fair price. Southern hospitality, nice facilities, fine cooking, and relaxing surroundings are what you'll find here. When you're not out hunting their 5,200 acres, you can fish in one of the five bass ponds or relax in a rocking chair on the front porch with a cup of coffee. The family works year-round at wildlife management to offer the best opportunities to harvest game. They plant deer and turkey food to enhance the size and number of game as well.

There are seven miles of pipeline and powerlines on the ranch where rye grass, clover, and corn are planted. Half of the pipeline is planted in the highest protein corn available. The pipeline and power lines have permanent all-weather double shooting houses, and there are 50 food plots in the woods planted in rye grass, clover, and corn. Hunts are on tripods on the food plots. There are also two creeks with crossings where ladder stands are used (they are changed around regularly). Each year, persimmon trees, sawtooth, white oaks, and a bush called anthumn olive are planted for the deer and turkey.

"Although no hunt can be guaranteed, we'll do whatever we can to make your hunt with us as successful as possible," states McKenna.

Vital Statistics

THE LODGE:

16 guestrooms, 20 beds total, 7 private baths

SERVICES: Telephone, fax, copying, TV, laundry

HUNTS:

- $1,800 / 4-day rifle hunt
- $1,000 / 4-day bowhunt
- $1,600 / 4-day blackpowder hunt

PAYMENT: Check, cash

MEAL PLANS: 3 meals a day (steak, potatoes, salad, English peas, bread, tea, desserts)

SPECIAL DIETS: n/a

NEAREST AIRPORT: Meridian, MS

TRANSPORTATION TO LODGE (30 miles): Rental car; van from lodge

CONTACT:

Steve, Mark or Betty McKenna
McKenna Ranch Outfitters
741 C.R. 313
Pachuta, MS 39347
Ph: 601/727-4926 or 3085
Fax: 601/727-7943.
Email: sbmckenna@aol.com
Web: www.buckmasters.com

THE HUNT:

SEASON:

- bow: Oct. 1 - Nov. 17, Jan. 20 - 31
- rifle: Nov. 18 - Dec. 1, Dec. 16 - Jan. 19
- muzzleloader: Dec. 2 - 15

BEST TIME TO HUNT: The rut, between Dec. 16 - Jan. 31

TERRAIN: Hills and hollows, some swamps, pipeline/powerline right of way

LAND: 6,000 private acres

DRAW BLOOD POLICY? No

HUNTING METHODS: Stand hunting (lock-ons, metal tripods and quadpods, enclosed shooting houses, lean-to ladders), still-hunting food plots, calling, rattling

YEARS IN BUSINESS: 10

STAFF OF GUIDES: 5

HUNTERS SERVED BY EACH GUIDE: 1 - 2

NONHUNTER CHARGE: No

LICENSES: Over the counter or by phone (1-800 - 5GOHUNT)

GAME CARE: Dressed and packaged for $75

OTHER ACTIVITIES: Turkey hunting, fishing, bird watching, hiking, swimming, wildlife photography, wildlife safari

BOONE AND CROCKETT

- B&C book bucks taken from property: 37
- Average B&C score: 130 - 170
- B&C bucks from this part of state: Many, including the Fulton buck, the current world record

Rose Hill Plantation

Bentonia, Mississippi

TYPICAL TROPHY TAKEN AT ROSE HILL
Plantation is an 8-pointer with a 15-inch spread.
Whitetails with racks bigger than 16 points have also
been taken on the 6,000-plus acres owned by Tom
Shipp, and 16-point sheds found after the season.
The doe-to-buck ratio is better than two-to-one, making for a well-balanced
herd. During a three-day hunt, clients will usually see more than a dozen deer
that would earn bragging rights anywhere. The size of the deer is so amazing to
many bowhunters that they sometimes lose their cool and blow reasonably easy
shots. That's okay, though, because chances are they'll get other opportunities
during their stay at Rose Hill.

One key to the good hunting at Rose Hill is that it is bowhunting only. A
few years ago, of the 30 hunters in camp, five took major bucks. The kill ratio
would no doubt be higher if firearms were allowed, but that's not what Rose
Hill is about. This is for serious bowhunters only, and it's managed to ensure a
continuous supply of trophy-quality bucks. Shipp must be doing something
right, as he has a 60 percent return of hunters year after year.

Rose Hill, 30 miles north of Jackson, has been in Shipp's family since just
after the Civil War. Like most plantations in the area, it grew and shrank as the
economy prospered or declined. Today, about 2,000 acres of the property is
devoted to soybeans, corn, wheat, and cotton. Deer tend to eat the first two
crops when they can, then bed down in the cotton. At dusk, they slip out of
the cotton, woodlands, and grass fields, and head toward the grain fields,
inevitably passing stands that Shipp and his guides have placed in likely areas.
You can catch them moving to food anytime during the season, although during the rut, calling and rattling can also get their attention.

Whether you're successful or not on a given day, the return to the lodge
each evening is always enjoyable. Extremely comfortable, the modern southern-style lodge (red cedar and glass) has three bedrooms and two baths. After
a shower and a bit of relaxing, the home-cooked meals are sure to recharge you
and get you fueled for the next day afield.

Vital Statistics

THE LODGE:

Modern main lodge has 3 guestrooms, some have private baths, 6 beds total

SERVICES: Telephone, fax, TV, laundry

HUNTS: (bow hunts only)

- $1,200 / 4 days from Oct. 1 - Nov. 31
- $1,600 / 4 days from Dec. 1 - Jan. 1

PAYMENT: Cash, credit cards, checks

MEAL PLANS: All meals included (pre-dawn breakfasts are continental style; late-morning breakfasts are large southern-style meals, with eggs, biscuits and gravy, pancakes and more; dinners after the hunt include filet mignon, marinated pork tenderloin, grilled catfish, shrimp scampi on angel hair pasta, grilled chicken, vegetables, salads, rolls, desserts, tea, soda, milk, coffee)

CONFERENCE GROUPS? Yes

NEAREST AIRPORT: Jackson, MS

TRANSPORTATION TO LODGE (30 miles): Rental car; van from lodge (no extra charge)

CONTACT:

Tom Shipp
Rose Hill Plantation
1079 Passons Rd.
Bentonia, MS 39040
Ph: 662/755-8383 Lodge: 662/755-8300
Fax: 662/755-2020
Web: rosehillplantation.com

THE HUNT:

SEASON: October 1 - January 31

BEST TIME TO HUNT: December 15 - January 15

TERRAIN: Hardwoods, grass fields, creek drainages, farm field edges (grain), large irregularly-shaped grainfields

LAND: 6,000+ private acres

DRAW BLOOD POLICY? 2 blood = 1 deer

HUNTING METHODS: Stand hunting (80 percent lock-ons, 20 percent ladder stands), calling, rattling

YEARS IN BUSINESS: 6

STAFF OF GUIDES: 4

HUNTERS SERVED BY EACH GUIDE: 2

NONHUNTER CHARGE: $100/day, space permitting

LICENSES: Over the counter (can purchase before arriving or at the lodge)

GAME CARE: Dress, package (freeze and ship game $100 extra)

OTHER ACTIVITIES: Bird hunting (quail, dove), fishing, bird watching, hiking, wildlife photography

POPE & YOUNG

- P&Y book bucks taken from property: 6
- Average P&Y score: 135
- P&Y bucks from this part of state: 75+

Tara Wildlife, Inc.

Vicksburg, Mississippi

WILLOW POINT is comprised of two islands in the Mississippi River, each noted as a haven for considerable numbers of large whitetails. Willow Point North consists of 3,800 acres and accommodates 10 hunters. Willow Point South covers 6,500 acres and can easily accommodate up to 12 hunters. The newest bow-only addition, Tara Hunt Club, totals over 5,500 acres and can accommodate up to 13 hunters. All 16,000 acres of fertile bottomland habitat are owned and operated by Tara Wildlife, Inc., one of the nation's premier wildlife management teams. As part of an intensive management plan of controlled harvest and supplemental food planting, Willow Point and Tara Hunt Club's outstanding habitat effectively carries a sizable and healthy herd. Live weights of up to 320 pounds have been recorded, and bucks weighing in excess of 200 pounds are common. Since 1988, there have been well over 184 Pope & Young (gross scores) deer harvested from Tara properties, with at least 133 of those taken during the 1995 through 2000 seasons.

Hunter success rates have been excellent, and projections for the upcoming seasons are good. Tara hosts all different types of hunters, from the avid trophy hunter to women and children, and even seniors over the age of 70. Hunting is done primarily from Loc-on Tree Stands, but those preferring ground blinds or climbers can hunt successfully as well. No open-on-impact broadheads are allowed.

The facilities on both islands are spacious and comfortable. Large dining rooms, complete with TVs and telephones, are the centers of activity. Meals are southern home favorites. The morning starts with a continental-style breakfast and ends with a hearty brunch following the morning hunt. A plentiful Southern-style dinner is served following the afternoon hunt.

Vital Statistics

THE LODGE:

51 guest rooms, 88 beds total, some private baths; accommodations are modern/rustic

SERVICES: Telephone, fax, copying, TV, laundry

HUNTS:

- $1,100 / 3-day early-season bow hunt
- $1,700 / 3-day late-season bow hunt (during and after the rut)

PAYMENT: Cash, credit cards, check

MEAL PLANS: 3 meals a day (southern dishes; excellent cooks, a wide variety of choices)

SPECIAL DIETS: Heart healthy, vegetarian, salt/msg free

NEAREST AIRPORT: Jackson, MS

TRANSPORTATION TO LODGE (85 miles): Rental car; van ($150 round trip)

CONTACT:

Sidney Montgomery
Tara Wildlife, Inc.
6791 Eagle Lake Shore Rd.
Vicksburg, MS 39183
Ph: 601/279-4261
Fax: 601/279-4227
Email: tara@tarawildlife.com
Web: www.tarawildlife.com

THE HUNT:

SEASON: October 1 - January 31

BEST TIME TO HUNT: Mid-December

TERRAIN: Hardwood bottomlands along the Mississippi River

LAND: Tara owns approximately 30 miles of river frontage and approximately 20,000 acres of huntable land

DRAW BLOOD POLICY? No

HUNTING METHODS: Stand hunting (lock-ons), still-hunting, rattling

YEARS IN BUSINESS: 15

STAFF OF GUIDES: 6

HUNTERS SERVED BY EACH GUIDE: 3

NONHUNTER CHARGE: $100 / day

LICENSES: Sold at Tara upon arrival

GAME CARE: Dressed, packaged, frozen, and shipped for no extra charge

OTHER ACTIVITIES: Bird hunting, waterfowling, fishing, antiquing, biking, bird watching, boating, canoeing, hiking, swimming, wildlife photography

POPE & YOUNG

- P&Y book bucks taken from property: 51 (through the 1999-2000 season)
- Average P&Y score: 125
- P&Y bucks from this part of state: Many

Buffalo Creek Guide Service

Selma, North Carolina

B UFFALO CREEK LODGE is approximately 5,000 acres of beautiful hunting country. It is flat land with slight ridges of hardwood and pine thickets surrounded by vast tracts of cypress swamps. It also contains many fields of peanuts, which deer absolutely love. In fact, the high protein found in peanuts helps to grow some of the biggest racks in North Carolina. The deer leave the protection of the bottomlands to graze on peanuts and also on grain provided by Buffalo Creek.

Tree stands are the most productive way of hunting in this area. Buffalo Creek also has several shooting houses for hunters who don't want to climb. In total, there are more than 200 stands on the property. Many are baited with corn or located on feeders, while some are on hardwood ridges and at the edges of peanut fields. When you hunt here, you decide the type of area you want to hunt.

Buffalo Creek has two lodges: one is in Sampson County, where deer are totally managed for trophy quality; the other is in Bertie County, where you're likely to see bucks of any size. Bow, shotgun, rifle, or muzzleloader may be used.

The rut usually runs from the last week of October to the middle of November. This is the best time to take a really big buck. Deer are usually on the move during this time, and hunters are placed in stands with greater visibility to watch for bucks in search of does.

There are no size restrictions at the Bertie Camp, though minimal fines are imposed for taking button bucks.

According to one member of the North American Hunting Club, "You can't go wrong with Buffalo Creek Guide Service. Johnnie Dale is an excellent guide, who goes above and beyond what is expected. He and his other guides did their very best to put us in prime areas." That hunter awarded excellent ratings to the lodge, both for quality and quantity of game, and for good accommodations.

Vital Statistics

THE LODGE:

6 guestrooms, 2 have private baths, 15 beds total

SERVICES: Telephone, TV

HUNTS:

- $250 / day at Bertie County lodge
- $300 / day at Sampson County lodge

PAYMENT: Check, credit cards, check

MEAL PLANS: 3 meals a day (typical dinners feature venison, roast beef, chicken, port, steak, pasta)

SPECIAL DIETS: Heart healthy, vegetarian, salt/msg free

NEAREST AIRPORT: Raleigh/Durham, NC

TRANSPORTATION TO LODGE (75 miles): Rental car; van ($100)

CONTACT:

Johnnie Dale
Buffalo Creek Guide Service
1476 Old Moore Rd.
Selma, NC 27576
Ph: 800/868-6265 or 919/965-4014

THE HUNT:

SEASON:

- bow: Sept. 11 - Oct. 7 (either sex — 2 per day)
- rifle: Oct. 16 - Jan. 1 (4 bucks and 1 doe — 2 per day)
- muzzleloader: Oct. 7 - 9 (3 bucks and 2 does — 2 per day)

BEST TIME TO HUNT: Oct./Nov.

TERRAIN: 200 stands are placed in swamps, peanut fields, cornfields, cutovers, and hardwood or pine plantations

LAND: 2,000 acres at Sampson Lodge; 5,000 acres at Bertie Lodge

DRAW BLOOD POLICY? No

HUNTING METHODS: Stand hunting (enclosed boxes with chairs, ladders with shooting rails, ground blinds)

YEARS IN BUSINESS: 16

STAFF OF GUIDES: 5

HUNTERS SERVED BY EACH GUIDE: 3

NONHUNTER CHARGE: $75 / day

LICENSES: Sold over the counter

GAME CARE: None, but will arrange taxidermy services

OTHER ACTIVITIES: Other big game hunting (wild hogs, bobcats, black bears, wild turkey in spring), bird hunting, waterfowling, trapping school

BOONE AND CROCKETT

- B&C book bucks taken from property: None
- Average B&C score: 110 - 155
- B&C book bucks from this part of state: None

Occoneechee Lodge

Jackson, North Carolina

O CCONEECHEE LODGE is located in the heart of the peanut belt of northeastern North Carolina. The lodge's hunting area consists of 7,000 acres of family-owned land in Northampton County on the historical Roanoke River. Northampton has been the state leader in deer kills reported for the past several years. Directly across the river is Halifax County, the No. 2 deer kill county in the state.

Occoneechee offers one of the longest seasons in the country, with the bowhunting season beginning in early September, blackpowder in early October, and rifle season running from mid-October to January 1. The bag limit is very liberal, with six-deer-per-season and two-deer-per-day limits. There is a one-month-long either-sex season beginning December 1. However, two does may also be taken between October and December using special tags.

The lodge's experienced guides do their best to make each client's hunting experience as successful and enjoyable as possible. Occoneechee does not guarantee any kills because under some conditions, the deer just do not move as well. However, over the past several years, hunters have enjoyed a 100 percent success ratio.

On a guided hunt, guests are taken to their stands before daylight by an experienced guide and picked up around 10 a.m. After lunch, the hunters are taken back to their stands where they stay until dark. Handling the kill is included in a guided hunt. The deer will be dressed and quartered. Packaging and shipping is the hunter's responsibility. There is a cooler on the premises.

Hunters have the option of hunting a 2,500-acre trophy management area, which consists of three miles of riverbottom, crop fields, swamp, and hardwood ridges along the Roanoke River. Bucks with a minimum 15-inch outside spread or mature does may be taken from this area.

County law requires hunters to be elevated eight feet when firing a rifle. Guests have a variety of stand locations to choose from. Tripod, tower, and ladder treestands are selectively placed over peanut, corn, and soybean fields, as well as pasture land, standing timber, and logging trails over fall and winter food plots. In addition, many of the stands are baited with corn, with an average of about 2,000 pounds a week being fed. Shooting distances range from five to 300 yards. Portable stands are available, or guests are welcome to bring their own. There is a shooting range on the premises too.

Lodging at Occoneechee is not fancy. The lodge is a clean and comfortable three-bedroom farmhouse that accommodates eleven. The lodge has full kitchen facilities for guests who prefer to cook for themselves; linens and towels are also provided. There are several restaurants, motels and hotels in the area, all within a few minutes of the lodge.

Vital Statistics

THE LODGE:

Farmhouse contains 3 guest rooms, none with private bath, 11 beds total; also local hotels

SERVICES: Telephone, TV

HUNTS:

• bow/rifle/muzzleloader: $250 / day with meals and lodging; $200 / day without meals

PAYMENT: Cash or check

CONFERENCE GROUPS: No

MEAL PLANS: All meals included if opting for the meal plan (dinners include pork chops, fried chicken, beef stew, meat loaf, veggies and all the fixins')

SPECIAL DIETS: Heart healthy

NEAREST AIRPORT: Raleigh-Durham, NC, or Richmond, VA

TRANSPORTATION TO LODGE (1 1/2 hours): Rental car

BOONE AND CROCKETT

• B&C book bucks taken from property: None

• Average B&C score: 100-130; 156 best taken

• B&C bucks from this part of state: Some

CONTACT:

Gil Cutchin
Occoneechee Lodge
Rt. 1, box 435
Jackson, NC 27845
Ph: 252/583-1799

THE HUNT:

SEASON:

• bow: Sept. 8 - Oct. 12

• rifle: Oct. 18 - Jan. 1

• muzzleloader: Oct. 12 - 18

BEST TIME TO HUNT: November

TERRAIN: Riverbottom agricultural land along the Roanoke River, cutovers, hardwoods, swamps

LAND: 7,000 private acres

DRAW BLOOD POLICY? No

HUNTING METHODS: Stand hunting (tripods, towers and wood boxes)

YEARS IN BUSINESS: 10

STAFF OF GUIDES: Several

HUNTERS SERVED BY EACH GUIDE: 5 - 6

NONHUNTER CHARGE: No

LICENSES: Can be purchased over the counter or before arriving by calling NCWRC at 919/715-4091

GAME CARE: Kills are dressed and quartered; packaging and shipping are the hunter's responsibility

OTHER ACTIVITIES: Fishing, antiquing, biking, bird watching, boating, canoeing, golf, swimming, tennis, whitewater rafting

Roanoke Tar Guide Service

Littleton, North Carolina

LOCATED IN HALIFAX COUNTY, where some of North Carolina's biggest deer reside (note the No. 4 in the state typical deer, scoring 172 6/8, which was taken in 1999), Roanoke-Tar Guide Service hunts more than 2,000 acres of prime real estate. Head guide Jeff Wolgemuth, who runs the service, not only knows the property like the back of his hand, but is a registered forester, and knows just what the deer are feeding on, where, and when.

According to Wolgemuth, "Our deer hunting tactics are stand hunting from tree or tower stands. Most of our deer stands are enclosed, so bad weather will not hamper your hunt. We have a deer feeding program that consists of mineral feeding during the spring and summer months, and corn feeding during fall and winter. This is completely legal, and is very helpful in getting the deer close enough for a good shot. We prefer small groups of hunters, to increase your chance of a successful hunt."

The enclosed tower stands are excellent for young hunters in particular. They provide a shooting rest, plus they conceal movement and noise from the deer. These stands allow an adult and child to hunt together, since they are 4' x 4' on the inside.

The lodge is a two-story farmhouse. It has kitchen and bath facilities on the lower level, and three rooms upstairs for sleeping quarters. Depending on the hunting package, you can either cook for yourself or have Roanoke provide breakfasts, lunches, and dinners. The cooking facilities are perfect for hunters who like to do it on their own.

The North Carolina season is long and generous, too. The entire season is either sex hunting, with a six-deer-a-year limit. Each hunter is allowed two deer per day, with a four-buck maximum per year.

The farmhouse at Roanoke Tar Guide Service.

Vital Statistics

THE LODGE:

Farmhouse contains 4 guest rooms, 8 beds total, no private baths

SERVICES: TV, laundry

HUNTS:

- $200 / day (lodging, linens, no meals)

- $250 / day (lodging, linens, meals, game cleaning)

- $1,000 / 6 days (lodging, linens, no meals)

- $1,250 / 6 days (lodging, linens, meals, game cleaning)

PAYMENT: Cash or check

CONFERENCE GROUPS: n/a

MEAL PLANS: Hunters who choose the meal plan are served a hot breakfast, cold cut lunch, and dinners that feature bbq chicken, hamburgers, pork chops and fish

NEAREST AIRPORT: Rocky Mount, NC

TRANSPORTATION TO LODGE (25 miles): Rental car

THE HUNT:

SEASON:

- bow: mid-Sept. - Oct. 7 (approximately)

- rifle: mid-Oct. - Jan. 1

- muzzleloader: Oct. 7 - 14 (approximately)

BEST TIME TO HUNT: Mid-November

TERRAIN: Mostly pine plantations, some swamps

LAND: 2,050 private acres

DRAW BLOOD POLICY? No

HUNTING METHODS: Stand hunting (enclosed tower stands, mostly with swivel seats on pedestals)

YEARS IN BUSINESS: 2

STAFF OF GUIDES: 1

HUNTERS SERVED BY EACH GUIDE: Up to 4

NONHUNTER CHARGE: $25 / day

LICENSES: Over the counter before arriving

GAME CARE: Hunters do their own

OTHER ACTIVITIES: Fishing

BOONE AND CROCKETT

- B&C book bucks taken from property: 0

- Average B&C score: n/a

- B&C bucks from this part of state: #4 typical in state was taken in 1999, just 20 miles away

CONTACT:

Jeffrey D. Wolgemuth
Roanoke Tar Guide Service
3851 Sledge Rd.
Littleton, NC 27850
Ph: 252/586-5914
Fax: 252/586-0251
Email: wolge@schoolink.net

Bostick Plantation

Estill, South Carolina

HUNTING IN SOUTH CAROLINA CAN BE TOUGH. With hot weather and the accompanying insects at the beginning of the season (August), and with colder weather than a northerner might imagine in December and January, the whitetail hunter is faced with his share of challenges.

Hunting hardwood forests, swamps, pine forests, fields, and food plots, hunters at Bostick Plantation can cover the type of terrain they prefer. Most hunting is done from enclosed stands that can accommodate two people. Bucks here can grow big antlers, especially those that frequent the food plots. And as in most of the state, hunters can take more than one deer — doe or buck.

At the end of the day, hunters catch a ride back to the plantation where they fill up on sumptuous meals that include chicken, venison, pork, turkey, and ham — all cooked southern plantation style. Then it's off to the living area for some good conversation, followed by a comfortable bed. The next day, guests can hunt deer again — or hog or quail. This is a fun, Southern experience that every hunter should sample.

Vital Statistics

THE LODGE:

12 guest rooms, 24 beds total, 3 bathrooms

SERVICES: Telephone, cable TV

HUNTS: $325 / day

PAYMENT: Cash, credit cards, money orders, cashiers checks, travelers checks

MEAL PLANS: 3 meals a day (Southern plantation style meals with ham, turkey, pork, venison, chicken, and all the fixin's, huge desserts)

SPECIAL DIETS: Any requests are honored

NEAREST AIRPORT: Savannah, GA

TRANSPORTATION TO LODGE (50 miles): Rental car; van ($150 charge)

CONTACT:

Joe Bostick
Bostick Plantation
Box 728
Estill, SC 29918
Ph: 800/542-6913
Fax: 803/625-2038
Web: Http://www.Bostick-Plantation.com

THE HUNT:

SEASON:

• bow/rifle/muzzleloader: Aug. 15 - Jan. 1

BEST TIME TO HUNT: Aug., Oct., Nov.

TERRAIN: Hardwood forest, swamp, pine forest, fields, food plots

LAND: Leased

DRAW BLOOD POLICY? No

HUNTING METHODS: Stand hunting (enclosed stands for 1 or 2, lock-ons, tripods), still-hunting, calling, rattling

Years in Business: 22

STAFF OF GUIDES : 6+

HUNTERS SERVED BY EACH GUIDE: 4 - 6

NONHUNTER CHARGE: $100 / day

LICENSES: Over the counter

GAME CARE: Packaged, frozen, and shipped ($45)

OTHER ACTIVITIES: Other big game hunting (hogs, turkeys), quail hunting, waterfowling, fishing, golf, swimming, tennis, wildlife photography

BOONE AND CROCKETT

• B&C book bucks taken from property: None

• Average B&C score: 173

• B&C book bucks from this part of state: 3

Cedar Knoll Hunting Lodge

Allendale, South Carolina

FOUNDED IN 1985 BY Hayward and Dona Simmons as a full service hunting club providing quality hunting for friends and relatives, while emphasizing the importance of fellowship, tradition, and sound wildlife management, Cedar Knoll is comprised of 2,600 acres near the Savannah River in Allendale County. The annual sustained harvest is approximately 40 bucks per square mile — making this one incredible place to hunt.

All hunting is done from elevated stands situated over food plots, or in the woods along ridges, bottoms, and/or wild food sources. Stand placement affords shooting opportunities ranging from 50 to 400 yards, with the average distance being 150 yards. Most stands will accommodate two people, so you can take along a non-hunting spouse or novice, if you wish.

A bonus to hunting this area is a long season — from mid-August until January 1. Hunters can take one buck "per sitting," plus one doe per sitting. Add up the possibilities for that, and you'll be astonished. For a whitetail hunt that's a bit out of the ordinary, consider an August hunt for bucks still in velvet.

Aside from the great hunting, Cedar Knoll offers great accommodations and incredible dining. For a whitetail hunter, who could ask for more?

Vital Statistics

THE LODGE:

7 guest rooms, 32 beds total, 4 rooms have private baths

SERVICES: Telephone, fax, copying, TV, laundry, game room

HUNTS: $325 - $450 / day

PAYMENT: Check, credit cards

MEAL PLANS: Evening meal included (typical menu includes entree, starch, two vegetables, bread and dessert, such as glazed pork tenderloin over rice, squash, greenbeans, yeast rolls, and peach cobbler)

SPECIAL DIETS: Heart healthy, vegetarian, salt/msg free

NEAREST AIRPORT: Savannah, GA, or Augusta, GA

TRANSPORTATION TO LODGE (65 miles): Rental car; van ($150 charge)

CONTACT:

Hayward Simmons
Cedar Knoll Hunting Lodge
875 Cedar Knoll Road
Fairfax, VA 39827
Ph: 803/584-0689
Fax: 803/584-0689
Email: lakeviewplantation@barnwellsc.com
Web: Http://www.lakeviewplantation.com

THE HUNT:

SEASONS:

• rifle: August 15 - January 1

• muzzleloader: August 15 - January 1

BEST TIME TO HUNT: October and November

TERRAIN: Bottomland hardwoods, pine plantations, cutovers, food plots

LAND: 2,600 leased/private acres

DRAW BLOOD POLICY? No

HUNTING METHODS: Stand hunting (12-foot metal tower stands with canvas skirts and tops, with padded rails), shooting houses with plexy windows

YEARS IN BUSINESS: 16

STAFF OF GUIDES : 2

HUNTERS SERVED BY EACH GUIDE: 4 - 5 (guides typically only transport hunters to and from fields, and dress game)

NONHUNTER CHARGE: $35 - $100 / day

LICENSES: Sold at the lodge

GAME CARE: $50 - $75 processing; shipping depends on destination

OTHER ACTIVITIES: Wild turkey hunting, shooting range

BOONE AND CROCKETT

• B&C book bucks taken from property: None

• Average B&C score: 110

• B&C book bucks from this part of state: 1

Cowden Plantation

Jackson, South Carolina

PREHISTORIC HUNTERS, Native Americans, an esteemed governor, and a master rifle craftsman all share a common bond here. A love of a land laced with flowing creeks, shadowed by tall pine forests and cypress swamps, and boasting an abundance of wildlife. Simply put — a love of Cowden Plantation. Ancient artifacts, left behind tens of thousand of years ago, tell the tale of tribes of hunters who relied on this land for their survival. Vast swamplands and flowing waters provided generously for Native Americans several hundred years ago. Antebellum days brought King Cotton to Cowden under the ownership of James Henry Hammond, a South Carolina governor whose home, Redcliffe, still stands proudly. Cowden Plantation today offers the same beauty and wildlife that people throughout history have cherished, and is home to Kenny Jarrett, the master craftsman of the renowned Jarrett rifle. A 10,000-acre wildlife and game preserve, Cowden Plantation is dedicated to the conservation and management of wild game and their natural habitat. You'll find Carolina forests filled with trophy whitetail deer, along with wild boar and turkeys, sparkling waters filled with bass and bream, and a variety of waterfowl. This is nature at its finest — hunted for centuries and still unspoiled today.

South Carolina enjoys the longest deer season in the nation, and at Cowden, under trophy management for the past 16 years, you'll find the game truly wild. On unfenced land, Cowden offers a fair chase hunt. You'll have a chance at a trophy buck, or you may want to stake out in one of the 110 deer stands that overlook food plots. Roofed and equipped with shooting rails and chair, these stands are something you'll like. Special areas of the property are managed for trophy bucks, and on others there's no restriction on size. The plantation contains 11.5 square miles laced with 145 miles of roads that run past fields, through oaks draped with moss, and across creeks that lead to a thick cypress swamp. The wild boar that roam these parts are hunted from stands over bait.

Clean and comfortable accommodations are found in an old farmhouse. When it comes to food, guests have three options. You can do you own cooking, eat at the Buckhead Diner in town, or make sure there are at least three hunters in your party. Then Kenny Jarrett and his crew will lay on a cook who will fatten you with her first platter of buttery biscuits. Hunting rates here are by the day.

Vital Statistics

THE LODGE:

Farmhouse has 1 guest room, no private baths, 10 beds total

SERVICES: TV

GUN HUNTS:

- $300 / night August 15 - October 30
- $4000 / night in November

PAYMENT: Cash, credit cards, check

CONFERENCE GROUPS: Yes

MEAL PLANS: Meals are included and are the hunters' preference; country cooking can be arranged

NEAREST AIRPORT: Augusta, GA

TRANSPORTATION TO LODGE (25 to 30 minutes): Van from lodge at no additional charge

CONTACT:

Jay Jarrett
Cowden Plantation
383 Brown Rd.
Jackson, SC 29831
Ph: 803/471-3616
Fax: 803/471-9246
Email: jarrett5@mindspring.com
Web: www.jarrettrifles.com

THE HUNT:

SEASON: August 15 - January 1

BEST TIME TO HUNT: Anytime

TERRAIN: Mixed hardwood and pines; 4,500 acres of property is flood plain swamp

LAND: 10,500 private acres

DRAW BLOOD POLICY? No

HUNTING METHODS: Stand hunting (wooden/enclosed/approximately 8 feet off the ground), still-hunting

YEARS IN BUSINESS: 20

STAFF OF GUIDES: 2

HUNTERS SERVED BY EACH GUIDE: Up to 4

NONHUNTER CHARGE: No

LICENSES: Sold at the lodge

GAME CARE: Dress, package, freeze, and ship game for an average of $100

OTHER ACTIVITIES: Other big game hunting (wild boar, turkeys), fishing

BOONE AND CROCKETT

- B&C book bucks taken from property: None
- Average B&C score: 173
- B&C bucks from this part of state: 3

Deerfield Plantation

St. George, South Carolina

D EERFIELD PLANTATION is situated in the heart of South Carolina's low country "deerbelt," and is a working plantation with corn, soybeans, peas, wheat, oats, rye, and coastal bermuda fields. The plantation has 300 permanent deer stands in two main hunting areas. In the "regular" hunting area (more than 7,000 acres), all bucks must have a minimum of 4 points that are also at least one inch long. In the trophy management area (more than 3,000 acres), any buck harvested must have 8 points and a 15-inch spread. The trophy area is hunted only in the afternoons. Beginning September 15, hunters may harvest a buck or doe in the regular hunting area.

All stands are selectively placed in highly active deer areas. Deerfield offers more than 80 shooting houses. Most are overlooking agriculture fields, food plots, and supplemental feeding stations. In addition to the shooting houses, there are more than 100 12-foot-high tripods with shooting rails. Some stands are located in cutovers and pine plantations. Others are strategically placed in hardwood swamps and runs. The balance of the stands are mostly movable lean-up stands with shooting rails.

A typical day at Deefield starts with a wakeup call at approximately an hour and a half before sunrise. A continental breakfast is offered at this time. Afterwards, an experienced guide will take you to your stand before the morning hunt. Between 10 and 11, depending on the time of year, you will be picked up and brought out to the lodge for lunch. The afternoon hunt begins between 2 and 4, again, depending on the time of year. You will hunt until dark, when one of Deerfield's guides will pick you up and return you to the lodge.

Deerfield Plantation follows the guidelines and recommendations of the South Carolina Department of Natural Resources, The Quality Deer Management Association, and its own independent biologist.

Visiting Deefield Plantation is a bit like taking a trip back in time, with Southern hospitality and traditional plantation-style cooking the usual fare. Moss-laden, winding, sandy roads help ease the stress from your body as you enter this region, a world of antebellum tranquility. Deerfield is an excellent place to bring your overworked mind, your appetite, and your hopes for a "Low Country" trophy buck.

Vital Statistics

THE LODGE:

8 guest rooms (6 in the plantation house, 2 in cabins), 3 have private baths, 30 beds

SERVICES: Telephone, fax, copying, TV

GUN HUNTS: $295 / day per person, 3-day minimum

PAYMENT: Cash or credit cards

Conference Groups: Yes

MEAL PLANS: All meals included (dinners of beef, pork chops, chicken, venison)

NEAREST AIRPORT: Charleston, SC

TRANSPORTATION TO LODGE (50 miles): Rental car; van from lodge $200 round-trip

CONTACT:

Hugh Walters III
Deerfield Plantation
709 Gum Branch Road
St. George, SC 29477
Ph:843/563-7927
Email: deerfield@infoave.net
Web: www.huntersnet.com/deerfield

THE HUNT:

SEASON:

• bow/rifle/muzzleloader: Aug. 15 - Sept. 14, one buck per day; Sept. 15 - Jan. 1, one deer morning hunt, one deer afternoon hunt

BEST TIME TO HUNT: Sept. 15 - Nov. 10

TERRAIN: Swamps, planted pines, food plots, agricultural fields

LAND: 10,000 private acres

DRAW BLOOD POLICY? Yes

HUNTING METHODS: Stand hunting (tripods, basket lean-ups, houses), still-hunting, calling, rattling

YEARS IN BUSINESS: 11

STAFF OF GUIDES : 4

HUNTERS SERVED BY EACH GUIDE: 4 - 5 (one-on-one hunts $100 additional per day)

NONHUNTER CHARGE: $100 / day

LICENSES: Sold at the lodge

GAME CARE: Dressed, packaged, frozen, and shipped, $50 plus shipping

OTHER ACTIVITIES: Wild hog hunting, bird hunting (turkeys, quail), fishing

Little River Plantation

Abbeville, South Carolina

L ITTLE RIVER PLANTATION controls and manages several thousand acres of prime white-tailed deer and turkey habitat. All of the land is situated in the South Carolina Piedmont in Abbeville and McCormick counties, about five miles from the Georgia border. This is the area of South Carolina where the vast majority of trophy bucks inhabit. There are a lot of deer, too, as the success rate is better than 85 percent. There are so many deer, in fact, that a hunter could actually take 10 deer in a season (no more than two a day) that runs from early bow in September to late rifle in January.

Hunters coming to Little River can sign up for three- or six-day hunts. All three-day hunts begin either on Mondays or Thursdays, while all six-day hunts begin on Mondays. Hunters should plan to arrive a day before the hunt begins, however, in order to buy licenses and get settled in.

Little River Plantation, under the leadership of owner Jim Edens, has been involved with a quality deer-management program for a number of years, with client/hunters only allowed to shoot bucks that are 6 points or better. Thanks to this program, younger bucks are getting the chance to grow to trophy size. Hunters saw twice as many rack bucks in 1996 as than they did in 1995, and that trend has been continuing with each passing year ever since.

The lodge itself, a 1930s-era barn that's been refurbished, overlooks a sprawling yard dominated by old oaks and sycamores, with an understory of dogwoods, redbud, and honeysuckle. To complete the classic Southern setting, dining is pure South: beef, potatoes, and vegetables, to be sure, but also barbecued offerings, fried chicken and peas, and biscuits and gravy with grits for breakfast.

Vital Statistics

THE LODGE:

4 rooms in main lodge, 4 in cabins, 23 beds total, some have private baths

SERVICES: Telephone, fax, TV, laundry

HUNTS:

• $995 / 3-day hunt

• $1,780 / 6-day hunt

PAYMENT: Cash, check, credit cards

CONFERENCE GROUPS: Yes

MEAL PLANS: Breakfast, lunch, and dinners — assorted fare

NEAREST AIRPORT: Augusta, GA

TRANSPORTATION TO LODGE (65 miles): Rental car; van from lodge $50

CONTACT:

Jim Edens
Little River Plantation
P.O. Box 1129
Abbeville, SC 29620
Ph: 864/391-2300
Fax: 864/391-2304
Email: L.R.Plantation@wctel.com
Web: www.littleriverplantation.com

THE HUNT:

SEASON:

• bow: September 15 - October 10

• rifle: October 11 - January 1

• muzzleloader: October 1 - 10

BEST TIME TO HUNT: First week of November

TERRAIN: Hardwood forests, fields, swamps

LAND: 5,000+ acres

DRAW BLOOD POLICY? Yes

HUNTING METHODS: Stand hunting (enclosed, ladder stands, two-piece climbers), calling, rattling

YEARS IN BUSINESS: 16

STAFF OF GUIDES: 4 - 6

HUNTERS SERVED BY EACH GUIDE: 2 - 4

NONHUNTER CHARGE: $60 / day

LICENSES: Sold over the counter, or at the lodge

GAME CARE: Dress, package, freeze, and ship for $35

OTHER ACTIVITIES: Turkey hunting, bird hunting (quail, chukar, pheasant), waterfowling, fishing, canoeing, wildlife photography, sporting clays

BOONE AND CROCKETT

• B&C book bucks taken from property: 0

• Average B&C score: 177 plus

• B&C bucks from this part of state: 3

Paradise Valley Hunt Club

E h r h a r d t , S o u t h C a r o l i n a

PARADISE VALLEY SPECIALIZES in personal, friendly service, and it caters to a wide range of hunters. It is set up for serious trophy hunters, from one man to a group that wants a choice of hunting areas. The club encourages no time limits; you can use your ownstand or one of the club's. You can drive yourself, if you like, and owner/operator Brock Hook will even give you your own area to hunt and leave you alone, if that is what you like. Hook knows that many hunters are very serious, and want to walk and scout an area, check for sign, and put up their own climbers. Many other clubs won't let you drive on their property or determine your own stand, but Hook is happy to do so. He will also sit with a first-time hunter to help him or her get their first deer, and non-hunters are also welcome.

This area has a large concentration of deer that aren't pressured by cold winters or overhunting. With abundant food, a mild climate and lots of timberland, this is a great area to hunt whitetail deer.

Aside from good hunting for unpressured bucks, Paradise Valley has all the amenities that are sure to please. The main lodge has four bedrooms and two fireplaces. All other lodges are private and have two to three bedrooms; each has a country kitchen, and a living room complete with all the amenities of home — including a huge porch where guests can prop their feet up and talk about the day's hunt.

The main lodge at Paradise Valley Hunting Club.

© Paradise Valley Hunting Club

Vital Statistics

THE LODGE:

15 guest rooms, 6 separate lodges, 25 beds total, 8 private baths

SERVICES: Telephone, fax, TV, laundry

HUNTS: Rates vary from $150 - $275 / day, depending on size of group and length of stay

PAYMENT: Cash, credit cards, checks

MEAL PLANS: Use lodge kitchens or two restaurants in town

SPECIAL DIETS: Heart healthy, vegetarian

NEAREST AIRPORT: Columbia or Charleston, SC

TRANSPORTATION TO LODGE (65 miles from either airport): Rental car; van ($50 one way)

CONTACT:

Capt. Brock Hook
Paradise Valley Hunt Club
PO Box 318
Ehrhardt, SC 29081
Ph: 803/267-BUCK (2825)
Fax: 803/267-4803
Web: http://www.fish-hunt.net

THE HUNT:

SEASONS:

• bow/rifle/muzzleloader: Aug. 15 - Jan. 1

BEST TIME TO HUNT: First rut (Oct. 28 - Nov. 15); second rut (Nov. 28 - Dec. 20)

TERRAIN: Flat fields, swamps, and at slightly higher elevations, hardwood and pine forests, planted pine plantations, open savanna with sprawling live oaks, agricultural fields

LAND: 3,780+ private acres on 15 different tracts

DRAW BLOOD POLICY? No

HUNTING METHODS: Stand hunting (12 16-foot box stands that seat 2 and have roofs, and ground stands), still-hunting

YEARS IN BUSINESS: 14 (25 years hunting the area)

STAFF OF GUIDES : 2

HUNTERS SERVED BY EACH GUIDE: 1 - 3

NONHUNTER CHARGE: $50 / day

LICENSES: Sold in town

GAME CARE: Dressed, packaged, frozen and shipped at local processor ($35)

OTHER ACTIVITIES: Bird hunting, fishing, antiquing, biking, bird watching, golf, wildlife photography

BOONE AND CROCKETT

• B&C book bucks taken from property: 8 since opening

• Average B&C score: n/a

• B&C book bucks from this part of state: n/a

Snake River Hunting Lodge

Ehrhardt, South Carolina

HUNTERS WHO STAY at Snake River Hunting Lodge participate in classic-style Southern hunts — mostly from 16- to 19-foot tower stands located along planted, pine-lined roads and trails that lead to and from bean, corn, wheat and green fields. Hunters get to their stands before daylight, first being dropped off at the road or trail end and then hiking silently to their posts. It can be chilly in the morning, especially in the fall, but that's often what it takes to get these big southern bucks on the move. Hunters often use binoculars to watch far-off fields, then ready themselves when deer are spotted headed in their directions. While the bucks in this area may top out at 180 pounds, rack size is good, with thick-beamed 10-pointers common.

The lodge has nine private rooms, a spacious kitchen, and a social area. Hunters can bring their own food and cook for themselves, although breakfast and supper are provided. This is the perfect type of facility for a group of hunters who wants to get away from it all, have some good hunting, and not empty their bank accounts in the process!

Vital Statistics

THE LODGE:

9 guest rooms, 18 beds total, no private baths

SERVICES: Telephone, fax, copying, TV

HUNTS:

• $175 / day

• $100 / half day

PAYMENT: Check, cash

MEAL PLANS: Breakfast and supper provided (Southern-style cooking)

SPECIAL DIETS: Vegetarian, other

NEAREST AIRPORT: Savannah, GA, or Charleston, SC

TRANSPORTATION TO LODGE (95 miles from Savannah, 65 to Charleston): Rental car

THE HUNT:

SEASON:

• bow/rifle/muzzleloader: August 15-January 1

BEST TIME TO HUNT: September - November

TERRAIN: Edges of swamps, planted pine roads over farming fields (beans, corn, wheat, etc.)

LAND: 2,000 leased acres

DRAW BLOOD POLICY? No

HUNTING METHODS: Stand hunting (16- to 19-foot tower stands), still-hunting, calling, rattling

YEARS IN BUSINESS: 3

STAFF OF GUIDES: No

HUNTERS SERVED BY EACH GUIDE: n/a

NONHUNTER CHARGE: $25 / day

LICENSES: Sold over the counter, or by phoning the South Carolina Dept. of Natural Resources (888/434-7472)

GAME CARE: Local processor $45

OTHER ACTIVITIES: Turkey hunting, bird hunting, fishing, swimming in pool, wildlife photography

CONTACT:

Gary and Savannah Mahon
Snake River Hunting Lodge
P.O. Box 224
Ehrhardt, SC 29081
Ph: 803/267-9023

777 Ranch Inc.

Hondo, Texas

LOCATED IN SOUTH TEXAS in the heart of trophy buck country, the 777 is well known as a producer of record-book class whitetails. According to Kevin Christiansen, president, "Some whitetail operations manage for quality, others for quantity. When we first started the ranch, we decided to manage for both — quality and quantity. And, thanks to rigorous management, we've been able to do just that!

"One of the biggest challenges for the hunter is self-discipline," Christiansen continued. "You'll see a lot of trophy bucks here. To get the best one possible, you have to be patient."

With a large number of repeat clients, the 777 covers almost 15,000 acres of typical South Texas countryside — rolling hills covered with thick brush. Early in the morning, hunters are driven to enclosed ground blinds situated in likely areas, and are accompanied by a guide. Your guide will help you evaluate any buck you see so that you can be sure it's the one you really want before you pull the trigger. With an airport, plush lodge, gourmet food, and a large staff of skilled guides, the 777 is a top-notch operation where hunters can immerse themselves in their sport. The 777 also offers over 50 big game species, most available year-round.

Vital Statistics

THE LODGE:
22 guest rooms, 44 beds total (they prefer no more than 20 guests at a time), all rooms have private baths

SERVICES: Phone, fax, TV, laundry

GUN HUNTS: $250/day per person, based on double occupancy, which includes all meals, lodging, open bar, professional guide, and comfortable 4-wheel-drive Jeep; additional charges for trophies taken

PAYMENT: Cash, credit cards

MEAL PLANS: All meals included (dinners of steak, pork chops, chicken)

SPECIAL DIETS: Heart healthy

NEAREST AIRPORT: San Antonio, TX

TRANSPORTATION: (45 minutes) Van

THE HUNT:
SEASON:
• bow/rifle/muzzleloader: mid-Nov. - mid-Jan.

BEST TIME TO HUNT: December

TERRAIN: Rolling, brush-covered hills

LAND: 15,000 private acres; most of ranch is high-fenced

DRAW BLOOD POLICY? Yes

HUNTING METHODS: Stand hunting

YEARS IN BUSINESS: 35

STAFF OF GUIDES: 12

HUNTERS SERVED BY EACH GUIDE: 1-2

NONHUNTER CHARGE: $250/day

LICENSES: Sold over the counter or at lodge if pre-register

GAME CARE: Dressed, packaged, frozen for $150

OTHER ACTIVITIES: Other big game hunting (exotics, javelina), bird hunting (turkeys, doves, other), waterfowling, fishing, bird watching, boating, swimming, tennis, wildlife photography

BOONE AND CROCKETT
• B&C bucks taken from property: 4
• Average B&C score: 170

CONTACT:
Kevin Christiansen
777 Ranch Inc., P.O. Box 610
Hondo, TX 78861
Ph: 830/426-3476
Email: 777Ranch@777ranch.com
Web: http://www.777Ranch.com

Adobe Lodge

San Angelo, Texas

BASED IN SAN ANGELO about 250 miles west of Dallas, Adobe Lodge owner Skipper Duncan currently owns or leases six ranches totaling more than 50,000 acres, and outfits hunts from two separate camps. With help from the Texas Department of Parks and Wildlife, he manages deer on the ranches for quality hunts. Back in 1996, hunters took 32 mature bucks from just one of Duncan's ranches — this one a 15,000-acre spread. The success rate is usually around 90 percent for mature bucks.

This is classic Texas hunting, with hunters taking blinds or stands near mesquite trees that overlook grasses, cedars, catclaw, and cactus. Aside from deer, hunters are likely to see javelina, turkeys, jackrabbits, quail, doves, and even diamondback rattlers. The lodge itself is comfortable, with clean bunkhouses set near the Concho River. Good food (including steaks cooked over a mesquite fire) and a campfire pit in the middle of everything make this outfit a complete Texas experience. Adobe's guides are well known for not only being courteous, but knowledgeable as well.

According to Duncan, "We specialize in condensing lots of hunting into just a few days. By alternating blind hunting with walking/stalking/rattling hunts, we have been able to produce a tremendous success rate on bucks each year. And we can custom tailor the hunt to the physical abilities of each hunter. We do all the work. You enjoy hunting. We want you to experience the most enjoyable time possible with us."

And it's true. Hunters from rookies to veterans consistently describe their Adobe Lodge hunting experience the same way — a great big game hunt. You'll get V.I.P. treatment here, and you'll hunt in a game-rich area from long-established, well-managed camps.

(P.S. At the end of the 1999 season, the best buck taken scored 157 B&C!)

Vital Statistics

THE LODGE:

4 guest rooms, 10 beds total, no private baths

SERVICES: Telephone, TV, laundry

GUN HUNTS:

• $2,950 / 4-day hunt out of Adobe Lodge

• $2,350 / 4-day hunt out of McManus Camp

PAYMENT: Personal/company check

MEAL PLANS: All meals included (breakfasts of eggs, bacon, sausage & biscuits, pancakes, cereal, burritos; lunches of soup, stew, chili, sandwiches; suppers of pepper steak and rice, barbecue brisket, spaghetti, rib-eye steaks)

SPECIAL DIETS: Salt/msg free; can accommodate hunter requests

NEAREST AIRPORT: San Angelo, TX

TRANSPORTATION TO LODGE (10 miles): Van

CONTACT:

Skipper Duncan
Adobe Lodge
P.O. Box 60127
San Angelo, TX 76906
Ph: 915/942-8040
Email: skipper@adobelodge.com
Web: http://www.adobelodge.com

THE HUNT:

SEASON:

• bow/rifle/muzzleloader: first Saturday in November until first Sunday in January

BEST TIME TO HUNT: Anytime

TERRAIN: Mesquite, cedar, and live oak — rolling brushy prairie; elevation is 1,850' - 2,250'; river-bottoms, rocky canyons, mesquite savannahs

Land: More than 50,000 private acres (owned and leased)

DRAW BLOOD POLICY? Yes

HUNTING METHODS: Stand hunting (4' x 4' box blinds — most are not elevated)

YEARS IN BUSINESS: 15

STAFF OF GUIDES: 12

HUNTERS SERVED BY EACH GUIDE: 2

NONHUNTER CHARGE: n/a

LICENSES: Sold over the counter; $250 for non-resident license

GAME CARE: Dressed, packaged, no charge

OTHER ACTIVITIES: Other hunting (spring turkey, varmints, rabbits)

BOONE AND CROCKETT

• B&C book bucks taken from property: 0

• Average B&C score: 120

• B&C bucks from this part of state: Some

Comanche Spring Ranch

Eden, Texas

COMANCHE SPRING RANCH straddles the northern rim of the Texas hill country on the Edwards Plateau. Paleo-Americans first inhabited this area 13,000 to 18,000 years ago, but the ranch was named for its much later visitors, the fierce Comanche Indians. These supreme horse warriors camped in its pecan and live oak groves, hunted its game, and left arrowheads and artifacts near the old spring source on the ranch.

Year round, the ranch has 2,465 acres for hunting some of the finest exotic trophy animals in Texas. In deer season, hunters can also go after some of the big Texas bucks that roam the property. As is done in much of this area, whitetails are usually hunted by vehicle, with hunters driving the many roads on the property, glassing and looking. When a good buck is spotted, the hunter will try to put on a stalk, or if the situation is right, he'll try rattling.

According to head guide Terry Caffey, "We hunt our whitetails safari style. The whitetail deer are running in the same pastures as the exotics. We have approximately ten whitetail hunters per year, and usually each hunter will harvest a buck. As we manage for deer and antelope, mostly exotics, our whitetails are well-managed too."

These are big-racked bucks, typical for this part of Texas. If you're a northern hunter and have never tried hunting in Texas, you owe it to yourself to give it a try.

Hunters will enjoy staying on the ranch in complete comfort. The easily accessible, 1,350-square-foot, three-bedroom, two-bath lodge features central heat and air, TV, phone, and a full kitchen complete with coffee maker and microwave. There's a BBQ grill out back. Making's for a continental breakfast are provided. For other meals, hunters usually go to the nearby town of Eden for the famous Mexican food, fried catfish, steak, and local atmosphere. Meals can be catered on the ranch for a small extra charge.

Vital Statistics

THE LODGE:

3 guest rooms, 6 beds total, some rooms have private baths

SERVICES: Telephone, fax, TV

HUNTS: Average price is $1,000 plus $100 perday guide fee

PAYMENT: Credit cards, check

MEAL PLANS: Guests do their own cooking

NEAREST AIRPORT: San Angelo, TX

TRANSPORTATION TO LODGE (50 miles): Rental car

CONTACT:

Terry Caffey
Comanche Spring Ranch
PO Box 10
Eden, TX 76837
Ph: 915/869-3221
Fax: 915/869-5015
Web: http://www.comanchespringranch.com
Email: mail@comanchespringranch.com

THE HUNT:

SEASON:

• rifle/muzzleloader: Nov. 2 - Jan. 5

BEST TIME TO HUNT: December

TERRAIN: Gently rolling hills with live oak brush

DRAW BLOOD POLICY? Yes

HUNTING METHODS: By vehicle, rattling

YEARS IN BUSINESS: 17

STAFF OF GUIDES: Ranch manager

HUNTERS SERVED BY EACH GUIDE: 1 - 4

NONHUNTER CHARGE: No charge

LICENSES: Over the counter

GAME CARE: None provided

OTHER ACTIVITIES: Other big game hunting (exotics, turkeys)

Double C Ranch

Crystal City, Texas

I F YOU GO HUNTING WITH Jeff Myers in South Texas, you'll have your choice of hunting in three counties (Dimmit, Zavala, and Refugio), on more than 25,000 acres of prime habitat. Myers and his outfit hunt a number of ranches: the Double C, the Lambert Ranch, La Espuela Ranch, Hamilton Ranch and Mesquite Ranch. Myers owns the Double C Ranch, where he keeps his offices and oversees the operations on each of the other sites.

The Lambert Ranch consists of approximately 7,000 acres, and is located in Refugio County. This ranch was not hunted for more than 50 years until the 1999 season! It is surrounded by a 200,000-acre ranch on three sides, and has plenty of game, including whitetails, Rio Grande turkeys, and wild boars. The cost to hunt here is $2,500 per person plus $1,000 kill fee, and includes four days with three nights (three full days of hunting), lodging in a nearby hotel, meals served on the ranch, game cleaned and quartered, and guide service (one on two). Hunting is mostly done out of deer stands overlooking corn feeders, although there are times when rattling and stalking are extremely effective. Hunters can expect to see 15 to 30 bucks per day, with the average score of trophy bucks running around 135 B&C. There are bucks that will score 170 plus, but they are wary and hard to locate.

The Double C is the center of it all, and is the breeding ranch for big whitetails. The lodge accommodates up to 22 people, and includes swimming pool, two hot tubs, a lake stocked with largemouth bass, and game that includes mega whitetails plus a variety of exotics.

San Antonio is the nearest commercial airport, while Dimmit County airport is available for those flying privately who want to hunt the Double C Ranch or the La Espuela Ranch. The Refugio airport is available for those hunting the Lambert. Dinners feature steak, fish, chicken, and a huge variety of Mexican dishes. Specialties include company seminars, bachelor parties, reunions, dinner parties, and so on.

The costs of whitetail deer hunting vary, but most hunts are conducted with the hunter paying $1,600 for a four-day, three-night trip, plus a trophy fee. The trophy fees are based on gross B&C scores: each buck that scores 150 plus is $1,000, and bucks that score 149 and less are $2,500. The cost rewards the trophy hunter for being patient.

For a true Texas whitetail hunt, Jeff Myers' operations are clearly tough to beat!

A happy Double C hunter displays his trophy 10-pointer.

Double C Ranch offers ranch style lodging, a lake fully stocked with black bass, hot tub, covered patio area, clay target machines, satellite TV. . .

. . . and comfortable interiors to help you relax after a full day of hunting whitetails.

Vital Statistics

THE LODGE:

11 guest rooms, all with private baths, 22 beds total (8 rooms are in the main lodge, 3 in an adjoining cabin)

SERVICES: Telephone, fax, copying, TV, laundry, more (depends on location)

GUN HUNTS: Costs vary, depending on which ranch is hunted, and when; call for details

PAYMENT: Cash, check, credit cards

CONFERENCE GROUPS: Yes

MEAL PLANS: All meals included (dinners feature steaks, fish, chicken, Mexican plates of all varieties)

NEAREST AIRPORT: San Antonio, TX

TRANSPORTATION TO LODGE (2 hours): Rental car; van from lodge ($75)

CONTACT:

Jeff Myers
Double C Ranch
PO Box 86
Crystal City, TX 78839
Ph: 830/374-2744 or 830/374-2953
Fax: 210/219-2714
Email: jeff@huntingwithjeff.com
Web: www.huntingwithjeff.com

AGENT:

Andy Dyess
Pearl River Outfitters, Inc.
355 Long Cove
Madison, MS 39110
Ph: 601/856-0933
Email: adyess@pearlriver.com

THE HUNT:

SEASON: October – January

BEST TIME TO HUNT: Anytime

TERRAIN: Brush, flat to rolling

LAND: Approximately 25,000 acres (3,500 acres in high fence)

DRAW BLOOD POLICY? Yes

HUNTING METHODS: Stand hunting (tripods, wooden ground blinds), still-hunting, by vehicle, rattling

YEARS IN BUSINESS: 25

STAFF OF GUIDES: 10

HUNTERS SERVED BY EACH GUIDE: n/a

NONHUNTER CHARGE: $150 / day

LICENSES: Sold at lodge

GAME CARE: Dressed, packaged, frozen and shipped for clients

OTHER ACTIVITIES: Other big game hunting (boar, javelina), bird hunting (quail, dove), waterfowling, fishing, bird watching, boating, hiking, swimming, wildlife photography

BOONE AND CROCKETT

- B&C book bucks taken from property: Many
- Average B&C score: 140-150
- B&C bucks from this part of state: 50+

J-Bar-C Ranch Outfitters

Camp Wood, Texas

WITH 30 YEARS OF professional guiding and outfitting experience in Wyoming, New Mexico, and Texas, J-Bar-C specializes in world-class exotics and whitetails. More than 400,000 acres of privately-owned land in 24 Texas counties are available to this outfit's clients. J-Bar-C offers corporate, family, and military discounts on all hunts. They hunt free-ranging wild animals safari-style on 40 Texas ranches.

Exotics are, of course, the main fare at J-Bar-C, but you'll see plenty of trophy whitetails during the course of a day. Hunters generally scope at least 20 bucks per day, with an average buck scoring 120 or so. Success rate is just about 100 percent, as baiting is legal in most of Texas, assuring that bucks will come into range sooner or later. The key is waiting for the one you want. Even when you're seeing good bucks right out in front of your blind, take your time. Count the tines, try to figure out how long they are. Are the antler claws respectable? How are the G1s and G2s? Carry good binoculars, and check the deer out carefully. The really big bucks are often lurking in the thick stuff. The wise hunter is the one who waits and watches to see what's going to happen.

A Texas ranch hunt can be about as difficult or easy as you want to make it. Most ranches have mechanical feeders to supplement the diets of turkeys, white-tailed deer, and exotics. Blinds overlooing such feeders are used by many archers and some pistoleers. Safari-style hunting — driving around and glassing for game and then staking it on foot — is the most comon way to hunt. Let Barry Cox know how you want to hunt, and he'll accommodate.

Vital Statistics

THE LODGE:

12 hunters can be accommodated in the main lodge

SERVICES: Telephone, fax, copying, TV

GUN HUNTS: $200 - $250 / day; plus trophy fees

PAYMENT: Cash, American Express, travelers' checks

CONFERENCE GROUPS: Yes

MEAL PLANS: All meals included

SPECIAL DIETS: Heart healthy, Kosher and vegetarian diets can be provided

NEAREST AIRPORT: San Antonio, TX

TRANSPORTATION TO LODGE (50 to 100 miles depending on the ranch): Rental car; van from lodge for an additional fee

CONTACT:

Barry C. Cox
J-Bar-C Ranch Outfitters
Box 99
Camp Wood, TX 78833
Ph: 830/ 597-6102

THE HUNT:

SEASON:

- bow: October
- rifle: Noember. - January
- muzzleloader: November - January

BEST TIME TO HUNT: November - December

TERRAIN: Mountains and plains

LAND: 350,000 private acres; about 20 percent is fenced

DRAW BLOOD POLICY? Yes

HUNTING METHODS: Stand hunting, still-hunting, calling, rattling

YEARS IN BUSINESS: 37

STAFF OF GUIDES: Yes (number varies)

HUNTERS SERVED BY EACH GUIDE: 2

NONHUNTER CHARGE: $75 / day

LICENSES: Sold over the counter

GAME CARE: Dressing, packaging, freezing, and shipping for an additional charge

OTHER ACTIVITIES: Hunting for exotics, fishing, wildlife photography

BOONE AND CROCKETT

- B&C book bucks taken from property: Several
- Average B&C score: 150 to 160
- B&C bucks from this part of state: Hundreds

Morning Star Ranch

U v a l d e ,   T e x a s

MORNING START RANCH is a hunting operation "of integrity, that offers professional hunting experiences." The ranch is located approximately 90 miles west of San Antonio, in the
fabled Hill Country. Hunters who stay at the
ranch have access to more than 80,000 acres of land. Lodging is available on
the ranch for $35 per person, per night, in a two-story lodge that's rich in
character.

Rifle, bow, pistol, and muzzleloader hunters are welcome at the ranch.
Hunts are conducted by stand, stalk, and safari (vehicle). For the whitetails in
the region, standard deer calibers work fine, with the ranch recommending
270, 30-06, 7 Mag, and 300 Win Mag. Weather varies from 70° to 25°F during
hunting season, so plan to bring a variety of clothing for different types of
weather.

The hunting at Morning Star is geared toward trophy whitetails, with most
hunting zones restricted to bucks with 10 points or more, with 17-inch-plus
spreads. Bowhunters in the North Zone, which is north of Highway 90 in Real
County, may take bucks with spreads between 14 and 17 inches, 8 to 10 points
on average, plus a doe. Other hunt packages are available, depending on the
zone hunted, and type of weapon used.

Vital Statistics

THE LODGE:

3 guest rooms, 10 beds total, 1 private bath

Services: Telephone, fax, copying, TV, laundry

HUNTS:

• A variety of hunt packages are available, ranging from $150 / day gun hunts to $3500 / 3-day trophy hunts

PAYMENT: Cash, check

MEAL PLANS: All meals included (breakfasts of coffee, juice, cereal or pastries; lunches of sandwiches; dinners of Texas steaks, bbq chicken, vegetables and all the fixin's)

SPECIAL DIETS: Any thing the client wants

NEAREST AIRPORT: San Antonio, TX

TRANSPORTATION TO LODGE (90 miles): Rental car; van ($150)

CONTACT:

Russell James
Morning Star Ranch
HCR 32, Box 138A
Uvalde, TX 78801
Ph: 830/232-5830
Fax: 830/232-5859

THE HUNT:

SEASON: October - January

BEST TIME TO HUNT: Anytime

TERRAIN: Typical Hill Country terrain — canyons and rolling hills with cedar and hardwoods, plus South Texas native brush

LAND: 50,000 acres (half is under high fence)

DRAW BLOOD POLICY? Yes

HUNTING METHODS: Stand hunting (enclosed box blinds, tripods), drives, by vehicle, rattling

YEARS IN BUSINESS: 10

STAFF OF GUIDES: 2

HUNTERS SERVED BY EACH GUIDE: 1

NONHUNTER CHARGE: No

LICENSES: Sold over the counter

GAME CARE: Dress, packages, freeze, and ship game for clients

OTHER ACTIVITIES: Other big game hunting (turkey, exotics ranging from elk and red stag to feral hogs, Corsican rams, kudu, sable and bison), bird hunting, fishing, antiquing, biking, bird watching, canoeing, golf, hiking, swimming, wildlife photography

BOONE AND CROCKETT

• B&C book bucks taken from property: Many

• Average B&C score: 140

• B&C bucks from this part of state: Many

Oak Knoll Ranch

Menard, Texas

THE SAN SABA RIVER VALLEY of Texas has for centuries been home to a huge variety of indigenous wildlife species, including whitetail deer, turkeys, ducks, herons, birds of prey, bobcats, foxes, jackrabbits and more. Today, thanks to an ongoing habitat restoration program designed to perpetuate native wildlife species, there are more deer and turkeys in this area than ever.

The restoration plan includes revitalizing plants that were present on the ranch a century ago. Stimulating and replanting these grasses, browse, and forbs provides the high-quaility nutrition needed by deer to acquire good body growth and antler quality. The ranch utilizes modern game management techniques, including taking regular helicopter censuses — with the intention of keeping the number of animals in balance with the natural habitat.

Oak Knoll Ranch is located in the beautiful western hill country of Texas, an area designated by the U.S. Nature Conservancy as being "one of the last great places." Oak Knoll specializes in providing guests with a unique experience in the outdoors. Not only does the ranch provide premier hunting opportunities, but it also has abundant wildlife and superior amenities, including classic accommodations and first-class locally-flavored menus. Visitors here leave with a lasting experience.

Most hunters head out early in the morning, climbing into one of the many enclosed wooden stands on the ranch that overlook trails snaking through the mesquite and oak brush. Bucks here typically sport large antlers, though body weights tend to be smaller than bucks found in the northern states. This is typical of Texas deer, though, as the smaller bodies let them thrive and survive in the hot climate. Hunters are likely to see many deer during the course of a day, and waiting for the big buck can really test your patience. Just don't pull the trigger until you're sure that the buck is the one you want.

At the end of the day, hunters head back to the main lodge for an evening of relaxation and camaraderie. The lodge building is a restored rural school house. Large bedrooms have private baths and telephones, and feature antique furnishings, mohair blankets, and goose-down duvets. Furnished in the style of a European hunting lodge, the surrounding are aimed at making your stay unique and comfortable. The highlight of the living room is a massive stone fireplace fashioned from an old German wall that was built in the 1700s.

Cocktails are served at the bar, followed by gourmet meals featuring fresh ingredients. Oak Knoll specializes in game dishes such as venison and quail, and ranch-raised beef and lamb. A highlight of the hunt is a Texas-style barbeque prepared and served on the banks of the San Saba River.

Oak Knoll Ranch has been in the same family for five generations, and began as a stagecoach stop between San Antonio and El Paso. For a taste of old Texas, and a true Texas hunting experience, Oak Knoll is tough to beat, both for deer hunting and comfortable accommodations. It is also one of only two U.S. lodges endorsed by Holland and Holland.

Vital Statistics

THE LODGE:

3 guest rooms, 6 beds total, all rooms have private baths

SERVICES: Telephone, fax, copying, TV

GUN HUNTS:

- $2,500 / 3-day hunt, ranch #1

- $3,500 / 3-day hunt, ranch #2

PAYMENT: Cash, check

MEAL PLANS: All meals included (vary from continental cuisine served in courses to a rustic Texas barbeque on the river)

SPECIAL DIETS: None

NEAREST AIRPORT: San Angelo, TX

TRANSPORTATION TO LODGE (90 minutes): Van from lodge (no extra charge)

CONTACT:

G.K. Lundgren
Oak Knoll Ranch
HCR 84, Box 27A
Menard, TX 76859
Booking/info: 915/234-3350
Lodge: 915/396-4393
Fax: 915/396-4393
Web: http://www.oakknoll.superservers.net

THE HUNT:

SEASON: October 1 - January 31

BEST TIME TO HUNT: Anytime

TERRAIN: Gently rolling hills with areas of heavy mesquite and oak brush; cactus-proof boots are suggested

LAND: 6,000 private acres

DRAW BLOOD POLICY? n/a

HUNTING METHODS: Stand hunting (enclosed wooden stands), by vehicle, calling, rattling

YEARS IN BUSINESS: 13

STAFF OF GUIDES : As many as requested

HUNTERS SERVED BY EACH GUIDE: 2

NONHUNTER CHARGE: $1,000 / 3 days

LICENSES: Sold over the counter

GAME CARE: Guides quarter game; shipping is at hunter's expense

OTHER ACTIVITIES: Turkey hunting, antiquing, canoeing, ladies' program offered

BOONE AND CROCKETT

- B&C book bucks taken from property: n/a

- Average B&C score: Ranch #1 120 - 140 Ranch #2 130 - 150

- B&C bucks from this part of state: n/a

Rafter W Ranches

S o n o r a ,   T e x a s

W ITH MORE THAN 32,000 acres on a working ranch, and with a rule that allows only one buck to be taken per 500 acres per year, Rafter Ranches consistently produces bucks that score 130 B&C points and better. Hunter success on the Rafter W Ranches is 100 percent for deer, but the hunt is not guaranteed. Rather, the success rate is a reflection of a management system that the Wardlaw family, who own this spread, has had in place for about 20 years.

Early in the season, the most successful approach is to hunt from blinds that overlook feeders. Later in the season, during the rut (late November/early December), it's best to get into a stand that lets you watch bucks looking for hot does and rival bucks fighting in the mesquite and cedar breaks, then try to rattle and call them into range.

Hunters can also hunt Rio Grande turkeys at Rafter, and hunts can be arranged for javelina and exotic deer such as sitka, fallow and axis. Recommended firearms include flat-shooting rifles (such as .270s) topped with variable scopes. Good binoculars and spotting scopes also come in handy for antler evaluation.

Vital Statistics

THE LODGE:

Main lodge has 11 guest rooms, 9 with private bath

SERVICES: Telephone, fax, copying, TV

GUN HUNTS: $2,900 / 4 days

PAYMENT: Cash, check

CONFERENCE GROUPS: No

MEAL PLANS: All meals included (dinners feature steak, turkey breast, pork, vegetables, breads, desserts)

NEAREST AIRPORT: San Angelo, TX

TRANSPORTATION TO LODGE (85 miles): Van from lodge (no charge)

THE HUNT:

SEASON: Early November through first Sunday in January

BEST TIME TO HUNT: November

TERRAIN: Mesquite and cedar breaks, pastures (a working ranch)

LAND: 32,000 private acres

DRAW BLOOD POLICY? Yes

HUNTING METHODS: Stand hunting (blinds overlooking feeders and heavily used trails), rattling, calling

YEARS IN BUSINESS: 17

STAFF OF GUIDES: Yes

HUNTERS SERVED BY EACH GUIDE: 2

NONHUNTER CHARGE: n/a

LICENSES: Sold over the counter

GAME CARE: Done at ranch

OTHER ACTIVITIES: Other big game hunting (wild turkey, javelina), wildlife photography

CONTACT:

Jack Wardlaw
Rafter W Ranches
Box 944
Sonora, TX 76950
Ph: 915/387-3377
Fax: 915/387-3173
Web: www/rafterranchesguided-hunts.com

Reserve Ranch

Burnet, Texas

WITH DENSE CEDAR BUSH cover, some open meadows and food plots, along with slightly rolling terrain, the Reserve Ranch offers quality whitetail hunting that is getting better and better each year, thanks to careful management. Many trophy bucks are taken on the 8,500 acres owned and leased by the Ranch. In 1998, the ranch boasted a 100 percent success rate, with some clients taking two bucks. Forty percent of the bucks taken scored over 140 B&C points, with three over 150. These are big bucks too, with many weighing in excess of 200 pounds. With numerous 3- and 4-year-old bucks in the 130- to 140- class roaming the property, the odds of topping those incredible numbers are excellent.

Hunting at the Reserve Ranch is done from blinds, with rattling a favored tactic, especially just before and during the rut. Each client is accompanied by a guide to assess the quality of the trophy taken before the kill. Due to the nature of this hunt and the consistent quality of the trophies taken, the price is not fixed. Rather, the hunt cost is based on the quality of the trophy taken plus the basic hunt fee.

Vital Statistics

THE LODGE:

Farmhouse has 2 guest rooms, 6 beds total, 1 private bath

SERVICES: Phone, fax, TV, laundry

GUN HUNTS:

- $1,000 / 3-day one-on-one hunt, plus trophy fee

PAYMENT: Cash, credit cards, travelers checks

MEAL PLANS: All meals included (Southern-style breakfast; dinners feature steaks, fowl, side dishes, dessert; all prepared fresh to client's specifications)

SPECIAL DIETS: Anything requested

NEAREST AIRPORT: Austin, TX

TRANSPORTATION TO LODGE (60 miles): Van

THE HUNT:

SEASONS:
- bow: October 1 - 31
- rifle: Noember. 7 - Jan. 4

BEST TIME TO HUNT: Anytime

TERRAIN: Cedar brush cover with some open meadows and food plots

LAND: 8,500 private acres; 100 percent is fenced pastures

DRAW BLOOD POLICY? No

HUNTING METHODS: Stand hunting (enclosed and tall enough to stand in, accommodate up to 5 people), by vehicle, rattling

YEARS IN BUSINESS: 17

STAFF OF GUIDES : 2

HUNTERS SERVED BY EACH GUIDE: 1

NONHUNTER CHARGE: $75 / day

LICENSES: Sold over the counter

GAME CARE: Available locally

OTHER ACTIVITIES: Exotics hunting, bird hunting, fishing, biking, bird watching, golf, tennis, youth hunts

BOONE AND CROCKETT

- B&C bucks taken from property: 1 over 170, several in the 150- to 160- class
- Average B&C score: 140-150

CONTACT:

John Ed Stepan
Reserve Ranch
100 S. Pierce St.
Burnet, TX 78611
Ph: 512/756-6445
Fax: 512/756-7715
Email: dh2@discounthunts.com
www.discounthuntershotline.com

AGENT:

JES International Adventures
800-725-4537

Robby Robinson Ranches

Junction, Texas

ROBBY ROBINSON'S headquarters ranch is located 25 miles east of Junction on Ranch Road 385. On top of the Blue Mountains, high on the Edwards Plateau, the area is rich in limestone, a mineral that helps account for the large number of deer with trophy-sized racks.

Nestled in the scenic and world-famous Hill Country in the heart of Texas' best whitetail deer range, the ranch produces a good number of trophy bucks each year. During their stay, hunters will also see an abundance of other native game, including turkey, javelina, bobwhite quail, doves, bobcats, and coyotes.

Each party of hunters has a private lodge. One lodge, a duplex, accommodates six people on each side. Each half of the lodge has a tile shower, fireplace, electric kitchen, central heating and air-conditioning. The lodge will be stocked with all the food you'll need for your stay. Two other nearby lodges can accommodate up to 10 hunters apiece. They're also available in summer; from these lodges, you can swim and fish on two miles of the Llano River.

A guide in a ranch vehicle will take you to your stand each morning and evening, with a break in the afternoon for lunch and a nap. The blinds are house-type affairs on the ground. Each is eight feet square with concrete floors, sliding glass windows on all four sides, and two leather swivel chairs in each. One section of the ranch is set aside exclusively for bowhunters, who can either hunt out of a stand or still-hunt.

The ranch also has a walk-in cooler to take care of your game. Each hunter can take one whitetail buck, 8 points or larger, plus a turkey and small game such as bobcats, coyotes, and javelinas. An added attraction, if you so desire, is all the non-native game offered by the ranch — some behind a high fence, some free-roaming. These include mouflon and Corsican rams, black buck antelope, fallow, sitka and axis deer, plus aoudad.

Vital Statistics

THE LODGE:

Two 10-person lodges, two 6-person lodges; each lodge has 2 bathrooms

SERVICES: Telephone

GUN HUNTS:

• $1,500 / 3-day hunt; $500 for each extra day; exotic game is additional, with different species commanding different prices

PAYMENT: Cash, checks

MEAL PLANS: All meals included

SPECIAL DIETS: n/a

NEAREST AIRPORT: San Antonio, TX

TRANSPORTATION TO LODGE (100 miles): Rental car; van (additional charge)

CONTACT:

Robby Robinson
Robby Robinson Ranches
P.O. Box 274
Junction, TX 76849
Ph: 915/446-3165
Fax: 915/446-8821

THE HUNT:

SEASON:

• rifle: November 4 - December 31

BEST TIME TO HUNT: Anytime

TERRAIN: Mountainous

LAND: 20,000 private acres (1,000 acres under high fence)

DRAW BLOOD POLICY? No

HUNTING METHODS: Stand hunting (8' square houses with cement floors, swivel chairs, windows on all sides), rattling

YEARS IN BUSINESS: 45

STAFF OF GUIDES: 3

HUNTERS SERVED BY EACH GUIDE: Varies

NONHUNTER CHARGE: No

LICENSES: Sold over the counter

GAME CARE: Robinson will arrange for you

OTHER ACTIVITIES: Other big game hunting (turkey, bobcat, javelina, coyote, exotics), wildlife photography

Rockin' J Outfitters

San Angelo, Texas

ROCKIN' J OUTFITTERS offers hunts on three different ranches. All of the hunts are three- to four-day affairs, unless otherwise specified, and are fully guided with one guide for every one to two hunters. Hunts start in a four-wheel-drive vehicle, but are likely to progress to a blind, calling (rattling, grunting), or a spot-and-stalk tactic, depending on each situation.

The three ranches include The Borden/Garza County Ranch, which is a 40,000-acre ranch with trophy whitetail bucks and aoudad rams. It also offers excellent coyote, prairie dog, and quail hunting. Until last year, only the ranch owner and his family hunted the ranch. Now they are allowing Rockin' J Outfitters in on some of the best hunting in the country.

The Tom Green County Ranch is a 2,500-acre ranch that has had very little hunting pressure for the past several years. It offers trophy whitetail buck and turkey hunting from several heated blinds overlooking feeders. Hunting here is excellent.

The Irion County Ranch is a game ranch under high fence. It is just under 1,000 acres and offers excellent exotic hunting from blinds over feeders or through a spot-and-stalk tactic. The species available are axis, fallow, and sitka deer, blackbuck antelope, aoudad, mouflon, Corsican, Texas dall, and black Hawaiian sheep, and scimitar horned orxy.

In addition to these ranches, Rockin' J is continually acquiring other lands on which to hunt. Inquire about these spreads as well.

Vital Statistics

THE LODGE:

Farmhouse and cabins have 3 guest rooms, no private baths, 6 beds total

SERVICES: Telephone, TV

GUN HUNTS: $2,700 plus trophy fee ($500 extra if animal reaches gold medal status)

PAYMENT: Cash, credit cards, checks

CONFERENCE GROUPS: Yes

MEAL PLANS: All meals included (menu is derived by hunter request)

NEAREST AIRPORT: Mathis Field in San Angelo, TX

TRANSPORTATION TO LODGE (15 mile): Rental car; van from lodge (no charge)

CONTACT:

Jory Rector
Rockin' J Outfitters
933 E. 42nd
San Angelo, TX 76903
Ph: 915/653-2893
Email: jrec3@aol.com
Web: www.rockinj.com

THE HUNT:

SEASON: November 1 - January 7 (1 buck, 2 does)

BEST TIME TO HUNT: Around Thanksgiving

TERRAIN: Rolling hills with good cedar and live oak cover

LAND: 2,500 private acres; 800-acre tracts

DRAW BLOOD POLICY? Yes

HUNTING METHODS: Stand hunting (enclosed, heated and elevated stands, about 75 to 100 yards from feeders), still-hunting, by vehicle, calling, rattling

YEARS IN BUSINESS: 2

STAFF OF GUIDES: Guided by owner

HUNTERS SERVED BY EACH GUIDE: 1 - 2

NONHUNTER CHARGE: $75 / day

LICENSES: Sold over the counter, or can apply in advance

GAME CARE: Dress, package, freeze, and ship game for clients for $200

OTHER ACTIVITIES: Other big game hunting (exotics such as aoudad sheep, blackbuck antelope, sitka, fallow and axis deer, and Iranian red sheep, plus prairie dogs, javelina, coyotes, wild boar, turkey), bird hunting (quail), fishing

[S O U T H]

Texas Best Outfitters (Krooked River Ranch)

Haskell, Texas

DRIVING NORTHEAST out of Abilene, west Texas seems as flat as a table. But within 25 miles, the land begins to fall away to the valleys of the Brazos River and its tributaries. Gone are the vast cotton and peanut farms. In their place are gently rolling hills studded with mesquite and scrubby oaks and pine. This is big ranch land, and Texas Best Outfitters encompasses almost 42,000 acres of it.

The deer are big and numerous here. Roy Wilson, who runs the ranch, manages the herd for trophy bucks. Eight-pointers or better are the rule here. Ten-pointers are common, but bigger ones are also taken. Leaving the lodge in a pickup before dawn, you'll drive over rutted roads to the meadow you're going to hunt. Each meadow, where one guide and two guests hunt, covers more than 2,000 acres — a mixture of river bottom, wheat field, and mesquite woods that eventually climb to table-rock plateaus.

You'll spend a lot of time glassing the hillsides, looking for moving deer. Once you know that they're working an area, you'll move in, find a good hiding spot and wait. Dawn and dusk are the best times for this type of hunting, and rattling and grunting can be especially effective. If you call one into range, try to stay calm, as bucks in this country often aren't used to hunters, and may come in fast, ready to fight. Preferred calibers for this country include 270s, 7mms and 30/06s, standard deer calibers.

At the end of the day, you'll head back to the main lodge for family-style dinners. Roy and wife, Becky, and their kids all pitch in to provide a comfortable and well-run lodge. They love it when clients bring their kids; they take extra special care of them. If you fill your deer tags early, stick around for quail, ducks, geese, or wild boar.

Vital Statistics

THE LODGE:

Modern main lodge has 9 guest rooms, 25 beds total, all rooms have private baths

SERVICES: Telephone, fax, copying, TV

GUN HUNTS:

• From $2,000 / 4-day hunt, plus a kill fee, depending on the size of animals

PAYMENT: Credit cards, check

MEAL PLANS: All meals included (grilled lemon-pepper pork chops, sesame goose, mesquite-seasoned chicken, BBQ pork ribs, mesquite grilled steak, southern fried chicken, smoked brisket, a variety of Mexican food, wild game)

SPECIAL DIETS: Heart healthy, vegetarian, salt/msg free

NEAREST AIRPORTS: Lubbock, Abilene, Dallas-Fort Worth

TRANSPORTATION TO LODGE: From Abilene (55 miles) rental car, van from lodge (no extra charge); from Lubbock or Dallas/Ft. Worth (160 miles) rental car, van from lodge (extra charge)

CONTACT:

Roy Wilson
Texas Best Outfitters
P.O. Box 85
Haskell, TX 79521
Ph: 915/773-2457
Fax: 915/773-2541
Web: http://www.krro.net
Email: Krro@westex.net

THE HUNT:

SEASON:

• bow: Oct. (most hunts include 1 buck and 1 doe)

• rifle: Nov. - Dec. (most hunts include 1 buck and 1 doe)

BEST TIME TO HUNT: November or December

TERRAIN: Rolling hills falling off into a small river bottoms, small canyons and draws, mesquite, scrub oak, and other small brush

LAND: 42,000 private acres

DRAW BLOOD POLICY? No

HUNTING METHODS: Stand hunting (tripods, box stands, ladder stands), drives, still-hunting, by vehicle, calling, rattling

YEARS IN BUSINESS: 15

STAFF OF GUIDES: 22

HUNTERS SERVED BY EACH GUIDE: 2

NONHUNTER CHARGE: $100 / day

LICENSES: Sold over the counter

GAME CARE: Dress, package and freeze game; game is shipped back with client on plane

OTHER ACTIVITIES: Other big game hunting (hogs), bird hunting (quail), waterfowling, fishing, biking, hiking, wildlife photography, four-wheeling

BOONE AND CROCKETT

• B&C book bucks taken from property: 1

• Average B&C score: 120 - 160

• B&C bucks from this part of state: 3 - 5

Y.O. Ranch

Mountain Home, Texas

THE Y.O. RANCH is the most famous and largest private hunting ranch of its kind in the world. In the early 1950s, to meet the needs of a changing economy, Charlie Schreiner III pioneered exotic wildlife ranching at the Y.O, stocking the ranch with game animals from all over the world. As early as 1953, blackbuck antelope, axis deer, sitka deer, fallow deer, and aoudad sheep were introduced and have been running wild with the native whitetail deer ever since.

The Y.O. Ranch and brand remain part of 550,000 acres acquired in 1880 by Captain Charles Schreiner, a native of Alsace-Lorraine who immigrated to Texas with his family in 1852. He bought the Y.O. Ranch and its brand with profits from driving more than 300,000 head of Longhorn cattle along the Western Trail to Dodge City. Four generations later, the Schreiner family, including Charles Schreiner III and his four sons, Charlie IV, Walter, Gus and Louis, still proudly own and operate the sprawling 50-square-mile ranch located in the ruggedly beautiful Texas Hill country, just 100 miles northwest of San Antonio.

The hunting here is special, with huge whitetails roaming the premises with the other game animals. Hunting whitetails here is no piece of cake, though. When you get within range of them, they'll be gone in a heartbeat. No more than two hunters are assigned to one guide, unless requested. Most guides are ranchers and outdoorsmen with 20 or more years of experience. They will advise you about the best areas to hunt, aid you in finding the type of trophy you want, and help you evaluate its trophy potential. For whitetails, good bucks start at 7 points and move up from there. Hunters are billed based on the type of whitetail they take; your guide will let you know exactly what you're looking at before you pull the trigger.

Hunts begin when your guide meets you at the Chuckwagon before daybreak for a hearty breakfast. You will then proceed to the hunting area. Normally, you will return to headquarters for lunch and dinner. Sunset signals the return to the lodge, where a warm fire and libations on the house are accompanied by exotic game appetizers. Meals are family-style buffet, all you can eat affairs. Good food and plenty of it are the motto here — you won't go hungry at the Y.O. After dinner, most hunters like to unwind and relax at the lodge, discussing the day's hunt and planning for the next day.

Vital Statistics

THE LODGE:

Modern, rustic lodge has 14 guest rooms, all with private baths, 42 beds total

SERVICES: Telephone, fax, copying, TV

GUN HUNTS: From $1,000 / 7-pointer or less to $5,000 / 8 points or better

PAYMENT: Cash, credit cards, check

CONFERENCE GROUPS: Yes

MEAL PLANS: All meals included (home-cooked ranch-style)

NEAREST AIRPORT: San Antonio, TX

TRANSPORTATION TO LODGE (100 miles): Rental car; van from lodge $100 additional per person

CONTACT:

Louis Schreiner
Y.O. Ranch
Mountain Home, TX 78058
Ph: 830/640-3222
Email: Louie@yoranch.com
Web: yoranch.com

THE HUNT:

SEASON:

- bow: October
- rifle: November – December
- muzzleloder: year-round

BEST TIME TO HUNT: October – December

TERRAIN: Typical Texas hill country terrain, with oaks and cedars

LAND: 550,000 private acres (40,000 acres under high fence)

DRAW BLOOD POLICY? No

HUNTING METHODS: Stand hunting (tripods and box blinds), rattling

YEARS IN BUSINESS: 40

STAFF OF GUIDES: 5

HUNTERS SERVED BY EACH GUIDE: 2

NONHUNTER CHARGE: $100 / day

LICENSES: Sold at the lodge for $250

GAME CARE: Dress, package, freeze, and ship for about $100 / deer

OTHER ACTIVITIES: Other big game hunting (exotics), wildlife photography

BOONE AND CROCKETT

- B&C book bucks taken from property: Very few
- Average B&C score: 130-150
- B&C bucks from this part of state: Very few

Falkland Farms Hunting Plantation

Scottsburg, Virginia

ONCE A PRIVATE hunting retreat, one of Virginia's largest contiguous tracts of private land is now open to the public. Falkland Farms Hunting Plantation is a 7,673-acre family-owned farm nestled in the rolling hills of southern Virginia. Rich in hunting tradition and bountiful in game, the plantation offers an exclusive hunting experience. Bordering Kerr Reservoir, the farm is located on a peninsula of land formed by the Dan, Banister, and Staunton rivers. Five streams give the area the nickname of the "Falks" and the namesake of the farm. The "Falks" consists of various types of habitat managed to support the many varieties of game found in the Southeast. There are upland hardwoods, riverbottom timber and swamps, as well as managed plantation pine stands. These habitats and topography, combined with the property's extraordinary size, allow for flourishing whitetail populations.

Falkland Farms has a long tradition of hosting deer hunters on its huge spread. The thickly wooded areas and brushy cutovers harbor the biggest bucks in the southeast, just as they did around the turn of the century. Archery and muzzleloader hunters are welcome at Falkland Farms. The farm only hosts six bowhunters at a time, or eight muzzleloaders, permitting a low hunter-to-guide ratio of two-to-one. With so few hunters on 12 square miles of private land, it makes the hunts personalized, and gives the archer or muzzleloader a chance to hunt ground that hasn't received any pressure. Guides meet hunters prior to daylight and take them to their stands. Then it's up to you; you can take a bag lunch with you and stay out all day, or you can arrange to be picked up for lunch and a quick nap before heading out to a different stand for the afternoon watch. Most stands are shooting boxes on tripods overlooking food plots, game trails, or areas where recent buck activity has been observed.

The lodge at Falkland Farms is the center of activities. Built as a hunting lodge in the early 1900s and recently restored, the main house offers hunters the comfort of modern conveniences mixed with the antiques of the past. Porches on the first and second floors offer vantage points for viewing the tranquil countryside. The lodge is open year-round as a bed-and-breakfast, and hosts weddings, receptions, and other meetings. Combine these comfortable accommodations with a chef who puts out ample meals every day, and hunters are certain to have memorable visits here.

Vital Statistics

THE LODGE:

Vintage frame plantation house has 7 guest rooms, 14 beds total, all have private baths

SERVICES: Telephone, fax, coying, TV

HUNTS:

- bow: $200 - $250 / day, depending on time of year
- muzzleloader: $250 / day
- 10% discount for parties of 4+

PAYMENT: Cash, check

CONFERENCE GROUPS: Yes

MEAL PLANS: All meals included (dinners of cornish game hens, quail, oysters, vegetables, breads, desserts, beverages — guaranteed to put an extra notch or two on your belt)

NEAREST AIRPORT: Raleigh-Durham, NC; Greensboro, NC; Lynchberg, VA; private planes can fly into Tuck Airport, only 10 minutes from the lodge

TRANSPORTATION TO LODGE (1 1/2 hours): Rental car; pickup can be arranged

CONTACT:

Falkland Farms Hunting Plantation
1003 Falkland Landing
Scottsburg, VA 24589
Ph/fax: 434/575-1400
Email: falkland@halifax.com
Web: www.falklandfarms.com

THE HUNT:

SEASON:

- bow: early Ocober - December 1
- muzzleloader: early November 6 - December 1

BEST TIME TO HUNT: Anytime, although the rut in mid-Nov. is productive

TERRAIN: Thickly wooded areas, thin plantation pines, brushy cutovers; property also contains wet, swampy areas, especially where it fronts the upper reaches of Buggs Island Lake

LAND: 7,643 private acres

DRAW BLOOD POLICY? No

HUNTING METHODS: Stand hunting (box blinds on tripods, some portables)

YEARS IN BUSINESS: 14

STAFF OF GUIDES: 6

HUNTERS SERVED BY EACH GUIDE: 2

NONHUNTER CHARGE: B&B charge

LICENSES: Sold over the counter

GAME CARE: All processing no extra charge (gratuities appreciated)

OTHER ACTIVITIES: Wild turkey hunting, rabbit hunting, bird hunting (dove, quail), waterfowling, antiquing, biking, bird watching, boating, canoeing, golf, wildlife photography, sporting clays

BOONE AND CROCKETT

- B&C book bucks taken from property: 5 or 6
- Average B&C score: n/a
- B&C bucks from this part of state: n/a

Fort Lewis Lodge

Millboro, Virginia

L OCATED IN BATH COUNTY, Virgina's best for whitetail deer, Fort Lewis Lodge was founded in 1754 as Fort Lewis Plantation on 3,200 acres. The current owners, John and Caryl Cowden, have preserved the natural beauty of this mountain farm while providing one of the finest guest facilities in the East. The old mill is now the dining room, while the barn has become the lodge with 12 comfortable rooms decorated with handmade hardwood furniture. The main lodge room is an ideal den, a good place for hunters to sit down and swap stories.

As for the hunting areas, you'll hunt a combination of woodlands and agricultural fields — all great deer country. John Cowden is a farm management specialist — a fact that enhances the habitat development. Riverbottom fields of corn, alfalfa, and soybeans are surrounded by mountain forests, providing bedding and cover areas. The Cowdens hunt 3,200 nearby acres — all surrounded by hundreds of square miles of prime deer country. Laurel thickets and regenerating clearcuts scattered throughout Fort Lewis are used by the older bucks to their advantage. These areas provide the necessary cover for the bucks to survive and reach the older age classes. When the rut gets into swing, these deer move around quite a bit, and the patient hunter who's in the right place at the right time will have the chance at a shot. Ground blinds are located at many of these "right places."

Offering two weeks of bowhunting and then a week of muzzleloading before the gun season, Fort Lewis has something for everyone. Plush accommodations, a quality whitetail herd that's carefully managed, plus seasons for the weapon of your choice, make this the place to go for a classic Appalachian hunt.

Vital Statistics

THE LODGE:

13 guest rooms, all with private baths, 25 beds total (although the Cowdens like to keep the number of guests to 18)

SERVICES: Telephone, fax, TV, laundry

HUNTS:

- $750 / 3-day rifle or muzzleloader hunt
- $650 / 3-day bowhunt

PAYMENT: Check, credit cards (Mastercard, Visa)

MEAL PLANS: 3 meals a day (all "first class")

SPECIAL DIETS: Heart healthy, vegetarian, salt/MSG free

NEAREST AIRPORT: Roanoke, VA

TRANSPORTATION TO LODGE (1 1/2 hours): Rental car

CONTACT:

John Cowden
Fort Lewis Lodge
HCR 3, Box 21A
Millboro, VA 24460
Ph: 540/925-2314
Fax: 540/925-2352
Email: ftlewis@tds.net

THE HUNT:

SEASON:

- bow: late October to early November
- rifle: mid-November to early December
- muzzleloader: mid-November

BEST TIME TO HUNT: Mid-November

TERRAIN: Hardwood forests, mountains, riverbottom fields of corn, alfalfa, and soybeans

LAND: 4,400 private acres

DRAW BLOOD POLICY? n/a

HUNTING METHODS: Stand hunting (lock-ons, ground blinds), still-hunting, rattling

YEARS IN BUSINESS: 14

STAFF OF GUIDES: 4

HUNTERS SERVED BY EACH GUIDE: 4

NONHUNTER CHARGE: $70 / day

LICENSES: Sold at lodge

GAME CARE: Dressed, packaged, frozen, and shipped; taxidermy can be arranged

OTHER ACTIVITIES: Spring turkey hunting, pheasant hunting, fishing, antiquing, biking, bird watrching, canoeing, hiking, swimming, whitewater rafting, wildlife photography

Primland Resort

Meadows of Dan, Virginia

THE BLUE RIDGE PARKWAY runs down Virginia's backbone. To the west is the Shenandoah Valley and below that Roanoke and a high plateau that slides into the headwaters of the Tennessee Valley. The eastern part of the valley consists of steep foothills forested with oak, hickory, maple, and sweet gum. These hills are remote, and undeveloped.

Nested in the middle of the lush part of the valley is Primland, a 14,000-acre resort that's mostly managed for upland birds. But whitetails are here too, thriving on cover plots of sorghum and milo. Streams, ponds, and springs provide water, and the thick laurel high on the slopes of the foothills offers deer incredibly good cover. Hunting here is done from stands overlooking scrape lines, trails between bedding and feeding areas, and near food plots. An eight-point or better rule applies here, though hunters can also take does.

Primland is part of a network of resorts that range from Ireland to France. Accommodations are first class, with guests staying in immaculate cottages set in the woods. The meals served in the main lodge dining hall are first rate, but those who want can also cook their own meals in their cabins, or hire a personal chef. Hunting guides are, of course, also available.

© Primland Resort

A monster 10-pointer taken at Primland Resort.

Vital Statistics

THE LODGE:

13 guest cottages, 70 beds total, all cottages have baths; Primland accommodates 12 hunters at a time

SERVICES: Telephone, fax, copying, TV, laundry, gas grills, full kitchens with appliances and utensils

HUNTS:

• $1,500 / 3 days, lunches and dinner, 3 bucks (greater than 14-inch spreads) and up to 2 antler-less deer per day

PAYMENT: Cash, check, credit cards (Mastercard, Visa)

MEAL PLANS: Lunch and dinner (entrees range from fillet dinner to wild game, and include either steamed vegetables or salads, potatoes, and beverage)

SPECIAL DIETS: Most anything can be arranged

NEAREST AIRPORT: Greensboro, NC

TRANSPORTATION TO LODGE (70 miles): Rental car; van from lodge ($50)

CONTACT:

Stephen G. Helms
Primland Resort
4621 Busted Rock Rd.
Meadows of Dan, VA 24120
Ph: 540/251-8012. Fax: 540/251-8244.
Email: primland@swva.net
Web: www.primland.com

THE HUNT:

SEASON:

• bow: opens first Saturday in October

• rifle: third Monday in November, runs for 2 weeks

• muzzleloader: first Monday in November, runs for 2 weeks

BEST TIME TO HUNT: During the rut (second week of November, usually)

TERRAIN: Old growth woodland, clearcuts, cereal crops, cornfields, and green fields; terrain ranges from rolling piedmont to steep ridges and mountains; elevations run from 1,700' to 3,100'

LAND: 14,000 private acres

DRAW BLOOD POLICY? No

HUNTING METHODS: Stand hunting (ladder stands, permanent stands), still-hunting, calling, rattling

YEARS IN BUSINESS: 13

STAFF OF GUIDES: 8

HUNTERS SERVED BY EACH GUIDE: 3

NONHUNTER CHARGE: Yes

LICENSES: Sold at the lodge

GAME CARE: Dressed, packaged, frozen, and shipped

OTHER ACTIVITIES: Spring turkey hunting, pheasant hunting, waterfowling, fishing, biking, bird watching, hiking, tennis, sporting clays, ATV and horse-back riding

BOONE AND CROCKETT

• B&C book bucks taken from property: None yet

• Average B&C score: 130 - 150

• B&C bucks from this part of state: Few

MIDWEST

ARKANSAS, ILLINOIS, INDIANA, IOWA, KANSAS, MICHIGAN, MINNESOTA, MISSOURI, NEBRASKA, NORTH DAKOTA, OHIO, OKLAHOMA, SOUTH DAKOTA, WISCONSIN

MANY PEOPLE who hunt the Midwest hunt the abundant public and private lands without the services of a lodge and outfitter. That's fine, as there is much quality habitat open to the public. There are some lodges, such as the ones listed here, however, that offer even better hunting than that, with many controlling and carefully managing their property and deer herds for maximum trophy quality.

Whitetails abound throughout the Midwest. The deer range from big grainfield deer, those from blackwater swamps of northern woods, or trophy bucks from rolling hardwood plateaus. Bowhunters have long seasons, with generous bag limits in many areas, but rifle hunters also get their share. Muzzleloader hunters, too, enjoy a lengthy season. The choice of weapon is yours, and the number of good lodges to choose from is long. Some of the best you'll find here.

Lodges

Illinois

1 BIG BUCK OUTFITTERS
2 CARTER'S HUNTING LODGE
3 ILLINOIS TROPHY BOWHUNTERS, INC
4 ILLINOIS TROPHY WHITETAILS
5 ROCK HOUSE HUNT CLUB
6 TURKEY CREEK LODGE

Iowa

7 SCHAFER OUTFITTERS

Kansas

8 XI ADAMS RANCH
9 KANSAS UNLIMITED
10 VERDIGRIS VALLEY OUTFITTERS

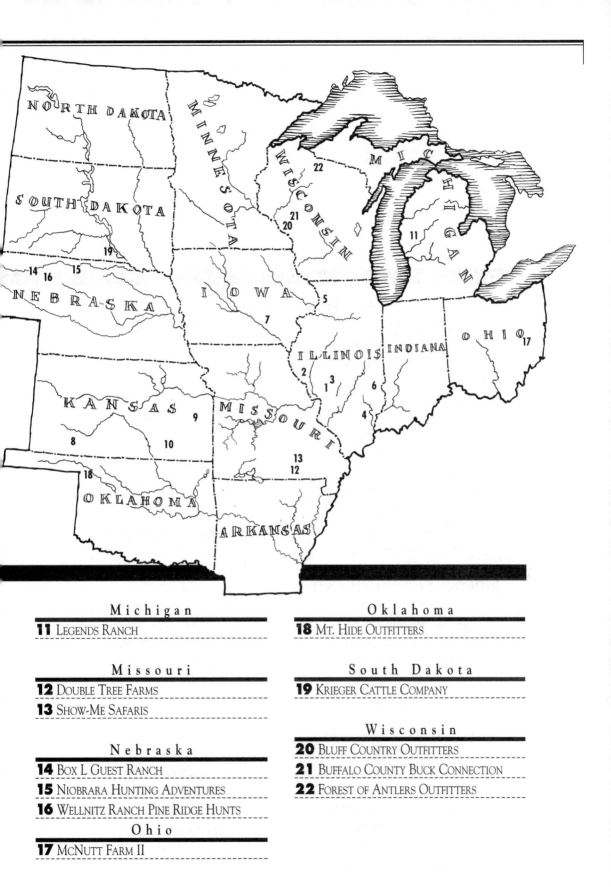

Michigan
11 LEGENDS RANCH

Missouri
12 DOUBLE TREE FARMS

13 SHOW-ME SAFARIS

Nebraska
14 BOX L GUEST RANCH

15 NIOBRARA HUNTING ADVENTURES

16 WELLNITZ RANCH PINE RIDGE HUNTS

Ohio
17 MCNUTT FARM II

Oklahoma
18 MT. HIDE OUTFITTERS

South Dakota
19 KRIEGER CATTLE COMPANY

Wisconsin
20 BLUFF COUNTRY OUTFITTERS

21 BUFFALO COUNTY BUCK CONNECTION

22 FOREST OF ANTLERS OUTFITTERS

Resources

ARKANSAS GAME AND FISH
COMMISSION
2 Natural Resources Dr.
Little Rock, AR 72205
Ph: 501/223-6300, 800/364-4263
Web: www.agfc.state.ar.us

ILLINOIS DEPT. OF NATURAL
RESOURCES
Lincoln Tower Plaza
524 S. Second St., Rm. 400
Springfield, IL 62701-1787
Ph: 217/785-6302
Web: Dnr.state.il.us

INDIANA DIV. OF FISH AND
WILDLIFE
402 W. Washington St.
Indianapolis, IN 46204
Ph: 317/232-4080
Web:
www.dnr.state.in.us/fishwild/index.htm

IOWA DEPT. OF NATURAL
RESOURCES
Wallace Bldg.
East Ninth and Grand Ave.
Des Moines, IA 50319-0034
Ph: 515/281-5145
Fax: 515/281-8895
Web: Sss.state.ia.us/wildlife

KANSAS DEPT. OF WILDLIFE
AND PARKS
900 SW Jackson St., Ste. 502
Topeka, KS 66612-1233
Ph: 785/296-2281
Fax: 785/296-6953
Web: www.kdwp.state.ks.us

MICHIGAN DEPT. OF NATURAL
RESOURCES
Wildlife Div.
Box 30444
Lansing, MI 48909-7944
Ph: 517/373-1263
Web: www.dnr.state.mi.us

MINNESOTA DEPT. OF
NATURAL RESOURCES
Div. of Fish and Wildlife
500 Lafayette Rd.
St. Paul, MN 55155-4001
Ph: 651/297-1308
Web: www.dnr.state.mn.lus

MISSOURI DEPT. OF
CONSERVATION
2901 W. Truman Blvd., Box 180
Jefferson City, MO 65102-0180
Ph: 573/751-4115
Web: www.conservation.state.mo.us

NEBRASKA GAME AND PARKS
COMMISSION
2200 N. 33rd St., Box 30370
Lincoln, NE 68503-0641
Ph: 402/471-0641
Web: www.ngpc.state.ne.us

NORTH DAKOTA GAME AND
FISH DEPT.
100 North Bismarck Expy.
Bismarck, ND 58501
Ph: 701/328-6300
Fax: 701/328-6352
Web: www.state.nd.us/gnf

OHIO DEPT. OF NATURAL
RESOURCES
DIV. OF WILDLIFE
Fountain Square
Columbus, OH 43224-1329
Ph: 614/265-6300
Web: www.dnr.state.oh.us/odnr/wildlife

OKLAHOMA DEPT. OF WILDLIFE
CONSERVATION
1801 N. Lincoln, Box 53465
Oklahoma City, OK 73152
Ph: 405/521-3851
Fax: 405/521-6535
Web: www.state.ok.us/-odwc

SOUTH DAKOTA GAME, FISH
AND PARKS DEPT.
523 E. Capitol
Pierre, SD 57501-3182
Ph: 605/773-3387
Web:
www.state.sd.us/state/gfp/index.htm

Big Buck Outfitters

Greenfield, Illinois

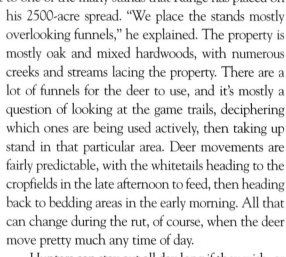

CCORDING TO OWNER Dennis Range, the year 2000 was a good one at Big Buck Outfitters. "Out of 10 hunters this season, all 10 saw good, shooting-size bucks," said Range. "And of those 10, three took good bucks, with the best one going in the 130 class." All 10 hunters were bowhunters, "although we do take some rifle hunters as well."

A typical day at Big Buck Outfitters begins with a wakeup call around 4:30 a.m., a light breakfast, then a ride out to one of the many stands that Range has placed on his 2500-acre spread. "We place the stands mostly overlooking funnels," he explained. The property is mostly oak and mixed hardwoods, with numerous creeks and streams lacing the property. There are a lot of funnels for the deer to use, and it's mostly a question of looking at the game trails, deciphering which ones are being used actively, then taking up stand in that particular area. Deer movements are fairly predictable, with the whitetails heading to the cropfields in the late afternoon to feed, then heading back to bedding areas in the early morning. All that can change during the rut, of course, when the deer move pretty much any time of day.

© Big Buck Outfitters

A heavy-beamed 10-pointer taken off Big Buck Outfitters' lands.

Hunters can stay out all day long if they wish, or can arrange to be picked up in the late morning, taken back to the lodge for a lunch and nap, then returned to their stands for the afternoon watch. Those staying out all day carry sack lunches and hot and cold drinks to keep them going during the day.

"We also tell them to take enough clothing," Range said. "Temperatures here can be anywhere from 80°F to freezing, so you have to be prepared."

Range, who farms the area, has lived in this part of Illinois all of his life, and knows the property like the back of his hand. Although he has been in the outfitting business for only three years, his is one of those little hunting gems that we all like to find and not let go.

"Well," he said in his Illinois drawl, "I do know that at least eight of the 10 hunters from 2000 are coming back in 2001." Of course, there's room for a few more, if you hurry.

Vital Statistics

THE LODGE:

5 guest rooms, 1 has private bath, 10 beds total (although Big Buck Outfitters prefers to take no more than 6 hunters at a time); all rooms are in a modern farmhouse attached to the main lodge, a large, modern country home

SERVICES: Telephone, fax, TV, laundry

HUNTS:

- pre- and post-rut archery hunts: $750 / 5-6 days
- rut archery hunts: $1,000 / 3 days
- gun (shotgun): $1,000 / 3 days
- $250 kill fee for all bucks taken

PAYMENT: Check

MEAL PLANS: 3 meals a day (typical dinner selection includes fried chicken, potatoes and gravy, salad, vegetables and dessert the first night; roast beef with vegetables, noodles, rolls, salad and dessert the second night; lasagna, salad, corn, garlic bread and dessert the third night; and grilled pork chops, baked potatoes, vegetables, salad, rolls and dessert the fourth; plus, tea, coffee, and beverages)

NEAREST AIRPORTS: Springfield, IL, or St. Louis, MO

TRANSPORTATION TO LODGE (60 miles): Van from lodge ($100)

CONTACT:

Dennis and Sara Range
Big Buck Outfitters
Rt. 2, Box 130
Greenfield, IL 62044
Ph: 217/368-2096
Fax: 217/368-3146
Email: range@accessus.net
Web: www.bigbuckoutfitters.com

THE HUNT:

SEASON:

- bow: October 2 - 21, October 23 - November 18, November 20 - January 10
- shotgun: November 17 - 19, Nov. 30 - Dec. 3
- muzzleloader: December 8 - 10

BEST TIME TO HUNT: During the rut (late October through mid to late November)

TERRAIN: Rolling oak timbers with small creeks running through them; small fields of corn, beans, wheat and clover

LAND: 2,500 private acres

DRAW BLOOD POLICY? Yes

HUNTING METHODS: Stand hunting (lock-ons), calling, rattling

YEARS IN BUSINESS: 3

STAFF OF GUIDES: 2

HUNTERS SERVED BY EACH GUIDE: Varies

NONHUNTER CHARGE: $50 / day

LICENSES: Bow licenses sold over the counter at lodge; gun licenses chosen in a state lottery

GAME CARE: Will help arrange processing and freezing

OTHER ACTIVITIES: Turkey hunting, mourning dove hunting

BOONE AND CROCKETT

- B&C book bucks taken from property: Several
- Average B&C score: 140
- B&C bucks from this part of state: Several

Carter's Hunting Lodge

Milton, Illinois

MOST BOWHUNTERS would agree that if you want to arrow a true trophy-class buck, one that's in the 150 class and up, west-central Illinois is the place to go. And if that's where you want to hunt, then Carter's Hunting Lodge should be high on your list of choices. The terrain in this area is ideally suited for growing trophy bucks.

From its junction with the LaMoine River, the Illinois River turns south and begins cutting through the plains. It forms the border between Pike County to the west and Scott County to the east, and scores of steep ravines lead from the high cropland to the river below. Creeks wind through the coulees, the sides of which are heavily timbered in oak and beech with occasional stands of cedar. Up on the plains, you'll find woodlots that are too wet or too rocky to plow. The rest of the country is planted in corn and soybeans with an occasional pasture for cows. Farmers here have been pretty good about setting aside Conservation Reserve Program (CRP) acreage. This land has everything needed to grow record-book bucks — and it does!

Dale and Nathan Carter, who operate a classic old farmhouse as a hunting lodge, lease 10,000 acres of CRP and cropland for archery hunts only. (2000 was the first year Carter's went to bowhunting only, and with great success as one client shot a 10-point buck that scored 198 1/8 points Pope and Young.)

In the morning, you'll hunt from stands strategically placed over scrape and rub lines. In the evening, you may find yourself watching a route from a bedding to feeding area. Your chances for a good buck are excellent here; the area has produced a number of Pope & Young deer over the years. And now, with archers required to shoot bucks that score 140 or better (shoot one under 130, and you'll pay a $500 fine), that ratio is going to soar.

There's one guide for every two hunters, with the guide making sure that the hunter is safely situated in a tree or portable stand well before daylight. Should a hunter hit a deer, the guide will track it. About 50 percent of Carter's hunters get a big buck during their stay.

Vital Statistics

THE LODGE:

Vintage farmhouse has 4 guest rooms, 24 beds total (though Carter's prefers to take 20 hunters at a time maximum)

SERVICES: Telephone, TV

HUNTS:

- $1,750 / 5 days during pre-rut
- $2,250 / 5 days during rut
- $1,500 / 5 days in December

PAYMENT: Cash or check

CONFERENCE GROUPS: No

MEAL PLANS: Family-style lunch and dinner

NEAREST AIRPORT: St. Louis, MO

TRANSPORTATION TO LODGE (two hours): Rental car or take the shuttle to the lodge at your expense

CONTACT:

Dale Carter
Carter's Hunting Lodge
P.O. Box 259
Milton, IL 62352
Ph: 217/723-4522
Email: DECO246@aol.com
Web: www.rockhousehuntclub.com

THE HUNT:

SEASON: Mid. October - January 15

BEST TIME TO HUNT: Second, third weeks of November

TERRAIN: Creek bottoms, timbered oak and beech stands with occasional cedar; corn, soybean fields, CRP land

LAND: Lease about 10,000 acres

DRAW BLOOD POLICY? No

HUNTING METHODS: Stand hunting (lock-ons and permanent stands), rattling, calling

YEARS IN BUSINESS: 3

STAFF OF GUIDES: Up to 12 (varies)

HUNTERS SERVED BY EACH GUIDE: 2

LICENSES: Sold over the counter

GAME CARE: Meat will be butchered/wrapped/frozen at local meat processing plant for $65

POPE AND YOUNG BOX

- Pope and Young book bucks taken from property: All bucks
- Average Pope and Young score: 140 plus
- Pope and Young bucks from this part of state: n/a

Illinois Trophy Bowhunters, Inc.

Springfield, Illinois

THE YEAR 2000 marked the 10th year of operation for Illinois Trophy Bowhunters (ITB), a guide service owned and operated by bowhunters. ITB's archery leases have been bowhunting-only for nine years, and are only hunted three weeks per year. With such light hunting pressure, it is easy to understand why ITB achieves an annual success rate of anywhere from 35 to 60 percent (much depends on weather and other variables, of course). ITB's total leases now exceed 18,000 acres, all of which are carefully managed for trophy whitetails. In fact, about 75 percent of the hunters who bowhunt with ITB see the biggest bucks of their lives during their stay! The best typicals taken from these leases run 180 to 200 class, while the best non-typicals are in the 180 to 240 class. With this type of world-class hunting, you can see why ITB has many repeat customers.

Central and western Illinois is a region that's well-known for producing monster whitetails. The topography contributes to ITB's success. The woods are small, and usually consist of long, narrow ridges of timber. The movement of deer to and from the corn, alfalfa, and soybean fields creates ideal funnel situations, which are perfect for bowhunting out of treestands. If you want to eat, breathe, and sleep trophy whitetails for six days, with bowhunters of the same dedication, come experience Illinois and hunt with ITB.

(Note: a free video is available upon request — you have to see this to believe it!)

Vital Statistics

THE LODGE:

8 to 10 camps throughout central Illinois; 3 camps have 10 beds apiece with private baths; the others use motels or let hunters set up their own camps

SERVICES: Telephone, TV

HUNTS:

- fully-guided 6-day bow hunt, 2 bucks: $1,800
- semi-guided 6-day bowhunt, 1 buck: $1,000
- semi-guided shotgun or muzzleloader hunt: $1,000
- archery/gun combo (6-day bow, plus 3-day gun): $1,800

PAYMENT: Check

CONFERENCE GROUPS: Yes

MEAL PLANS: Depends on the camp and the type of hunt; full hunt includes chicken, spaghetti, steaks, roasts, plus vegetables, breads, desserts

SPECIAL DIETS: Can accommodate most requests

NEAREST AIRPORT: Depends on camp location

TRANSPORTATION TO LODGE: Depends on camp location

CONTACT:

Brian Bergmann
Illinois Trophy Bowhunters, Inc.
825 Cherokee Drive
Springfield, IL 62707
Ph: 217/698-5798
Fax: 205/459-4479
Email: hunting@water-valley.com

THE HUNT:

SEASON:

- bow: October 30 - Noember. 21

BEST TIME TO HUNT: Third week in November

TERRAIN: A mixture of hardwoods, scrub, and agriculture (about 50/50 corn and beans)

LAND: Lease 18,000-plus acres

DRAW BLOOD POLICY? No

HUNTING METHODS: Stand hunting (lock-ons, some ladder stands), calling, rattling

YEARS IN BUSINESS:

STAFF OF GUIDES: 15

HUNTERS SERVED BY EACH GUIDE: 1 - 4

NONHUNTER CHARGE: n/a

LICENSES: Bow licenses sold over the counter; shotgun licenses must be drawn (the lodge will mail license applications to clients for both bow and shotgun well in advance of the deadline)

GAME CARE: Done by clients

OTHER ACTIVITIES: n/a

BOONE AND CROCKETT

- B&C book bucks taken from property: 20 - 30
- Average B&C score: 140
- B&C bucks from this part of state: Numerous

Illinois Trophy Whitetails / Campbell Resources, Inc.

O N MORE THAN 12,000 ACRES set between two rivers in the middle of prime deer hunting territory in southern Illinois, the Campbell family offers hunters a unique opportunity. Trophy whitetails are found on the wooded hillsides, creek bottoms, fencerows, swamp timber and food plots that are accessible from area crop lands. With the Campbell's extensive experience in the region, hunters have an excellent chance of taking one of the outstanding bucks that roam the property.

The Campbell family has been in the White County district since 1836. Their outfitting business, Campbell Resources Inc., includes a modern lodge with office facilities on the premises. The Campbell brothers, John and Matt, know the deer patterns well. They do the pre-hunt work for the hunters and offer fair chase hunting of free-ranging whitetails. Their guide-assisted leasing system allows hunters to use their own equipment and hunting tactics.

Upon arrival, hunters are met by a representative of Campbell Resources, Inc. Hunters are shown their lease areas and given up-to-date scouting reports on deer movements, bedding areas, feeding grounds, and suggested stand locations. The representative helps with information on obtaining extra permits (archery only), checking in of harvested game, deer processing facilities in the area, and other helpful information. He can also help with any equipment problems, retrieval of game, and trailing a wounded deer.

The Campbells strive to protect their younger bucks through a resource management program. Archery hunters are allowed one buck per hunt with a minimum 15-inch outside antler spread, and one doe. Firearm hunters are allowed either one buck (same minimum antler spread) or one doe. Archery hunters take Pope and Young bucks every year and several Boone and Crockett-class bucks have been taken.

"We're farmers here too," says John Campbell. "We have some leasing arrangements with neighboring farmers and we scout that land. Most of the other areas we have farmed, owned or hunted for several years, so we know the deer patterns. We do most of the prehunt work for the hunters, and when they come, we are ready to put them right on the deer.

"What we're actually doing is managing the resource on our property and providing people access so they can hunt the way they want to," he concluded.

Guests are welcomed into the comfortable rustic atmosphere of the hunting lodge. It has accommodations for eight with all the amenities of home. The full kitchen, dining room, and living room with a cozy fireplace offer a relaxing retreat from the day's hunt. A hot tub and tennis court are also available for the guests. Hunters may choose to stay in the comfortable bunkhouse that sleeps four hunters, complete with TV, VCR, separate changing room, bathroom and cooking facilities located above the hunting office.

© Illinois Trophy Whitetails

The main lodge at Illinois Trophy Whitetails.

Vital Statistics

THE LODGE:

4 bedrooms in the main lodge can accommodate 8 hunters; bunkhouse sleeps 4 hunters; no private baths

SERVICES: Telephone, fax, copying, TV, laundry

HUNTS:

• bow: guided hunts range from $900 / 3 days to $2,050 / 6 days

• firearms: guided hunts range from $1,850 to $2,350

• prices include lodging

PAYMENT: Cash

CONFERENCE GROUPS: No

MEAL PLANS: Guests cook for themselves

NEAREST AIRPORT: Evansville, IN

TRANSPORTATION TO LODGE (35 miles): Rental car

CONTACT:

John Campbell
Illinois Trophy Whitetails
Campbell Resources, Inc.
1327 County Road 800 N.
Carmi, IL 62821
Ph: 618/382-7939
Email: info@illinoisdeerhunting.com
Web: www.illinoisdeerhunting.com

THE HUNT:

SEASON:

• bow: Oct. 1 - Nov. 16, Nov. 20 - 29,
Dec. 4 - Jan. 13

• shotgun: Nov. 17 - 19, Nov. 30 - Dec. 3

• muzzleloader: Dec. 8 - 10

BEST TIME TO HUNT: November and December

TERRAIN: Farmland, river bottoms, hardwood forests, wooded ridgelines

LAND: Own and lease land in White, Wabash and Johnson counties (Illinois)

DRAW BLOOD POLICY? No

HUNTING METHODS: Stand hunting (portable climbers, lock-ons, ground blinds, ladder stands), calling, rattling

Years in Business: 4

Staff of Guides: 3

Hunters served by each guide: 4 (one-on-one hunts $150 / day additional)

Nonhunter Charge: $50 / day; lodging (based on availability)

Licenses: Sold at lodge

Game Care: Local processing, packaging, shipping available for extra fee

Other Activities: Waterfowling, tennis, wildlife photography

BOONE AND CROCKETT

• B&C book bucks taken from property: 3

• Average B&C score: mid 170s typical;
200 nontypical

• B&C bucks from this part of state: Many

Rock House Hunt Club

ROCK HOUSE HUNT CLUB is located in north-western Illinois two miles east of the Mississippi River, right in the middle of prime white-tailed deer habitat.

The club caters to experienced bow and gun hunters who come from areas where large, mature whitetail bucks may not exist. It offers a real chance for taking a Pope and Young or Boone and Crockett-class buck. With no fences or enclosures, all bucks shot at Rock House can indeed qualify for the record books. Hunters at Rock House are very particular about what they shoot. Many 120- to 130-class bucks were passed up last season. In fact, multiple, verified (videotaped) 180-class deer were seen. As it turns out, a number of hunters even got within range (one at full draw) of these bucks at some point during the season, but could not get clear shots. (Bucks that large have a habit of doing that, don't they?) The largest bow kill in the 2000 season was a 144-inch net 9-pointer with a 24-inch inside spread. Notable shotgun kills included a massive racked 170-inch-plus, 225-pound dressed buck. Two others were estimated 170- to 180-class bucks.

Success rates on archery kills of 120- class or better bucks have been in excess of 50 percent. According to Mike Novak of Rock House, "There are Boone and Crockett class bucks around too. Don't be brainwashed that Pike County in Illinois is the only place in the state that has monster bucks. It's just not true. We have the exact same habitat and genetics in our area of Carroll County. In addition, Pike County is receiving tremendous hunting pressure these days. We have a low density of hunters on our property, typically one hunter per 200 acres." Novak also pointed out that the No. 2 state with the most number of deer entered in the Boone and Crockett record books of North America is Illinois, and that twenty-five percent of the Boone & Crockett entries in recent years have come from Illinois. The club has approximately 3,000 acres managed carefully for whitetails. The property has everything, including cropland, CRP food plots, hardwood timber, bottoms, and more than 11 miles of river frontage along the Plum River and Camp Creek. This is a densely wooded, rolling area. The property is about one third tillable; the rest is timber and rough ground, with much of it being fairly rugged and hilly.

Lodging is provided for all hunts in the premier rustic lodge. Accommodations are also available in the Rock House, a stone home that is the oldest standing structure in the county, built in 1842. Meals are on your own, unless you're at Rock House during the height of the hunting season, at which point a cook is brought in.

A bow-hunter at Rock House Hunt Club displays his trophy.

The Rock House is the oldest standing structure in the county, and lodges visiting hunters.

Vital Statistics

THE LODGE:

Rustic farmhouse has 9 guest rooms, 20 beds total, no private baths

SERVICES: Telephone, TV, email

HUNTS:

• $1,500 / 5-day bow hunts

• $1,850 / 3- to 4-day gun hunts

PAYMENT: Cash, check

CONFERENCE GROUPS: No

MEAL PLANS: All meals included (At peak season, there is a cook on the premises. Other times guests do their own cooking. Minimal charge per day when cook is available. Dinner features prime rib, ham, pork roast, venison roast, chicken, lasagna, spaghetti, turkey, and all the fixings.)

NEAREST AIRPORT: Moline, IL

TRANSPORTATION TO LODGE (40 minutes): Rental car or pick up

CONTACT:

Mike Novak
Rock House Hunt Club
11599 Messmer Road
Savanna, IL 61074
Ph: 630/236-0669
Fax: 630/236-0652.
Email: nsasquatch@aol.com

THE HUNT:

SEASON:

• bow: Oct. 1 - Jan. 12

• shotgun: Friday, Saturday and Sunday prior to Thanksgiving; Thursday - Sunday after Thanksgiving

• muzzleloader: first weekend in December

BEST TIME TO HUNT: Last weekend in October - third week in November

TERRAIN: Eleven miles of river frontage, one-third agricultural land, the remainder river bluffs, deep draws, dense woods, river bottoms, cropfields, food plots, hardwood forests (oak, hickory, walnut)

LAND: 3,000 private acres

DRAW BLOOD POLICY? Allow one wounded deer

HUNTING METHODS: Stand hunting (ladder stands, hang-on treestands, ground blinds), still-hunting, calling, rattling

YEARS IN BUSINESS: 10

STAFF OF GUIDES: 2

HUNTERS SERVED BY EACH GUIDE: 2 - 4

NONHUNTER CHARGE: $50 / day (space permitting)

LICENSES: Apply by lottery for gun license; over the counter for bow

GAME CARE: Field dressing only; local butcher can cut, freeze, ship; taxidermy available

OTHER ACTIVITIES: Turkey hunting

BOONE & CROCKETT

• B&C book bucks taken from property: 2

• Average B&C score: 170

• B&C bucks from this part of state: 33 (including only Rock House's county — Carroll — and immediate adjacent county)

Turkey Creek Lodge

Newton, Illinois

T URKEY CREEK LODGE was created for the sole purpose of providing a high quality and exclusive hunting experience for clients. The concept for this family-owned and operated lodge was developed when the owners realized that there were few options for hunters who wanted a quality, all-around hunting experience in this part of the country — an area well-recognized for its trophy whitetails. Being avid hunters themselves, the owners of Turkey Creek Lodge have hunted at many different lodges and with many different guide services. Turkey Creek Lodge is a combination of the best aspects of each of these facilities. The result? An operation devoted to providing customers with the best possible hunting experience. Turkey Creek Lodge can accommodate the needs of most any group or organization.

As any hunter knows, access to quality hunting grounds is a key to repeat success. Since the owners of Turkey Creek are native to Jasper County and farm many of the acres that are hunted, they are able to identify and access the best hunting properties.

Central Illinois offers some of the best whitetail habitat in the country. Add this to the fact that Turkey Creek's owners and guides live and work in this habitat year round, and you've got a hunting combination that's tough to beat. They are able to track the size and quality of the area's whitetail deer well before hunting season, thus giving clients the best possible opportunity for a trophy buck once the season does open. Clients have more than 7,000 total acres to hunt, and when they're finished at the end of a long day, return to the modern, log cabin lodge that can accommodate 12 hunters at a time. With hearty home cooking and comfortable beds waiting after dinner, clients won't go wrong booking with Turkey Creek.

Vital Statistics

THE LODGE:

Lodge has 5 guest rooms, 1 with private bath, 12 beds total

SERVICES: Telephone, fax, laundry, TV

BOWHUNTS: $1600 / 5-day hunt

PAYMENT: Cash, check, MasterCard, Visa

CONFERENCE GROUPS: Yes

MEAL PLANS: All meals included; home-cooked

NEAREST AIRPORT: Indianapolis, IN, or St. Louis, MO

TRANSPORTATION TO LODGE: Van from lodge at no additional cost

CONTACT:

Turkey Creek Lodge
13388 N. 875th Street
Newton, IL 62448
Ph: 877/660-6602
Fax: 618/783-4402
Email: info@turkeycreeklodge.com
Web: www.turkeycreeklodge.com

THE HUNT:

SEASON: October 1 - January 13

BEST TIME TO HUNT: Late October to beginning of November

TERRAIN: Hardwoods, creek bottoms, small woodlots, funnel areas, agricultural fields

LAND: 7,000 acres privately owned or leased

DRAW BLOOD POLICY? No

HUNTING METHODS: Stand hunting (lock-ons, portables), calling, rattling

YEARS IN BUSINESS: 2

STAFF OF GUIDES: 3

HUNTERS SERVED BY EACH GUIDE: 1 - 3

NONHUNTER CHARGE:

LICENSES: Sold over the counter or at the lodge

GAME CARE: Freeze and package but do not ship

OTHER ACTIVITIES: Turkey hunting, bird hunting, waterfowling, fishing, bird watching, wildlife photography

Schafer Outfitters

Fairfield, Iowa

S CHAEFER OUTFITTERS leases more than 2,000 acres of prestigious hunting grounds in Van Buren and Jefferson counties in southeast Iowa. This land has a proven track record of producing Boone and Crockett deer for family members and friends, but it has never been leased for commercial hunting until now. These lands have not been hunted hard in the past, the deer are not heavily pressured, and your chance of getting a shot at a super buck are good.

All deer hunting is done from tree stands. Hunters may bring their own stands, or use one provided by Schafer Outfitters. Bowhunters are welcome, and the opportunity for a Pope and Young size buck here is realistic. Hunts can be guided or unguided depending on each hunter's needs. Transportation to and from tree stands is provided, as are tracking and field dressing.

The weather in Iowa during hunting season is unpredictable, so hunters are advised to pack clothing for anything from warm to cold, dry or wet conditions.

© Schafer Outfitters

A monster with drop tine, taken off the lands hunted by Schafer Outfitters.

Vital Statistics

THE LODGE:

Local motel or log cabins on Lake Segonia; can accommodate 3 hunters

SERVICES: Telephone

HUNTS:

• shotgun and bow: $1,500 / 5 days

• muzzleloader: $1,200 / 5 days

• public ground hunts: $1,500 / 5 days

PAYMENT: Check or cash

MEAL PLANS: Breakfast only; buffet style

NEAREST AIRPORT: Burlington or Cedar Rapids, IA

TRANSPORTATION TO LODGE (50 miles):Van from lodge

BOONE AND CROCKETT

• B&C bucks taken from property: 2 or 3 per year

• Average B&C score: 165 typical, 200 nontypical

• B&C bucks from this part of state: Many

CONTACT:

Jack Schafer
Schafer Outfitters
2326 Salina Road
Fairfield, IA 52556
Ph: 515/662-2393
Web: huntguide.com/mossyoak.com
Email: Jackschafer@lisco.com
Web: www.huntcamp.com (go to Iowa)

THE HUNT:

SEASON:

• bow: October 14 - December 1, December 17 - January 10

• shotgun: December 9 - 16

• muzzleloader: December 17 - January 10

BEST TIME TO HUNT: During the rut for bowhunters, late in the season for muzzleloaders

TERRAIN: Some small woodlots, rolling timber with corn and bean fields; no fences

LAND: Leased land totals 2,000 acres; access to 5,000 acres of public hunting ground

DRAW BLOOD POLICY? No

HUNTING METHODS: Stand hunting (portables, lock-ons, some permanent stands), still-hunting, calling, rattling, by vehicle

YEARS IN BUSINESS: 1 (new operation)

STAFF OF GUIDES: Owner

HUNTERS SERVED BY EACH GUIDE: 1

NONHUNTER CHARGE: None

LICENSES: Must apply for licenses ahead of time; contact Iowa Fish & Wildlife Division

GAME CARE: Dress, package, freeze and ship; cost varies, depending on service

OTHER ACTIVITIES: Bird hunting, fishing, antiquing, biking, bird watching, boating, canoeing, hiking, wildlife photography

XI Adams Ranch

Plains, Kansas

WHEN YOU HUNT out of the Adams Ranch, you give yourself the opportunity to get in on some of the finest Midwestern/Southwestern whitetail hunting available. The Adams Ranch controls more than 37,000 acres of privately-owned land in Texas and Kansas. The property is loaded with prime cover and forage, ideal for whitetails that can grow to trophy size in just two to three years.

The Texas and Kansas ranches are only 90 miles apart, meaning you can shuttle between both if you desire. But if you're in prime Texas or Kansas deer hunting country, why would you want to leave it? The only good reason would be if you filled out your tag in one state; then you'd have more than enough reason to head to the other state and try for a double!

The Texas hunts take place in the scenic, caprock country of Roberts and Ochiltree counties, with the southern edge of the property bordering the Canadian River. This privately owned working cattle ranch contains ideal habitat not only for whitetails (check those river bottoms), but for mulies as well. The ranch also has many standing waterholes and natural springs scattered throughout its 17,000 acres.

If you opt to hunt for a Kansas buck, you'll be hunting a prime area right along the Oklahoma border, a quick car ride from the Texas Ranch, down Route 83. The Kansas property is located along the Cimarron River in Seward and Meade counties. This is also privately held land, and prime trophy country. The Adams Ranch owns and controls approximately five miles of river property in Unit 18 — and if you're from this area, you know what that means! Big whitetails, in numbers. In 1998, a whitetail scoring 205 1/8 was shot in Seward County on property adjoining the Adams tract. Where do you think that monster's offspring are now?

Lodging for guests at both ranches is comfortable and clean, in modern guesthouses. All meals are provided — you'll need the energy, as the up-and-down terrain here can keep you working!

Vital Statistics

THE LODGE:

Kansas: 2 guest rooms with 2 beds; Texas: 3 guestrooms with 6 beds (although owner H.G. Adams prefers to have no more than 2 hunters in each camp at a time); there are no private baths; accommodations are modern ranch houses

SERVICES:

- Kansas: telephone, fax, copying, TV and laundry
- Texas: there are no public phones available on the premises

HUNTS:

- rifle: $3,250 / 5 days
- bow: $3,000 / 5 days

PAYMENT: Cash or check

MEAL PLANS: 3 meals a day (home-cooked meals including beef as the main course on many occasions)

SPECIAL DIETS: "We can work with our guests to accommodate."

NEAREST AIRPORT: Amarillo, TX

Transportation to Lodge: Rental car (Texas ranch is 90 miles, Kansas ranch is 180 miles)

CONTACT:

Wanda and H.G (Kell) Adams IV
XI Adams Ranch
8051 CC Road
Plains, KS 67869
Ph: 316/563-9266
Fax: 316/563-6160
Web: www.rahab.net/xiadams

THE HUNT:

SEASON:

- Texas rifle: November 20 - January 7
- Texas bow: September 30 - October 29
- Kansas rifle: November 29 - December 10
- Kansas bow: Oct. 2 - Nov. 28, Dec. 11 - 31

BEST TIME TO HUNT: Anytime is good; the rut is ideal

TERRAIN: Sharp hills and coulees, riverbottoms; there are no high fences

LAND: Adams owns 33,400 acres and leases 3,600 acres

DRAW BLOOD POLICY? Yes

HUNTING METHODS: Stand hunting (blinds on ground, lock-on tree stands), still-hunting, rattling

YEARS IN BUSINESS: New operation

STAFF OF GUIDES: 3

HUNTERS SERVED BY EACH GUIDE: 1 - 2

NONHUNTER CHARGE: $100 / day

LICENSES: Texas licenses are over the counter; Kansas licenses must be drawn in a lottery ahead of time

GAME CARE: Mostly done by clients

OTHER ACTIVITIES: Mule deer hunting, turkey hunting

Kansas Unlimited

Garnett, Kansas

KANSAS HAS A well-deserved reputation as the place for big whitetails. Hunters can expect to see mature bucks with heavy bases and tines in the six-to nine-inch range. Many deer score in the 120- to 160-Boone and Crockett point range with an occasional 180-point animal. Kansas is also known for non-typical racks, and it is not unusual to see a white-tail with drop tines. Deer from this area are big bodied and healthy due to year-round feeding on the vast variety of row crops grown in the area.

Hunters who book with Kansas Unlimited stay in either small, local motels or the Kansas Unlimited lodge, depending on the exact location of the hunt. Hot showers and warm beds are available every night. Weather will vary from T-shirt temperatures in early October to extreme cold in November and December. Hunters should be prepared for a variety of conditions.

With rifles, most deer will be taken at 150 yards or less, so any of the traditional deer calibers are acceptable. Scopes are recommended for improved accuracy. Archers can use traditional or compound equipment. Kansas requires a minimum 40-pound pull.

The drawing for out-of-state whitetail permits in Kansas is conducted in late spring. Contact Kansas Unlimited about details and procedures.

This outfit is located on the eastern edge of the historic Flint Hills of Kansas, which offer a mixture of tall prairie grass, rich cropland and treed waterways, creating the important edge habitat so important to great whitetail hunting. Fields are lined with endless hedgerows planted in the 1920s and 30s as windbreaks, and waterways and drainages are lined with a mix of cedar and hardwood timber. These areas serve as important travel lanes for deer on the move.

All hunts are fair chase only; there are no high fences. Hunts take place from permanent or portable ground or tree stands. Stands are located along primary travel lanes and feeding areas to allow the hunter the greatest opportunity at a trophy animal. A variety of stand locations will be available to each hunter to allow for changes in whitetail patterns. KU welcomes both gun and archery hunters.

Vital Statistics

THE LODGE:

Main lodge has 4 guest rooms, 12 beds total; also local motels, depending on location of the hunt

SERVICES: Telephone, TV, laundry

GUN HUNTS:

- rifle: $3,500 / 5 days
- bow: $2,250 / 5 days
- muzzleloader: $2,500 / 5 days

PAYMENT: Cash or check

CONFERENCE GROUPS: Yes

MEAL PLANS: All home-cooked meals

NEAREST AIRPORT: Kansas City International, MO

TRANSPORTATION TO LODGE: (Three hours) Rental car; van from lodge ($80 one way)

CONTACT:

Wes Traul
Kansas Unlimited
11464 NW 2100 Road
Garnett, KS 66032
Ph: 785/448-3239

THE HUNT:

SEASON:

- rifle: Dec.1 - 11
- bow: October – December
- muzzleloader: September

BEST TIME TO HUNT: During the rut in November with a bow

TERRAIN: Farmland and grassland

LAND: 33,500 private acres

DRAW BLOOD POLICY? No

HUNTING METHODS: Stand hunting (ladders, tripods, lock-ons), rattling

YEARS IN BUSINESS: 4

STAFF OF GUIDES: 3

HUNTERS SERVED BY EACH GUIDE: 2

NONHUNTER CHARGE: $200 / day

LICENSES: Apply in spring

GAME CARE: Dress, package, freeze and ship for about $150 additional

OTHER ACTIVITIES: Bird hunting (quail, pheasant), waterfowling, fishing, antiquing, biking, bird watching, golf, hiking, wildlife photography

BOONE AND CROCKETT

- B&C book bucks taken from property: 22
- Average B&C score: 180
- B&C bucks from this part of state: Many

Verdigris Valley Outfitters

Neodesha, Kansas

BASED IN southeastern Kansas about 100 miles east of Wichita, Verdigris Valley Outfitters offers quality hunts for big Kansas whitetails. Hunts take place on leased private farms throughout the area. The total acreage hunted each year varies from 8,000 to 10,000, although owner Doug Arnold and his crew are constantly on the lookout for new acreages to ensure that all of their clients get quality experiences.

Last year, rifle hunters at Verdigris Valley had an almost 80 percent success rate, with 15 rifle hunters taking 12 bucks. Bucks ranged from the 130 to 163 range — and Arnold will tell you that there are definitely bigger bucks out there. Muzzleloaders get a crack at deer first, starting in September. Bow season picks up in October and runs through November; then rifle hunters get their shot in the first two weeks of December.

This is classic Midwestern hunting, with land of mixed hardwoods near crop-fields, plus pastures, creek and river bottoms — all perfect habitat for whitetail bucks to feed and grow. The way to get them is from stands, and Arnold has a bunch located near trails leading into and out of fields, and in crossing areas near water.

Vital Statistics

THE LODGE:

3 guest rooms in a comfortable farm house, 2 with private baths, 9 beds total

SERVICES: Telephone, TV, laundry

HUNTS:

• rifle: $3,000 / 5 days

• bow: $2,000 / 5 days

PAYMENT: Cash, money orders

MEAL PLANS: All meals included (dinners of turkey, roast beef, ham, ribs, rib eye steaks)

SPECIAL DIETS: Heart healthy, Kosher, vegetarian, salt/msg free

NEAREST AIRPORT: Tulsa, OK

TRANSPORTATION TO LODGE (1 hour 40 minutes): Van from lodge (no extra charge), rental car

THE HUNT:

SEASONS:

• bow: Oct. 1 - Nov. 30

• rifle: Dec. 1 - 12

• muzzleloader: Sept. 23 - 30

BEST TIME TO HUNT: 1st of Nov. for bow

TERRAIN: Some hardwoods, pasture, creekbottoms, riverbottoms

LAND: Approximately 9,000 acres of private leased land

DRAW BLOOD POLICY? No

HUNTING METHODS: Stand hunting (ladders and box blinds), calling, rattling

YEARS IN BUSINESS: 6

STAFF OF GUIDES: 3

HUNTERS SERVED BY EACH GUIDE: 2 - 3

NONHUNTER CHARGE: $100 / day

LICENSES: Must apply in a draw

GAME CARE: Dressed, packaged, frozen and shipped for $50

OTHER ACTIVITIES: Turkey hunting, quail hunting, wildlife photography

BOONE AND CROCKETT

• B&C bucks taken from property: 2

• Average B&C score: 150 - 155

• B&C bucks from this part of state: n/a

CONTACT:

Doug Arnold
Verdigris Valley Outfitters
Rt. 2, Box 324
Neodesha, KS 66757
Ph: 316/325-2708
Fax: 316/325-2585
Email: VValley@hit.net

Legends Ranch

Bitely, Michigan

I F YOU'RE AFTER TRULY mammoth whitetails, the stuff that dreams are made of, then Legends Ranch in Michigan is the place to go. Legends Ranch is the ultimate whitetail hunting experience, run by a team of wildlife professionals who really know whitetail management. From the moment you arrive at the airport in Grand Rapids and are picked up in the lodge's custom limo, Legends looks after the client's every need. Legends Ranch sets the standard when it comes to accommodations, with a beautiful, sprawling, modern log lodge. First-class service "is just how things are done around here," states Bettis.

The help is trained to make sure that clients are comfortable and that everything they want is provided. Clients unanimously agree that the food is first class (and with as much as you can eat, be prepared to gain a few pounds). Where Legends equally shines is when you head out to the woods with a seasoned guide to help you find that buck of a lifetime.

"One thing I noticed about the deer here," states one client, "is that they come in one size, and that's big!"

And it's true. With many Pope & Young and Boone and Crockett class deer roaming the property, your chances of getting a monster are excellent.

"We begin the management hunts in early September," states Bettis. "But nothing can compare with the heart-pounding hunts that occur during the rut, in November-December. If you're looking for action and excitement, this is the time."

"Quick thinking, quick shooting, rut fights. . . it's incredible." And unforgettable.

© Legends Ranch

Jo Ann Nadler, a guest at Legends Ranch, proudly displays her trophy.

Vital Statistics

THE LODGE:

Modern log lodge with 8 guest rooms, 4 with private baths, 20 beds total

SERVICES: Telephone, fax, copying, TV

GUN HUNTS:

• $2,800/person /5-day pre-rut "buddy" hunt (Sept. - Oct.), 2 hunters/guide $1,000 trophy fee

• $4,400 / 5-day pre-rut (Sept. - Oct.), one hunter/one guide, $2,000 trophy fee

• $6,400 / 5-day hunt in Nov. - Dec., one hunter/one guide, $3,000 trophy fee

PAYMENT: Credit cards, check

CONFERENCE GROUPS: Yes

MEAL PLANS: All meals included

NEAREST AIRPORT: Grand Rapids, MI

TRANSPORTATION TO LODGE (80 miles): Pick up and drop off by Legends limo at no additional charge

CONTACT:

Skipper Bettis
Legends Ranch
2022 West 14 Mile Road
Bitely, MI 49309
Ph: 800/972-9092; 231/745-8000
Fax: 231/745-9000
Web: www.legendsranch.com

THE HUNT:

SEASON:

• rifle, bow, muzzleloader: Sept. - Dec.

BEST TIME TO HUNT: The rut (Nov. - Dec.)

TERRAIN: Mixed hardwoods, ridges, some swampy areas

LAND: 5 square miles of enclosures

DRAW BLOOD POLICY? Yes

HUNTING METHODS: Stand hunting (enclosed permanent stands), still-hunting, rattling

YEARS IN BUSINESS: 25

STAFF OF GUIDES: 10

HUNTERS SERVED BY EACH GUIDE: One-on-one hunts

NONHUNTER CHARGE: $200 / day

LICENSES: Lodge provides in cost of hunt

GAME CARE: Client's responsibility

OTHER ACTIVITIES: Turkey hunting, pheasant hunting, fishing, antiquing, biking, bird watching, golf, wildlife photography, tower shoots, cross-country skiing

BOONE AND CROCKETT

• B&C book bucks taken from property: Numerous

• Average B&C score: 140+

• B&C bucks from this part of state: n/a

Double Tree Farms

L i c k i n g ,   M i s s o u r i

A T DOUBLE TREE, you'll hunt more than 1,200 acres of privately-owned Ozark hardwoods and riverbottoms from tree stands or ground blinds. Some overlook food plots, others watch well-used trails. Average whitetails run 160 pounds, dressed, from this part of the country. The bow season opens October 1, breaks for a two-week rifle season in mid-November, then picks up again and runs until January 15. The limit is two whitetails of either sex.

Owners Jim and Shari Ludan bought this old farm and converted it into a relaxing retreat almost 10 years ago. The two bedrooms accommodate eight guests, although only four stay at a time during the deer season. Shari is a gourmet cook, and if you don't believe it, try her pork crown roast when you come back to the lodge after a long day of hunting. You'll want to spend the rest of the week near the kitchen!

Vital Statistics

THE LODGE:

3 guest rooms, 7 beds total, some with private baths; accommodations are modern/rustic, in farmhouse

SERVICES: Telephone, fax, copying, TV

HUNTS:

• bow/gun/muzzleloader: $1,350 / 4-day hunt

PAYMENT: Cash, check

MEAL PLANS: All meals included (dinners of pork crown roasts, duck, chicken, prime rib, venison roasts)

SPECIAL DIETS: Double Tree sends a questionnaire prior to the hunt to find out favorite foods, drinks, special dietary needs

NEAREST AIRPORT: St. Louis (140 miles) or Springfield, MO (90 miles)

TRANSPORTATION TO LODGE (1 hour 45 minutes): Rental car

THE HUNT:

SEASON:

• bow/rifle/muzzleloader: mid-Nov. - mid-Dec.

BEST TIME TO HUNT: Oct. 15 - Dec. 15

TERRAIN: Hardwoods, riverbottoms, food plots

LAND: 1,200 private acres

DRAW BLOOD POLICY? No

HUNTING METHODS: Stand hunting (permanent platforms, Blackwater and Big Oak ladder stands), drives, still-hunting, calling, rattling

YEARS IN BUSINESS: 8

STAFF OF GUIDES: 4

HUNTERS SERVED BY EACH GUIDE: 2

NONHUNTER CHARGE: $50 / day

LICENSES: Over the counter

GAME CARE: Dressed, packaged, frozen and shipped (cost varies)

OTHER ACTIVITIES: Turkey hunting, bird hunting, waterfowling, fishing, antiquing, biking, bird watching, boating, canoeing, golf, hiking, swimming, wildlife photography

BOONE AND CROCKETT

• B&C book bucks taken from property: 4

• Average B&C score: n/a

• B&C bucks from this part of state: n/a

CONTACT:

Jim Ludan
Double Tree Farms
18463 Dixon Rd.
Licking, MO 65542
Ph: 573/674-4142.
Fax: 573/674-4018

Show-Me Safaris

Summersville, Missouri

SHOW-ME SAFARIS offers a quality and challenging hunting experience for the entire family. This large private ranch provides the sportsman a unique opportunity to enjoy hunting a multitude of free-roaming non-indigenous big game — including trophy-class whitetails.

The Ozarks of southern Missouri (the location of Show-Me Safaris) is one of the most scenic, beautiful, and compelling regions of mid-America. You'll be hunting in Texas County, one of the top areas in the state for native white-tailed deer. The ranch is interspersed with ridges and hollows, heavily forested with oak and pine trees, and full of cedar glades and some open fields that provide ideal natural habitats for game. The landscape is ideally suited for a challenging hunt, and a quality outdoor experience.

Outfitter Mark Hampton grew up and still resides in rural south Missouri, having spent most of his life hunting and fishing. He has hunted on four continents, taking more than 80 different species of big game. Hampton has been a paying client on many hunting trips and knows firsthand what hunters expect. This Missourian has also written numerous articles on hunting and shooting for a variety of outdoor publications. Further, he serves on the Handgun Hunting Advisory Council for Safari Club International. Hampton's knowledge and experience will help assure you of an exciting, successful, and rewarding hunting experience.

The guides at Show-Me are competent and avid outdoorsmen, natives of the area, who are most concerned about your care, comfort, and enjoyment. They will provide a safe and memorable hunting adventure with Ozark-style hospitality. They take pride in the individual attention and satisfaction given to the guests.

The accommodations will be arranged according to your wishes — from a ranch house to a fine local motel. Show-Me does not provide food, but there are many local restaurants that serve great meals and will appreciate your patronage.

Vital Statistics

THE LODGE:

Main lodge contains 3 guestrooms, no private baths, 15 beds total; also local motels

SERVICES: Telephone, TV

GUN HUNTS:

• $850 and up for whitetails, depending on rack size

• $20 / night lodging

• $50 / day guide fee

PAYMENT: Cash, credit cards

CONFERENCE GROUPS: No

MEAL PLANS: No meals at lodge; clients eat at local restaurants

NEAREST AIRPORT: St. Louis, MO

TRANSPORTATION TO LODGE (2 1/2 hours): Rental car

CONTACT:

Mark Hampton
Show-Me Safaris
PO Box 108
Summersville, MO 65571
Ph: 417/932-4423
Fax: 417/932-6634

THE HUNT:

SEASON: Private preserve — whitetails may be hunted anytime of year

BEST TIME TO HUNT: September - December

TERRAIN: Gently rolling hills in the Ozarks, some low ridges, vegetation mostly consists of cedar, pine, and oak

LAND: 1,000 private acres (half is fenced)

DRAW BLOOD POLICY? Yes

HUNTING METHODS: Stand hunting, drives, still-hunting, by vehicle

YEARS IN BUSINESS: 8

STAFF OF GUIDES: 2

HUNTERS SERVED BY EACH GUIDE: 1 - 2

NONHUNTER CHARGE: n/a

LICENSES: Over the counter, or at the lodge

GAME CARE: Skin, quarter, and caping of trophies ($15)

OTHER ACTIVITIES: Other big game hunting (wild boar, exotics such as fallow deer, aoudad, nilgai, elk, bison and Barbarossa rams)

Box L Guest Ranch

THE BOX L RANCH is one of the most beautiful private ranches in the state. Located in the scenic Pine Ridge area of northwestern Nebraska, the ranch is more than 25,000 acres and has been owned and managed by the same family since it was homesteaded in 1884. The ranch land includes wooded ridges and hills, miles of river beds, and a 26-acre lake where anglers can try for largemouth and smallmouth bass, perch, and bluegills.

Hunts on the Box L are strictly limited each year to a very few hunters so that the competition for the game is light and the access is outstanding. The ranch specializes in whitetail and mule deer hunting, although some antelope hunting is also available.

The hunting conditions vary; during deer season, temperatures range from -20°F to the mid-60s. Hunters should plan for extreme temperatures and dress appropriately. The best approach is to dress in layers so you can shed clothing if the temperature is warm, or add layers if the temperature is cold. Good polarfleece is always a solid recommendation, especially if you are hunting later in the season when cold temperatures are probable.

Deer hunting on the Box L allows hunters to experience the wildest and remotest parts of northwestern Nebraska, one of the top buck-producing areas in the country. According to Nebraskalands Guide to Public Hunting Lands, "No area of the state has a wider variety of terrain than the panhandle. There are high plateaus, scarred badlands, huge, rugged escarpments and canyons cloaked in dark pines, all in direct contrast to the Oglala National Grasslands also located in the district. Traditionally a good deer hunting area, the Panhandle also has good numbers of wild turkey, especially in the Pine Ridge."

Much of the deer hunting is done from tree stands, natural blinds, and canyon overlooks. Box L guides will also put on small, two- or three-man drives, but they have found that the greatest success and the greatest hunter enjoyment comes from allowing the deer to go about their natural movements, while hunters watch trails, scrapes, and river crossings. Because the guides live in this area all year, they have the opportunity to study the deer's daily behavior patterns and their eating habits. They can put clients into hot areas, giving them a better chance of taking the trophy of their dreams.

Vital Statistics

THE LODGE:

Modular home with 4 guest rooms, 8 beds total

SERVICES: Telephone, copying, laundry, TV

GUN HUNTS: $1,500 / 3 days

PAYMENT: Cash or check for deposit; balance in cash

CONFERENCE GROUPS: No

MEAL PLANS: Guests do their own cooking

NEAREST AIRPORT: Rapid City, SD

TRANSPORTATION TO LODGE (1 1/2 hours): Rental car; van from lodge at an additional cost

CONTACT:

Andrea Isham Voss
Box L Guest Ranch
835 Chadron Avenue
Chadron, NE 69337
Ph: 308/432-3275
Email: boxlhunt@netscape.net
Web: www.BoxLRanch.com

THE HUNT:

SEASON:

• rifle: Nov. 12 - 20

BEST TIME TO HUNT: Anytime

TERRAIN: Wooded ridges, riverbeds, cedar breaks, canyons

LAND: Over 25,000 private acres

DRAW BLOOD POLICY? No

HUNTING METHODS: Stand hunting, drives, still hunting, calling, rattling

YEARS IN BUSINESS: 10

STAFF OF GUIDES: Yes

HUNTERS SERVED BY EACH GUIDE: One-on-one

NONHUNTER CHARGE: Negotiable

LICENSES: Sold over the counter or over the Internet before arriving

GAME CARE: Dress, freeze, and ship game; price varies

OTHER ACTIVITIES: Other big game hunting (mule deer, buffalo, antelope), small game hunting, turkey hunting, waterfowling, fishing, antiquing, arrowhead hunting, biking, bird watching, boating, canoeing, hiking, swimming, wildlife photography

Niobrara Hunting Adventures

NIOBRARA HUNTING ADVENTURES is owned and operated by Joel Gothard and his cousin, David Galloway. They offer fully-guided hunts for white-tailed deer, mulies, turkeys and grouse. They can accommodate up to three hunters at a time, thus ensuring a high-quality, personalized hunt.

With more than 8,000 acres of mixed habitat and access to much more, Gothard and Galloway can take their hunters to areas where the deer receive little if any hunting pressure, making for a natural hunt with hunters stalking deer in their natural environment.

On the hunting, one client had this to say: "Basically, they get you up early and put you on a stand from about one hour before light to about 9:30 or 10 in the morning. From there they will go to other places where they will try to drive deer to you . . . In that time, they also have a lunch usually served picnic style out of a cooler. Then, before the evening hunt, there's dinner back at the ranch, which is outstanding, then back out to sit the evening stands.

"I saw deer under my stand every single day, and bucks under the stand almost every day [i.e. under 25 yards]. I saw some huge bucks in the 130 to 150 class, but never got close enough for a shot at one. I passed on a number of bucks, including a really nice 8-pointer at about 12 yards that was bigger than anything I have taken yet. I don't regret not taking the shot, as I felt I could really score on some of the bigger ones I was seeing.

"My buddy missed a HUGE 10-point 145- to 150-class buck that almost ran him over! That same evening, just before dark, he arrowed a beautiful 8-pointer that we recovered soon after. That buck scored around 130."

Clients can choose to book a hotel room in Valentine, Nebraska, or be pampered at the ranch house instead (highly recommended). According to one client who stayed at the ranch house recently, "The accommodations were great. We stayed at the ranch house, where you truly feel like family from the second you walk in. Joel and his father even played piano and fiddle for us. We always had pies and desserts ready for us after the evening hunts, and our dinners included roasts, venison, elk and other great home-cooked meals."

The guest continued, "I also can't say enough about the guides. We have been on many hunts, but have never experienced this type of hard work and dedication. Bottom line, we all re-booked."

In addition to big game and upland birds, Niobrara has expanded its operation to include exciting hunts for coyotes, where the guides call them in, and for
prairie dogs across the state line in South Dakota. Niobrara also offers summer
and winter fishing trips for bass, perch, bluegills, and walleyes.

© Niobrara Hunting Adventures

A pleased group of hunters at Niobrara Hunting Adventures.

Vital Statistics

THE LODGE:

Main lodge/farm house has 3 guest rooms, 4 beds total, no private baths

SERVICES: Telephone, TV, laundry

HUNTS: $2,125 - $2,375 / 5-day hunts

PAYMENT: Check

MEAL PLANS: All meals included (dinners feature roast beef, pork, wild turkey, grouse, pheasant, ham salads, casseroles, desserts, pies, cakes)

SPECIAL DIETS: Heart healthy, salt/msg free

NEAREST AIRPORT: Rapid, SD

TRANSPORTATION TO LODGE (180 miles): Rental car

BOONE AND CROCKETT

- B&C book bucks taken from property: About 3 per year
- Average B&C score:165
- B&C bucks from this part of state: Several every year

CONTACT:

Joel Gothard or David Galloway
Niobrara Hunting Adventures
809 Craig Street
Valentine, NE 69201
Ph: 334/843-3168
Fax: 205/459-4479.
Email: gothardj@inetnebr.com
Web:www.huntguide.com/niobrara.htm

THE HUNT:

SEASON:
- bow: Sept. 15 - Nov. 11, Nov. 21 - Dec. 31
- rifle: Nov. 12 - 20
- muzzleloader: Dec. 2 - 31

BEST TIME TO HUNT: Oct. - Nov. 25

TERRAIN: A mixture of pine-filled canyons, hardwood river bottoms, swamps and sloughs; most of the land hunted runs along the Niobrara River

LAND: Some public, but access to 180,000 acres adjacent to the lodge's land

DRAW BLOOD POLICY? No

HUNTING METHODS: Stand hunting (mostly API lock-ons), drives, still-hunting, calling, rattling

YEARS IN BUSINESS: 3

STAFF OF GUIDES: Owners are the guides

HUNTERS SERVED BY EACH GUIDE: 1 - 2

NONHUNTER CHARGE: $50 / day

LICENSES: Archery and muzzleloader licenses are sold over the counter (clients must purchase before arriving at camp); firearms license are picked through a lottery

GAME CARE: Dress, package, and pack in ice for travel — complementary

OTHER ACTIVITIES: Other big game hunting (turkeys, coyotes), small game hunting (prairie dogs), bird hunting (grouse), fishing

Wellnitz Ranch Pine Ridge Hunts

Hay Springs, Nebraska

WELLNITZ IS A NEW hunting operation that opened up just recently (2000). But owner Dale Wellnitz has been guiding whitetail hunters for years, and he thoroughly knows their behavior. That, plus the fact that his ranch located smack in the middle of prime whitetail country, means your chances of getting a good buck, prairie style, are high.

The terrain in this area is perfect for whitetails: Ponderosa pine-covered slopes and deep canyons. Wellnitz also hunts riparian areas filled with hardwood trees and brush-covered bottomlands. The whitetails generallly find cover in these areas, which also feature alfalfa and millet fields interspersed along the creek bottoms. The whitetails tend to feed in these areas from late afternoon to early morning, and then move to the cool areas in the pine timber to bed down for the day. Hunters are placed in blinds in strategic spots, although some still-hunt as well. Weather during the hunting season can range from September highs in the 80s to November lows of 0°F or below, with snow.

Last fall's whitetail hunts were very successful, with three whitetails taken — a 10-point nontypical, a 10-point typical, and an 8-point. This, with just a limited number of hunters.

The ranch offers two rifle buck hunts and two archery buck hunts. In order to keep the herd in balance, Wellnitz also offers a limited number of blackpowder or bow doe hunts. Additionally, only two hunters per hunt are booked.

This is a small operation that specializes in attention to personal detail. If you want a classic Midwestern type of hunt — sitting in stands watching trails leading to and from fields, or setting up stands over creekbottoms and meadows — then this hunt is for you.

Vital Statistics

THE LODGE:

Newly remodeled bunkhouse has 1 guest room with private bath; 2 beds total

SERVICES: Telephone, TV

GUN HUNTS:

- $2,000 / 5-day bow or gun hunt (buck)
- $1,000 / 3-day bow or gun hunt (doe)

PAYMENT: Cash or certified check

CONFERENCE GROUPS: No

MEAL PLANS: All meals included; Western ranch-type meals

NEAREST AIRPORT: Chardon or Rapid City, SD

TRANSPORTATION TO LODGE: Van from lodge at no additional cost

CONTACT:

Dale Wellnitz
Wellnitz Ranch Pine Ridge Hunts
HC 70, Box 35
Hay Springs, NE 69347
Ph: 308/327-2986
Email: lazy@gpcom.net
Web: huntguide.com

THE HUNT:

SEASON:

- bow: September 16 - October 20
- bow (doe): September - November 7
- rifle: November 11 - 19
- blackpowder (doe): December

BEST TIME TO HUNT: Anytime

TERRAIN: Rugged pine ridges along creekbottoms, fields, meadows

LAND: 2,000 private acres

Draw Blood Policy: No

HUNTING METHODS: Stand hunting (ladder stands and blinds), still-hunting, calling, rattling

YEARS IN BUSINESS: 1

STAFF OF GUIDES: 1

HUNTERS SERVED BY EACH GUIDE: 2

NONHUNTER CHARGE: $125 / day

LICENSES: Outfitter pre-purchases from game commission

GAME CARE: A local locker plant is available for processing game for an additional cost of about $50 - $60; taxidermy services are available in the area

OTHER ACTIVITIES: Bird hunting, biking, bird watching, wildlife photography

McNutt Farm II / Outdoorsman Lodge

Blue Rock, Ohio

THE MCNUTT FARM II/Outdoorsman Lodge is located in southeastern Ohio, in Muskingum County, long known for a high harvest of quality white-tailed bucks, wild turkeys, and a variety of small game animals. One of the few remaining family-owned and operated hunting lodges in this part of the country, the McNutt Farm prides itself on offering quality hunts for both bow and rifle hunters at affordable rates.

On an Ohio white-tailed deer hunt at McNutt Farm II/Outdoorsman Lodge, you will hunt mainly on 5,000 acres of publicly-owned lands under a wildlife management program run by the Ohio Division of Wildlife. You may hunt as long or as short as you want, although the more time you spend afield, the better your chances of success. While many hunters like to hunt the mornings, then come in for lunch and a nap, heading out again for an evening watch, savvy hunters stay afield between 10 a.m. and 3 p.m., a time when whitetail bucks are often on the move.

Guides at McNutt Farm also use the Poli Wheel to assist them in determining game movement. Developed by Marcel Poli and put on the market in 1993, the Poli Wheel lets you dial in environmental factors (times of day, moon phases, weather) and then determine the major and minor feed periods of game animals. It shows the approximate time the animals will begin moving in to the peak period, the length of that period, and the approximate time the animals will begin bedding down. It also shows activity periods of the animals, and allows you to figure out the best times to be in your stand, giving you the best opportunity for success.

Aside from the quality hunting, hunters will also enjoy comfortable quarters in either the log cabin, carriage house, or the main lodge itself. Home-cooked meals are available to all, although hunters staying in the log cabin can also cook for themselves. Another cabin, called the "cellar cabin," is also available for do-it-yourselfers. Located in a remote area, this dwelling has game available from the moment you step out the front door. A shooting range is also available to clients who stay at this and the other dwellings, as it's imperative to sight in and tune your equipment before your hunt.

Vital Statistics

THE LODGE:

Modern log lodge has 3 guest rooms, all with private baths, 10 - 12 beds total

SERVICES: Telephone, TV

GUN HUNTS: $300 / week / hunter, or any part thereof

PAYMENT: Cash, check

CONFERENCE GROUPS: Yes

MEAL PLANS: Guests do their own cooking

NEAREST AIRPORT: Columbus, OH

TRANSPORTATION TO LODGE (60 miles): Rental car

CONTACT:

Patty L. McNutt
McNutt Farm II/Outdoorsman Lodge
6120 Cutler Lake Road
Blue Rock, OH 43720
Ph: 740/674-4555

THE HUNT:

SEASON: The lodge operates under state laws, with the season determined annually by the Ohio Division of Wildlife

BEST TIME TO HUNT: Anytime

TERRAIN: In the foothills of the Appalachian Mountain Range — hills and hollows, with hardwoods and pines of forested areas; small crop fields are on the perimeter of the forested areas and are private (no hunting); forested areas are publically-owned, with hunting allowed

LAND: Combination of private and public

DRAW BLOOD POLICY? No

HUNTING METHODS: Stand hunting (clients bring their own stands if they choose to tree stand hunt), still-hunting, calling, rattling

YEARS IN BUSINESS: 26

STAFF OF GUIDES: 20

HUNTERS SERVED BY EACH GUIDE: Guide placement service

NONHUNTER CHARGE: Same as hunter

LICENSES: Sold over the counter, although non-resident hunters should purchase by mail

GAME CARE: Dress game; processing is available nearby

OTHER ACTIVITIES: Small game hunting, fishing, antiquing, biking, bird watching, canoeing, golf, hiking, swimming, wildlife photography

Mt. Hide Outfitters

Laverne, Oklahoma

MT. HIDE OUTFITTERS is a big operation with hunting leases in three states, yet they limit their number of hunters to ensure quality, personalized hunts for each client. The outfitter offers some of the best private deer hunting available in Oklahoma, Texas, and Kansas. They specialize in trophy whitetails, but also offer trophy hunts for mule deer, antelope, and turkey. Because they take a limited number of hunters, their success rate remains very high.

Steve Purviance, owner of Mt. Hide, has personally taken a number of bucks that have made the Oklahoma record books. His best was a huge buck, taken in 1997 with a .54 caliber muzzleloader, that scored 197 7/8. That buck still stands as the fourth best blackpowder buck ever taken in the state. Purviance is dedicated to using his knowledge about deer, and hard work ethic, to help his clients get trophy deer too.

"I am a hunter myself, and come from a hunting family. I have lived and breathed hunting everyday since I was very young, and know better than anyone the habits and movements of our wildlife, especially our whitetails and turkeys. My guides are all experienced hunters, and I will guarantee that they are hard workers, and will do what they need to do to make a hunt enjoyable and successful. I spend 20 to 25 days a month scouting and glassing. I do my best to pattern our wildlife, to help assure my hunters success, and it definitely pays off."

Purviance offers a variety of hunts for different weapons and in different areas. In Oklahoma, rifle and muzzleloader hunters are positioned overlooking rugged canyon country, thick river bottom openings, and dense cedar shooting lanes, all of which are funnels between feeding and bedding areas. Last year, Mt Hide hunters ended up having a 90 percent success rate on trophy bucks, a rate that's tough to beat anywhere.

The hunts in Texas are equally good, as Purviance has gained access to some excellent ranches in the Panhandle. These areas have had little or no hunting pressure over the years, and are starting to produce some real monster bucks — particularly for hunters who are placed in stands overlooking dense river and creek bottoms, which are primary travel routes for deer in this open country.

Finally, it's no secret that Kansas offers great trophy opportunities. Unit 16, where Purviance hunts, ranks number two in the state for trophy bucks. When muzzleloader season starts in September, the bucks are still found in their bachelor groups and are very predictable. Later, when the rut begins, rifle season opens, giving hunters an opportunity for bucks that are roaming far and wide, searching for estrus does. "I highly recommend putting in for these hunts," says Purviance. "Hunters will have a great chance at taking a trophy on this hunt. The application deadline is the first of June, so if you're interested, call me!"

© Mt. Hide Outfitters

A Texas buck taken off the property hunted by Mt. Hide Outfitters.

Vital Statistics

THE LODGE:

Mt. Hide can accommodate up to 10 hunters at a time; lodging is at a nearby motel

SERVICES: Telephone, fax, copying, TV, laundry, deer check station

HUNTS:

• 4-day hunts for bow, rifle and muzzleloader are offered in parts of Kansas, Texas and Oklahoma

• all hunts are $3,000 - $4,000 / 4 - 5 days, depending on the hunt, and include everything from lodging to food

PAYMENT: Check, money orders

CONFERENCE GROUPS: Corporations book hunts for clients and employees, but there is no lodge for conferences.

MEAL PLANS: All meals included (breakfasts feature bacon and eggs, biscuits and gravy; lunch is at a local cafe or restaurant, or a box lunch that hunters can eat while staying on stand; dinner is at a restaurant or when homemade includes noodles, potatoes, corn, chili or venison dishes, lasagna, casseroles, garlic bread, more)

SPECIAL DIETS: Hunters are asked about their needs and preferences before their hunt

NEAREST AIRPORT: Oklahoma City, OK; private planes can be flown into Woodward Airport

TRANSPORTATION TO LODGE (120 miles): Rental car

CONTACT:

Steve Purviance
Mt. Hide Outfitters
P.O. Box 587
Laverne, OK 73848
Ph: 580/921-2555
Email: mthide@yahoo.com
Web: www.mthide.com

THE HUNT:

SEASON:

• bow: October 1 - December 31

• muzzleloader: October 28 - November 5 in Oklahoma, September 23 - October 1 in Kansas

• rifle: Nov. 18 - 26 in Oklahoma, Nov. 4 - Dec. 31 in Texas, Nov. 29 - Dec. 10 in Kansas

BEST TIME TO HUNT: During the rut, which begins around November 1 and peaks November 10 - 30; and December 5 - 31

TERRAIN: Thick riverbottom hardwoods and brush country; big, rugged cedar canyons filtering into wheat, rye and milo fields; also a lot of CRP (Conservation Reserve Program) ground bordered by wheat fields

LAND: Private leases; approximately 22,000 acres in Oklahoma, 11,500 in Texas, and 8,800 in Kansas

DRAW BLOOD POLICY? No

HUNTING METHODS: Stand hunting (many box blinds and towers, tripods, lock-ons and ground blinds), still-hunting (with a guide)

YEARS IN BUSINESS: 3

STAFF OF GUIDES: 10 - 12

HUNTERS SERVED BY EACH GUIDE: 2

NONHUNTER CHARGE: Yes; it varies

LICENSES: Oklahoma and Texas are sold over the counter; Kansas is a draw, although the lodge may also be able to provide

GAME CARE: Dress, package, and pack; processing is done for a small extra charge

OTHER ACTIVITIES: Other big game hunting (mule deer, antelope, wild turkey), wildlife photography

BOONE AND CROCKETT

• B&C book bucks taken from property: 7

• Average B&C score: Approximately 180 gross

• B&C bucks from this part of state: 20+ in past 3 yrs

Krieger Cattle Company

KHE KRIEGER CATTLE COMPANY is a privately-owned ranch located where the Missouri River breaks in Gregory County, South Dakota. The ranch land consists of rolling hills, cedar and oak ridges, canyons, and creek bottoms interspersed with croplands. This makes for an absolute deer paradise! Ken Krieger and his group hunt the south and north forks of the Whetstone Creek area, which has consistently produced trophy bucks. The ranch has 10 years of trophy deer management, limited hunting, and selective harvests (only bucks over 125 B&C may be shot), which all makes for some of the best whitetail hunting in the country. There are no fenced areas on the ranch, and the whitetails that come and go across the property are free-ranging, experience-hardened deer — the ultimate hunting challenge.

Krieger Cattle Company is one of those great places that offers the hunter a chance to take the trophy deer of his dreams. By hosting a limited number of exclusive quality hunts, Krieger can provide its clients with exceptional service and personalized attention.

According to Ken Krieger, "When you hunt on our ranch, you can expect to see many 130- to 150-class whitetails, with the opportunity to see the big guys in the 160- to 170-and-up class for a heart-pounding, memory-making experience you won't forget. Please keep in mind that the big guys didn't get that way by being dumb! They will test your hunting skills and keep you coming back to Krieger Cattle Company for the challenge of a lifetime."

Krieger continues, "Not only do we offer a quality hunting experience, but you will leave our ranch with stories and memories of a challenging hunting adventure and new friendships you have gained. And this, we believe, is the true joy of hunting."

Add that philosophy to great accommodations in a rustic, 1906 ranch house with all the modern conveniences, great food, and a wide porch overlooking an area where trophy deer may be seen wandering by, and you have as good a deer hunter's heaven as you're ever going to find.

© Krieger Cattle Company

Two sisters show that hunting at Krieger's is for kids too!

© Krieger Cattle Company

Owner Ken Krieger took this 11-pointer (note the drop tine) off their private lands.

Vital Statistics

THE LODGE:

A comfortable, rustic ranch house, built in 1906, has 4 guest rooms, 8 beds total, with 2 spacious, shared bathrooms

SERVICES: Telephone, TV, laundry

HUNTS:

• $1,600 / 5-day bowhunt, semi-guided

• $2,000 / 4-day rifle hunt, fully-guided

• trophy fees (for rifle only): $1,200 for any buck under 170 B&C, $2,000 for any buck over 170 B&C

PAYMENT: Cash, check, money orders; deposit required

CONFERENCE GROUPS: Yes

MEAL PLANS: Two meal plans: all meals, or breakfast and supper. "We raise the best Hereford beef in the world, so most home-cooked main meals feature tender, great-tasting Hereford beef such as grilled hamburgers, steaks or pot roasts, with potatoes and gravy, vegetables, salads, desserts. No one ever goes away hungry, and most guests gain weight!"

SPECIAL DIETS: On request

NEAREST AIRPORT: Sioux Falls, SD; there is also a 3,300-foot lighted and paved runway in Gregory, SD, for small planes

TRANSPORTATION TO LODGE (165 miles to Sioux Falls): Rental car; pickup can be arranged for an extra charge; Gregory airport is 16 miles away and pick-ups can be arranged

CONTACT:

Ken Krieger
Krieger Cattle Company
RR2, Box 119
Burke, SD 57523
Phone: 605/775-2113

THE HUNT:

• bow: Sept. 23 - Dec. 31

• rifle: Nov. 4 - 26

• muzzleloader: for residents only (doe only)

BEST TIME TO HUNT: Anytime

TERRAIN: Rolling hills, cedar and oak ridges, canyons and creek bottoms interspersed with croplands

LAND: 3,000-plus private acres

DRAW BLOOD POLICY? Yes

HUNTING METHODS: Stand hunting (lock-ons, Summit tree stands, bale blinds, some fully-enclosed and heated blinds on 10-foot stands, if needed), drives, still-hunting, spot-and-stalk, by vehicle (4x4 pick-up), calling, rattling

YEARS IN BUSINESS: 10

STAFF OF GUIDES: 2

HUNTERS SERVED BY EACH GUIDE: 1 - 2

NONHUNTER CHARGE: Yes

LICENSES: Apply and draw format, with application deadline

GAME CARE: Dress, package, and pack for travel for extra fee

OTHER ACTIVITIES: Other big game hunting (mule deer, turkey, coyote), small game hunting (prairie dogs), bird hunting (pheasant, sharp-tailed grouse, prairie chickens), fishing (bass, bluegill), antiquing, biking, bird watching, hiking, swimming, wildlife photography, horseback trail rides

BOONE AND CROCKETT

• B&C book bucks taken from property: 2

• Average B&C score: 140-170

• B&C bucks from this part of state: Numerous

Bluff Country Outfitters

A l m a ,   W i s c o n s i n

LOCATED ALONG THE MISSISSIPPI RIVER, the bluff country in Buffalo County is an area that escaped glaciation during the Ice Ages. This left the soil exceptionally fertile and rich in minerals, which is why, according to Bluff Country Outfitters, "It's no coincidence that this area produces more recordbook bucks per square mile than any other area in the world."

In Wisconsin alone, the number of recordbook bucks from Buffalo County more than doubles that of the county that is in second place. Bluff Country Outfitters hunts are conducted on privately-owned land in the heart of this area.

© Bluff Country Outfitters

Buffalo County in Wisconsin produces the most B&C bucks in the state.

This hunting isn't for the faint of heart, as 125-class deer are considered to be on the small size in the area, with many bucks taken scoring 150 and up. Hunting is done from stands or by stalking. The rut is always a prime time to hunt here, although any time during the season can produce a decent rack. According to head guide Tom Indrebo, the key is to hunt the hot sign whenever you find it.

Tom also promises the following: "You will be hunting free-roaming bucks in their natural environment [no fences]. We promise a good hunt with an experienced guide, good, hot food, and plenty of it, a dry, warm camp, hot showers; and good old hunting camaradie."

Vital Statistics

THE LODGE:

5 guest rooms in modern lodge, 1 in cabin, 18 beds total, no private baths; 1 handicapped-accessible room

SERVICES: Telephone, fax, copying, TV, laundry

HUNTS:

• bow: $1,450 / 3 days, $1,850 / 5 days
• gun: $2,150 / 4 days

PAYMENT: Personal/company check; no credit cards

MEAL PLANS: All meals included (good home cooking, with meat and potatoes, fruit, etc.)

SPECIAL DIETS: Heart healthy, Kosher, vegetarian, salt/msg free

NEAREST AIRPORT: LaCross, WI

TRANSPORTATION TO LODGE (50 miles): Rental car; van from lodge (no extra charge)

CONTACT:

Tom Indrebo
Bluff Country Outfitters
S. 1751 St. Road 88
Alma, WI 54610
Ph: 608/685-3755
Fax: 608/685-4232.
Email: buffbuck@win.bright.net
Web: www.visi/com/—Bluff

THE HUNT:

SEASONS:

• bow: Sept. 20 - Nov. 15, Dec. 5 - 31
• rifle: Nov. 20 - 29
• muzzleloader: Nov. 30 - Dec. 5

BEST TIME TO HUNT: Sept. 20 - 30; Oct. 10 - Nov. 15

TERRAIN: Hardwood ridges with farm fields in the valleys; 400- to 500-foot ridges along the Mississippi River

LAND: Approximately 5,000 acres of private land owned and leased, all of it managed for trophy bucks

DRAW BLOOD POLICY? No

HUNTING METHODS: Stand hunting (portables), calling, rattling

YEARS IN BUSINESS: 12

STAFF OF GUIDES: 1

HUNTERS SERVED BY EACH GUIDE: 2; one-on-one hunts are available at no extra charge

NONHUNTER CHARGE: $100 / day

LICENSES: Over the counter; 3-day waiting period on bow licenses

GAME CARE: Dressed, packaged, frozen and shipped for $75

OTHER ACTIVITIES: Bird hunting, fishing, antiquing, biking, bird watching, boating, canoeing, golf, hiking

BOONE AND CROCKETT

• B&C book bucks taken from property: 8
• Average B&C score: 170s to 200
• B&C bucks from this part of state: Approximately 100

Buffalo County Buck Connection

Mondovi, Wisconsin

BUFFALO COUNTY is located along the upper Mississippi River. After many years of quality deer management, it has earned a well-deserved reputation for producing trophy bucks, and is recognized as one of the best trophy areas in the Midwest.

The Buck Connection specializes in offering semi-guided hunts during the September through December seasons. Clients hunt wild whitetails in their natural habitat on 1,600 areas of privately-owned land in a quality deer management area. The land offers many different types of rough terrain, including bluffs, ridges, valleys, coulees, thick and thin woods, and open fields. Overall, the land is approximately 70 percent woods and 30 percent open fields, offering a variety of places to hunt. The late-season hunting is excellent, especially near the 10-acre food plots, which are left unharvested in order to provide food for deer and other wildlife. Crops include corn, alfalfa, oats, and soybeans. Seven ponds also dot the area, and some hunters prefer to set stands and watch the water, looking for bucks coming to drink.

A limited number of hunters are allowed on the land each year, and consequently the late-season hunting is excellent. In recent years, bucks scoring from 135 to 167 have been taken from the property. The high quality of the bucks can be traced to adequate feed and careful management of the herd.

Wildlife biologists in the state have developed population models for the deer. The models depend on information gathered mostly from hunters. Such information includes the actual number of deer taken annually, along with the sex and age of each animal. When applied to a specific geographical unit, it is possible for biologists to accurately estimate the number of deer living there. They can then estimate the numbers that may be harvested to keep populations at healthy levels. Other factors, such as habitat changes that have seen the land altered from farming to logging or urban expansion are also taken into account.

The hunting package includes the hunt, lodging, all meals, and use of tree stands. The lodging is in a new and comfortable cabin that includes a refrigerator, stove, heat — everything you need to feel at home. Food is also included as part of the package. Home-cooked dinners are served nightly, while groceries are also provided for make-your-own breakfasts and sack lunches during the day.

Vital Statistics

THE LODGE:

A large, modern cabin next to the main lodge has 4 guest rooms, 8 beds total, no private baths

SERVICES: Telephone, TV

HUNTS:

- bow: range from $1,000 - $1,500 / 4- to 5-day hunts
- rifle: range from $1,500 - $2,600 / 4- to 9-day hunts
- hunts are semi-guided; prices vary based on pre-rut, rut or post-rut
- last-season muzzleloader: $1,000 / 4 days

PAYMENT: Cash, check

MEAL PLANS: Breakfast and supper (dinners include chicken, roast beef, vegetables, potatoes, coffee, soda, pie, cake, fresh fruit)

SPECIAL DIETS: Heart healthy, salt/msg free

NEAREST AIRPORT: Minneapolis, MN

TRANSPORTATION TO LODGE (100 miles): Van from the airport to Eau Claire, WI, then picked up ($35); rental car; shuttle flight

CONTACT:

Jeffrey Peil
Buffalo County Buck Connection
S1226 State Road 88
Mondovi, WI 54755
Ph: 715/946-3211
Email: buckhunt@buckconnection.com
Web: www.buckconnection.com

THE HUNT:

SEASON:

- bow: September 16 - December 31
- rifle: November 18 - 26
- muzzleloader: November 27 - December 2

BEST TIME TO HUNT:

- Rifle: November
- bow: October 31 - November 16
- muzzleloader: November

TERRAIN: Hardwood hills (coulees, mixed with farm fields)

LAND: Own/lease 1,600 acres

DRAW BLOOD POLICY: No

HUNTING METHODS: Stand hunting (lock-ons, permanent stands), calling, rattling

YEARS IN BUSINESS: 4

STAFF OF GUIDES: No; owners guide

HUNTERS SERVED BY EACH GUIDE: 4

NONHUNTER CHARGE: $35 / day

LICENSES: Sold over the counter, purchase before arrival; Wisconsin has a 3-day prior on bow, which can be bought through the mail

GAME CARE: Local butcher for an extra fee

Other Activities: Bird hunting, bird watching, wildlife photography, snowmobiling

BOONE AND CROCKETT

- B&C book bucks taken from property: 1 (most are Pope and Young)
- Average B&C score: 150s
- B&C bucks from this part of state: 4 in 1997

Forest of Antlers Outfitters

Minocqua, Wisconsin

HUNTERS WHO ARE LOOKING for that trophy in a lifetime, that one wallhanger above all others, should look no further than Forest of Antlers Outfitters. Located deep in Wisconsin's Northwoods, three hours from Madison and 25 minutes from the Rhinelander airport, FOA is a 1000-acre enclosed preserve — a hunter's paradise filled with some of the most magnificent whitetail bucks you'll ever see. There are a lot of them, too, with sightings of 20 to 40 bucks per day a regular occurance. Racks of 10 to 12 points are common, but there are bigger ones (including a lot of non-typicals) roaming the property as well. Methods include hunting out of enclosed elevated stands, tree stands, ground blinds, or scouting from 4X4s.

Hunters arrive in the morning the day before their hunt begins. The next three days are spent hunting mornings and evenings, with a typical day beginning with an exciting and exhilarating early morning hunt. Then hunters return to the lodge for a late-morning breakfast and a period of free time until mid-afternoon. Then it's back to the field for the evening hunt. The day ends with dinner in the rustic lodge.

FOA offers up to three of days of hunting, with hunts running from September 15 through December 31. This outfit books fewer hunters than bucks available, creating a 100 percent success rate for every hunter, every year. Hunt with the weapon of your choice, be it bow, rifle, shotgun, pistol or muzzleloader. When packing, make sure to bring warm clothes (Wisconsin can get cold, especially in the late season), leather boots, raingear (including rubber boots), binoculars, and a camera with lots of film.

Forest of Antlers provides beautiful and modern comforts in a northwoods atmosphere. The lodge sleeps 8 and is fully handicapped accessible.

Vital Statistics

THE LODGE:

Main lodge is modern/rustic with 4 guest rooms, 8 beds total, no private baths

SERVICES: Telephone, TV, laundry, VCR

GUN HUNTS:

• from $2,250 - $6,000 / 3 days; price depends on size of buck taken

PAYMENT: Check, money order

CONFERENCE GROUPS: Yes

MEAL PLANS: All meals included (roast beef, chicken, meat loaf, pork chops, potatoes, vegetables, breads, desserts)

NEAREST AIRPORT: Rhinelander, WI

TRANSPORTATION TO LODGE (20 minutes): Van from lodge (no extra charge)

CONTACT:

Ronald Lee
Forest of Antlers Outfitters
PO Box 1188
Minocqua, WI 54548
Ph: 715358-7574
Fax: 715/356-3694
Web: www.forestofantlers.com

THE HUNT:

SEASON: September through December

BEST TIME TO HUNT: Mornings and evenings

TERRAIN: Hardwood ridges, spruce swamps, riverbottoms, jackpine, aspens and small fields

LAND: 1,000 private acres

DRAW BLOOD POLICY? Yes –

HUNTING METHODS: Stand hunting (most stands are 12' high, 6' x 8'; bow stands are generally 18' high, 4' x 4' platforms with rails)

YEARS IN BUSINESS: 4

STAFF OF GUIDES: 5

HUNTERS SERVED BY EACH GUIDE: 1

NONHUNTER CHARGE: $150 / day

LICENSES: Included

GAME CARE: Dress, package and freeze game at no extra charge

OTHER ACTIVITIES: Wildlife photography

BOONE AND CROCKETT

• B&C book bucks taken from property: 4 to 5 per year
• Average B&C score: 150 to 160
• B&C bucks from this part of state: n/a

WEST

ARIZONA, CALIFORNIA, COLORADO, IDAHO, MONTANA, NEVADA, NEW MEXICO, OREGON, UTAH, WASHINGTON, WYOMING.

UNTIL RECENTLY, WHITETAIL HUNTING in the West wasn't much of a big deal. The mule deer was king when it came to deer — unless, of course, you wanted to go for something bigger, such as elk. But lately, whitetail numbers have been exploding across the West. And with that explosion has come an increased interest in hunting them by residents and non-residents alike. The whitetails haven't been usurping mulies in many areas, but instead have moved into voids. In much of the West, you can find the mulies up in the high country and the whitetails down along the riverbottoms. Most of the trophy whitetails, like whitetails everywhere, hole up during the day, then come out at night to feed. Hunters down along the riverbottoms should watch the edges of fields, in particular. Right at dusk, that's when the big boys come out. Of course, if you are hunting during the peak of the rut, all that can be thrown to the wind. If there is a doe in estrus, most bucks are going to throw caution to the wind too, and go tend to that doe.

We have combined a large number of states, and a vast region, into this one chapter, as many western lodges are still devoted to elk or mule deer, with whitetails almost an afterthought. Those lodges listed in this section are just a bit more devoted to whitetails, a bit more concentrated. Try one of them. You'll find hunting whitetails in the West to be a totally different experience than hunting them anywhere else. And if you have the right tags, you might just be able to get a mule deer while you're at it. And if you have a shotgun with you, you can go after sharptails or Hungarian partridge once your big game tag is filled.

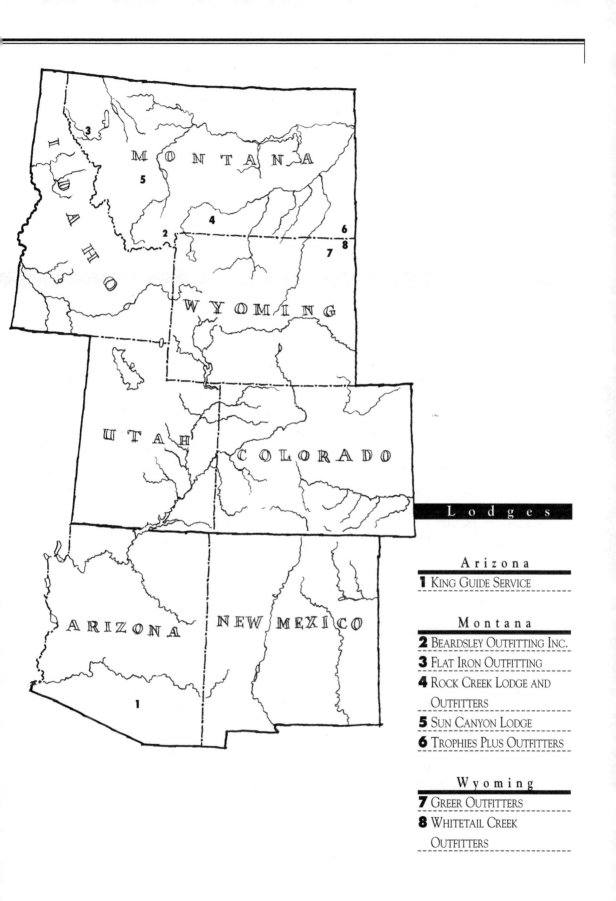

Lodges

Arizona
1 KING GUIDE SERVICE

Montana
2 BEARDSLEY OUTFITTING INC.
3 FLAT IRON OUTFITTING
4 ROCK CREEK LODGE AND OUTFITTERS
5 SUN CANYON LODGE
6 TROPHIES PLUS OUTFITTERS

Wyoming
7 GREER OUTFITTERS
8 WHITETAIL CREEK OUTFITTERS

Resources

ARIZONA GAME AND FISH
DEPT.
2221 W. Greenway Road
Phoenix, AZ 85023-4312
Ph: 602/942-3000
Web: www.gf.state.az.us

CALIFORNIA DEPT. OF FISH &
GAME
1416 9th St.
Box 944209
Sacramento, CA 95814
Ph: 916/653-7664
Fax: 916/653-1856
Web: www.dfg.ca.gov

COLORADO DIV. OF WILDLIFE
6060 Broadway
Denver, CO 80216
Ph: 303/297-1192
Fax: 303/294-0894
Web:www.dnr.state.co.us/wildlife

IDAHO FISH AND GAME DEPT.
Box 25, 600 S. Walnut St.
Boise, ID 83707
Ph: 208/334-3700
Fax: 208/334-2114
Web: w/state.id.us/fishgame

MONTANA DEPT. OF FISH,
WILDLIFE, AND PARKS
1420 E. 6th Ave., PO Box 200701
Helena, MT 59620-0701
Ph: 406/444-3186
Fax: 406/444-4952
Web: fwp.state.mt.us

NEVADA DIV. OF WILDLIFE
1100 Valley Rd.
Reno, NV 89512
Ph: 775/688-1500
Fax: 775/688-1595
Web: www.state.nv.us/cnr/nvwildlife

NEW MEXICO DEPT. OF
GAME AND FISH
Box 25112
Santa Fe, NM 87504
Ph: 505/827-7911
Web: www.gmfsh.state.nm.us

OREGON DEPT. OF FISH AND
WILDLIFE
2501 SW 1st Ave.
Portland, OR 97207
Ph: 503/872-5310
Web: www.dfw.state.or.us/

UTAH DIV. OF WILDLIFE
RESOURCES
1594 W. North Temple,
Suite 2110
Box 146301
Salt Lake City, UT 84114-6301
Ph: 801/538-4700
Fax: 801/538-4709
Web: www.nr.state.ut.us/dwr/!home-
ytg.htm

WASHINGTON DEPT. OF FISH
AND WILDLIFE
600 Capitol Way North
Olympia, WA 98501-1091
Ph: 360/902-2200
Fax: 360/902-2947
Web: www.wa.gov/wdfw/

WYOMING GAME AND FISH
DEPT.
5400 Bishop Blvd.
Cheyenne, WY 82006
Ph: 307/777-4600
Fax: 307/777-4610
Web: www.gf.state.wy.us

King Guide Service

Tucson, Arizona

I T'S PRETTY EASY to be enthusiastic about Coues white-tail hunting, especially if you've read Jack O'Connor's writings. However, the diminutive Coues deer is a big-game animal that's hard to hunt on your own, especially if you live in another part of the country. Where do you go to hunt them? How do you hunt them when you find them? A good outfitter can answer all of those questions for you, and one top-notch guide service is King Guide Service, out of Tucson.

Personal and enthusiastic, Dan King scouts his areas thoroughly before the season, helps his clients get drawn for a permit, and gets them pointed in the right direction if they've booked an on-your-own hunt. Booking a guided hunt means that Dan or Monica King, or one of their guides, will take you to a productive area where you'll spend a lot of time glassing locations known to hold good-size Coues deer. If one is spotted, the drill is to stalk within range. Like any whitetail, Coues are ever-alert, with good eyesight and an excellent sense of smell. Getting within range can be a challenge.

The effort King puts in before the season to find clients trophy deer is legendary. Once he locates a potential record-book contender, he studies and patterns its characteristics, including social interactions, feeding and browsing corridors, and its rut cycle.

King cautions that many true trophy bucks never really develop routines (which could account for why they live to be trophy bucks), but may simply remain bedded all season in thick cover where they have access to food and water. Such a situation may mean that King has to sit and wait for movement, for the buck to stand up and stretch during the day, giving his client an opportunity to site the buck in the crosshairs for a shot.

King hunts prime areas in both Mexico (Sonora and Chihuahua states) and southern Arizona. Guests stay at the King's lodge, which is comfortable, spacious, and modern, with belt-loosening meals served breakfast, lunch, and dinner.

Vital Statistics

THE LODGE:

4 guest rooms (2 in main lodge, 2 in guest house), 6 beds total, no private baths

SERVICES: Telephone, fax, copying, TV, laundry

HUNTS:

• Coues whitetail: $2,500 / mature specimens; $3,500 / trophy

PAYMENT: Money orders, cashiers checks, PayPal.com

MEAL PLAN: 3 meals a day included (dinners of porterhouse steak, salmon, traditional southwestern fare, appetizers, side dishes, desserts)

SPECIAL DIETS: Heart healthy, Kosher, vegetarian, salt/msg free with advance notice

NEAREST AIRPORT: Tucson, AZ

TRANSPORTATION TO LODGE (45 minutes): Van pickup at no extra charge

BOONE AND CROCKETT

• B&C book bucks taken from property: 264

• Average B&C score: 114 typical, 130 nontypical

• B&C bucks from this port of state: 171 in rest of the area

CONTACT:

Dan or Monica King
King Guide Service
13005 W. Castle Dr.
Tucson, AZ 85736
Ph: 520/822-1195
Fax: 520/822-5493
Email: danmking@aol.com
Web:
http://members.aol.com/dandmking/index.html

THE HUNT:

SEASON:

• Arizona rifle: Oct. - Dec.

• Arizona bow: Aug. - Sept., Dec. - Jan.

• Arizona muzzleloader: Oct. - Dec.

• Seasons in Mexico are open through January

BEST TIME TO HUNT: Dec. - Jan. hunts are best; although B&C bucks have been taken on all rifle hunts

TERRAIN: Low, easy rolling hills to steep rocky mountains

LAND: Public land in Arizona; private ranches in Mexico

DRAW BLOOD POLICY? No

HUNTING METHODS: Stand hunting (one stand in Mexico, aluminum tripod with camo blind), still-hunting; the majority is done by glassing with high-powered binoculars from a vantage point, then stalking

YEARS IN BUSINESS: 15

STAFF OF GUIDES: Independent guides hired as needed

HUNTERS SERVED BY EACH GUIDE: 1

NONHUNTER CHARGE: $100 / day

LICENSES: Rifle is by drawing, archery is over the counter (purchased prior to arrival or at a sporting goods store near lodge)

GAME CARE: Dress and freeze game for no extra charge; shipping extra

OTHER ACTIVITIES: Other big game hunting (desert mule deer, mountain lions, javelina, coyotes, foxes, antelope, elk, desert or Rocky Mountain bighorn sheep, bison, bear, turkey), small game hunting (rabbits), bird hunting (quail, doves), waterfowling, antiquing, bird watching, hiking, wildlife photography

© King Guide Service

A trophy 10-point Coues whitetail taken in southern Arizona.

Beardsley Outfitting Inc.

Ennis, Montana

TIM BEARDSLEY OWNS a 100-acre ranch up on Jack Creek Bench overlooking Ennis, on the Madison River and the lake beyond. You wouldn't call this ranch tiny, not with its rustic main lodge and two guest cabins, but it's small compared with some of the 10,000-acre-plus ranches in the neighborhood. The Lee Metcalf Wilderness, which contains most of the western side of the Madison Mountains, is practically out the back door of the ranch.

Most of Beardsley's hunters go for elk, riding out each morning, with bow or rifle, searching for bugling bulls coming out of their high-country dark-timber cover. There is limited whitetail hunting available, however. Most whitetails are found in the riverbottoms and areas that Beardsley has permission to hunt on neighboring ranches. This is mostly early morning or late evening hunting, with hunters taking up positions that overlook trails leading in and from cropfields. The big bucks, in particular, are most likely to be seen in the closing hour of the day, either sneaking out to the edge of a field to grab a bite to eat, or following an estrus doe as she does the same.

You can use the same rifle you'd use for mulies for this type of hunting, with 270, 280, 30-06, or 7mm being ideal. Using an elk rifle such as a 300 or 338 Win Mag would be overgunning it, however.

Beardsley's is a laid-back type of operation. Its fishing program has received Orvis' endorsement, and 80 percent of the hunters are repeat customers. The hunting is good, and the food — with seafood and pasta, grilled chicken breasts and fresh green salads — stands head and shoulders over most.

Vital Statistics

THE LODGE:

5 guest rooms, some private baths, 10 beds total; accommodations are in the lodge and guest cabins

SERVICES: Telephone, fax, TV

GUN HUNTS:

• $3,300 / week 2-on-1 for elk or deer

• $4,200 / week 1-on-1 for elk or deer

PAYMENT: Cash, check

CONFERENCE GROUPS: n/a

MEAL PLANS: All meals included (dinners include rib eye steaks, chicken breasts, pastas and more)

NEAREST AIRPORT: Bozeman, MT

TRANSPORTATION TO LODGE (60 miles): Rental car; van from lodge ($50)

CONTACT:

Tim Beardsley
Beardsley Outfitting Inc.
PO Box 60
Ennis, MT 59729
Ph: 406/682-7292
Fax: 406/682-5756
Email: tbbigsky@3rivers.com
Web: www.beardsleyfishhuntmt.com

THE HUNT:

SEASON:

• bow: September 2 - October 8

• rifle: October 22 - November 26

BEST TIME TO HUNT: Anytime

TERRAIN: Riverbottoms, cropland edges

LAND: Own 2,000 acres, have access to 12,000 acres of national forest land, plus a number of area ranches

DRAW BLOOD POLICY? n/a

HUNTING METHODS: Stand hunting, drives, rattling

YEARS IN BUSINESS: 15

STAFF OF GUIDES: 3

HUNTERS SERVED BY EACH GUIDE: 2

NONHUNTER CHARGE: $1,000 / week

LICENSES: Must apply

GAME CARE: Dress, freeze, and ship game for additional fee

OTHER ACTIVITIES: Other big game hunting (mule deer, elk), bird hunting, waterfowling, fishing, biking, bird watching, whitewater rafting, wildlife photography

Flat Iron Outfitting

Thompson Falls, Montana

JERRY SHIVELY, the head guy at Flat Iron Outfitting, has a different philosophy than a lot of outfitters who pack hunters into remote wilderness camps miles from the nearest road. Shively puts his clients up in local motels, and has them dine in area restaurants. Each morning, they drive to permit areas 121, 123, and 124 of the Lolo National Forest, or to the 2,500-acre ranch that he leases for hunting.

His system works like this. Hunters may move at a moment's notice into areas where deer are concentrated. He can change his hunting strategies to take advantage of changes in the weather, then tune his hunts to the desires and abilities of his hunters. At the end of the day, they head back to their motels for hot showers, then on to a restaurant for some dinner.

Most whitetail hunting takes place on the private ranch where Shively has had exclusive access for the past decade. The ranch is flat, with a few deep gullies, and butts up against a national forest. No hunting is allowed on the adjacent properties, which means the deer here are totally unpressured, and move about naturally. Big whitetails — over 150 points B&C — have come from the ranch. And there are more roaming around out there. In fact, many say the ranch has some of the finest whitetail habitat in Montana. The land is located on a working ranch, under the management of a rancher who is actively concerned about the wildlife. His grain and alfalfa fields provide ample feed during the summer, fall, and early winter. Careful management practices are observed.

Flat Iron limits the hunting on the leased land to only eight hunters per week. If you want the chance to hunt trophy whitetail with the possibility of an elk as well, this hunt is for you.

Vital Statistics

THE LODGE:

2 guest rooms, 2 beds total, private baths; plus nearby motels

SERVICES: Telephone, TV

HUNTS:

• $1,995 / 7-day hunt

PAYMENT: Cash, check

MEAL PLANS: Nearby restaurant

SPECIAL DIETS: n/a

NEAREST AIRPORT: Missoula, MT

TRANSPORTATION TO LODGE (100 miles): Rental car

CONTACT:

Jerry C. Shively
Flat Iron Outfitting
3 Golf Course Road
Thompson Falls, MT 59873
Ph: 406/827-3666
Email: flatiron@montana.com

THE HUNT:

SEASON:

• bow: first Saturday in Sept. to third Sunday in Oct.

• rifle/muzzleloader: fourth Sunday in Oct. to Thanksgiving

BEST TIME TO HUNT: Anytime

TERRAIN: Private lease is flat timbered ranchland; national forest is steep mountains and heavy timber

LAND: Lease is 2,500 acres; Lolo National Forest is 100,000 acres plus

DRAW BLOOD POLICY? No

HUNTING METHODS: Stand hunting (lock-ons, ladder stands), drives, still-hunting, calling, rattling

YEARS IN BUSINESS: 14

STAFF OF GUIDES: No

NONHUNTER CHARGE: None

LICENSES: Nonresident application deadline is March 15

GAME CARE: Processing is available locally

OTHER ACTIVITIES: Other big game hunting (elk, bear, mountain lion, mule deer), bird hunting, fishing, wildlife photography

BOONE AND CROCKETT

• B&C book bucks taken from property: Several

• Average B&C score: 130 class

• B&C bucks from this part of state: Several

Flat Iron Outfitting: Tracy Miller shows the largest whitetail taken on a guided hunt in Montana, 1995.

© Flat Iron Outfitting

A beautiful 8-pointer taken by a Rock Creek Lodge bowhunter.

© Rock Creek Lodge and Outfitters

Rock Creek Lodge and Outfitters

Hillsdale, Montana

A T ROCK CREEK LODGE, you'll be visiting one of the most remote locations in Montana, but you won't be roughing it. Your room in the three-year-old lodge will be warm, comfortable, and comes with a private bath. The home-like atmosphere offers comfort and privacy. Three bedrooms are just off the lobby, dining room and kitchen area where meals are prepared. Owners Dean and Patti Armbrister take great pride in their country cooking, specializing in homemade bread, baked goods, and Montana beef.

Hunters don't go to Rock Creek just for the comfortable accommodations and family-type atmosphere, of course. They go for the hunting, and Rock Creek has excellent hunting for both whitetails and mule deer. Most of the whitetail hunting takes place along the Rock Creek drainage and in the oat, millet, and alfalfa field bottoms of the Milk River, where hunters set up in portable tree stands or ground blinds that overlook trails that connect bedding and feeding areas. Bowhunters in total camouflage sometimes have success by hiding in one of the ditches along the river, where they watch trails along the oxbows and sloughs for deer moving to feed. Rifle hunters, on the other hand, should be prepared to make 100- to 200-yard shots across the fields or through the trees along the river. Dean and his guides scout this area all summer and into the fall, so they'll know exactly where to put you for your best chance at success. They'll also make sure that you go out to the rifle range and triple-check your firearm to make sure it's still dead-on after your trip. The last thing you want is to get a shot at a nice buck, only to miss because your gun wasn't sighted in properly.

Western whitetail hunting has become increasingly popular in recent years, in part because the deer get so large here, and in part because the hunting pressure is relatively light. For a serious chance at a trophy whitetail, Rock Creek should be right up there on your list.

Vital Statistics

THE LODGE:

3 guest rooms, all have private baths, 7 beds total

SERVICES: Telephone, fax, TV, laundry, hot tub

HUNTS:

• $2,250 / 5 days

PAYMENT: Cash, check

MEAL PLANS: All meals included (menu includes buttermilk pancakes, bacon, eggs, homemade toast, omeletes, roast beef, homemade noodles, homemade bread, fried chicken, steak (ranch raised), ham with new potatoes and creamed peas)

SPECIAL DIETS: Heart healthy, or will accomodate requests

NEAREST AIRPORT: Billings, MT

TRANSPORTATION TO LODGE (45 miles): Rental car; shuttle flight

CONTACT:

Dean and Patti Armbrister
Rock Creek Lodge and Outfitters
P.O. Box 152
Hillsdale, MT 59241
Ph: 406/648-5524
Email: rock-creek-lodge@juno.com
Web:
www.Finditlocal.com/Rock Creek

THE HUNT:

SEASON:

• bow: Sept. 5 - Oct. 23
• rifle/muzzleloader: Oct. 23 - Nov. 28
• allowed to take one buck, whitetail or mule deer, plus one whitetail doe

BEST TIME TO HUNT: Bow: mid-season; rifle: mid- to late season

TERRAIN: Milk River areas, alfalfa fields, oat fields, and native grasses, riverbottoms, oxbows and wasteland

LAND: Most private property; lease sizes vary

DRAW BLOOD POLICY? No

HUNTING METHODS: Stand hunting (steel ladders, portable canvas blinds), still-hunting, calling, rattling

Years in Business: 7

STAFF OF GUIDES : 2

HUNTERS SERVED BY EACH GUIDE: 2

NONHUNTER CHARGE: $150 / day

LICENSES: Nonresident application dead-line is March 15; should book before December of the preceding year

GAME CARE: Processing is available for $35; shipment is the hunter's responsibility

OTHER ACTIVITIES: Other big game hunting (elk, antelope, mule deer), bird hunting (pheasants), waterfowling, bird watching, hiking, wildlife photography

BOONE AND CROCKETT

• B&C book bucks taken from property: n/a
• Average B&C score: 120 - 160
• B&C bucks from this part of state: n/a

Sun Canyon Lodge

A u g u s t a ,   M o n t a n a

S
UN RIVER CANYON is an eastern gateway to the vast
Lewis and Clark Forest and the unique Bob Marshall
Wilderness Area. The majestic Rocky Mountains suddenly end the otherwise rolling foothill country of western Montana. The high rock walls rise up abruptly in
majestic grandeur to welcome those who venture into the last of the true
mountain wilderness areas.

Located in the canyon, Sun Canyon Lodge offers elk, mule deer, and some
whitetail hunting. According to lodge owner Lee Carlbom, the majority of people who hunt with him hunt for elk as well as whitetails. "The price is virtually the same for hunting two animals as it is for only elk," Carlbom said.

Elk hunting comes in three categories: early season, which opens
September 15, on the west side of the Continental Divide; regular season,
which generally opens the last Sunday in October, with the main camp being
Cabin Creek; and bowhunting, which starts in early September and runs into
late October.

"Our main whitetail camp is Cabin Creek," stated Carlbom, "but each year
hunters also pick up some nice whitetails hunting out of the main lodge. We
also hunt elk in the Juliet area during the early rifle season, and bowhunt for
whitetails on private land that we have access to."

According to Carlbom, the only area that has mule deer only is the Black
Tail camp. Otherwise, hunters are apt to run into a good buck almost anywhere.

Vital Statistics

THE LODGE:

6 guest log cabins, 6 to 8 beds per cabin, 30 beds total, 4 cabins have private baths

SERVICES: Telephone, laundry

HUNTS:

• $2,500 / 6-day hunt

PAYMENT: Cash, check, credit cards

CONFERENCE GROUPS: No

MEAL PLANS: 3 meals a day (dinners feature rib-eye steaks with shrimp, sirloin steaks, hamburgers, halibut, chicken, soup, salad, bread, baked potatoes, hash browns, french fries)

NEAREST AIRPORT: Great Falls, MT

TRANSPORTATION TO LODGE (85 miles): Van from lodge ($100 round-trip)

CONTACT:

Lee Carlbom
Sun Canyon Lodge
P.O. Box 327
Augusta, MT 59410
Ph: 406/562-3654
Fax: 406/562-3603.
Email: suncanyn@3rivers.net
Web: www.suncanyonlodge.com

THE HUNT:

SEASON:

• bow: Sept. 2 - Oct. 14
• rifle: Oct. 24 - Nov. 26

BEST TIME TO HUNT: Mid-November for rifle; September and October for bow

TERRAIN: River valleys, moderate to steep hillsides

LAND: Over 10,000 acres (private and public)

DRAW BLOOD POLICY? No

HUNTING METHODS: Stand hunting (treestands, ground blinds), drives, still-hunting, by vehicle, calling, rattling

YEARS IN BUSINESS: 18

STAFF OF GUIDES: 8

HUNTERS SERVED BY EACH GUIDE: 2

NONHUNTER CHARGE: Half price

LICENSES: Must buy through a draw — guaranteed only until March 15

GAME CARE: Dress, package, freeze and ship game

OTHER ACTIVITIES: Other big game hunting (elk, mule deer), bird hunting, fishing, boating, hiking, wildlife photography, horseback riding

BOONE AND CROCKETT

• B&C book bucks taken from property: A few each year.
• Average B&C score: 130-160
• B&C bucks from this part of state: n/a

Trophies Plus Outfitters

Alzada, Montana

I F YOU DON'T HAVE ACCESS to prime national forest land, you're pretty much relegated to hunting private land when you're in the outfitting business. And make no mistake about it, hunting on private leases can be excellent. The trick is to find the land, lease it from the landowner for a price you can live with, then patrol and manage it well. Successful outfitters are always looking to sign up new properties, while at the same time hanging onto the good ones they already have.

With tracts of prime game country in Montana, Wyoming, and South Dakota, Trophies Plus hunts where the game goes. They do it with a good attitude, too.

"We operate where South Dakota, Montana, and Wyoming come together, to provide us the opportunity to hunt all three states," states Mike Watkins, owner of Trophies Plus. "We specialize in deer, antelope, and turkeys, and only hunt private ranches to assure quality hunts."

"We believe each hunt should be a quality hunting experience," he says. "It should be remembered long after the trophy mounts have faded and lost their luster. To this end we strive to make each hunt a totally satisfying experience, so much so that the only easing of the pain as the hunt ends is the knowledge that next year's hunt has already started counting down. Our hunts are 100 percent fair chase, with no game fences or guaranteed kill situations." Watkins concludes. "The only guarantee that we do make is that we will do everything possible to make your hunt a success, and an experience you will want to enjoy again and again.

"Our guides are professionals who have put in countless hours over the years to achieve the level of success in their field. They give 110 percent to ensure that you have the hunt of your dreams."

Trophies Plus runs antelope hunts from three to seven days, and combines them with deer hunts. Hunters stay either in motels or tent camps on private ranches. In Wyoming, they hunt 11 different management areas in three general regions: the Shirley Basin, north of Laramie; east central, northwest of Lusk; and the northeastern corner near the town of Colony. In Montana, TP hunts the 700 region in the southeastern corner of the state, near Alzada. Success rates run between 95 and 100 percent, with bucks averaging more than 14 inches.

For mule and white-tailed deer, hunters stay in motels, ranch houses, and tent camps on private ranches in east-central Wyoming, northeastern Wyoming, southeastern Montana, and western South Dakota. Big bucks of both subspecies are plentiful in these regions. And if you can shoot out to 200 yards with accuracy, your chances of getting a trophy-class animal are good. A 270, 7mm or 30-06 are the calibers of choice out here.

Just tell Trophies Plus what you're looking for, and they'll make it happen. Archery seasons generally open in September and run into October for deer and antelope, with rifle season running the month of November for deer, mid-October into mid-November for antelope.

Vital Statistics

THE LODGE:

Private ranch houses have 9 rooms, 15 beds total; also tent camps, motels

SERVICES: Vary

HUNTS:

- $2,250 / 3-day hunt
- $2,700 / 4-day hunt
- $4,000 / 6-day 2-state hunt (South Dakota, Wyoming, Montana)

PAYMENT: Cash, check

CONFERENCE GROUPS: Yes

MEAL PLANS: All meals included (dinners feature roast beef, lasagna, chicken, served family-style)

NEAREST AIRPORT: Rapid City, SD

TRANSPORTATION TO LODGE (120 miles): Vehicle from lodge, $150 round-trip

CONTACT:

Mike Watkins
Trophies Plus Outfitters
Box 44
Alzada, MT 59311
Ph: 800-248-6899; 406-828-4512
Web: www.trophiesplusoutfitters.com
Email: info@trophiesplusoutfitters.com

THE HUNT:

SEASON:

- bow: September - October
- rifle: early through late November

BEST TIME TO HUNT: Anytime

TERRAIN: Varied — raws, arroyos, sage brush flats, river bottoms

LAND: Leased tracts throughout three states, plus hunt management areas

DRAW BLOOD POLICY: n/a

HUNTING METHODS: Still-hunting, glass and stalk

YEARS IN BUSINESS: 11

STAFF OF GUIDES: 10

HUNTERS SERVED BY EACH GUIDE: 1 - 2

NONHUNTER CHARGE: n/a

LICENSES: Mostly over the counter

GAME CARE: n/a

OTHER ACTIVITIES: Other big game hunting (turkey, mule deer, antelope), wildlife photography

Greer Outfitters

Gillette, Wyoming

GREER OUTFITTERS is a family-run operation. Established in 1952 by Jack Greer, it was passed on to his son Randy in 1977. Randy has operated it since then with the help of his wife, Lora, and his four sons. Greer Outfitters strives to provide a quality hunt, and continually produces trophy animals equaling those taken in the 1950s and 1960s. They still maintain their original lease, with an excess of 200,000 additional acres of private property, some of which is exclusively for archery. Their lasting success can be attributed to their strict game management, limited number of hunters, knowledgeable guides, and exceptional number of trophy game animals.

Vital Statistics

THE LODGE:
Farmhouse has 3 guest rooms, 6 beds total, some private baths; also nearby motel

SERVICES: Telephone, laundry

HUNTS:
- $2,500 / 4 days (motel)
- $2,750 / 4 days (farmhouse)
- $3,250 (motel) and $3,500 / 4 days (farmhouse) for whitetail/antelope combo hunts

PAYMENT: Cash, check

MEAL PLANS: 3 meals a day included

SPECIAL DIETS: Heart healthy, Kosher, vegetarian, salt/msg free, other

NEAREST AIRPORT: Gillette, WY

TRANSPORTATION TO LODGE (70 miles): Rental car; van

THE HUNT:
SEASON:
- bow: Sept. and Nov.
- rifle: November
- muzzleloader: November

BEST TIME TO HUNT: Anytime

TERRAIN: Black Hills area — cedar, pines, some creek bottoms

LAND: More than 200,000 leased acres

Draw Blood Policy? No

HUNTING METHODS: Stand hunting (lock-ons, wooden), drives, still-hunting, vehicle (car), calling, rattling

YEARS IN BUSINESS: 24

STAFF OF GUIDES: 6

HUNTERS SERVED BY EACH GUIDE: 2

NONHUNTER CHARGE: $250

LICENSES: Must apply ahead of season

GAME CARE: None provided at lodge

OTHER ACTIVITIES: Other big game hunting (mule deer, antelope, buffalo, exotic sheep and goat, elk, turkey); fishing, wildlife photography

BOONE AND CROCKETT
- B&C bucks taken from property: 0
- Average B&C score: 130 to 140
- B&C bucks from this part of state: Few

CONTACT:
Randy and Lora Greer
Greer Outfitters
P.O. Box 38
Gillette, WY 82717
Ph/fax: 307/687-7461
Email: hunt@greeroutfitters.com
Web: http://greeroutfitters.com

© Rock Creek Lodge and Outfitters

Marion Garret took this 158 B&C buck from the Milk River area in Montana in 1995.

Whitetail Creek Outfitters

Hulett, Wyoming

J UST WEST OF THE BLACK HILLS National Forest in northeastern Wyoming, the Tumbling T Ranch consists of 8,000 acres, surrounded by more than 100,000 acres of other private ranches. Devil's Tower, America's First National Monument, can be seen from most parts of the ranch. There are approximately 400,000 additional leased acres available to Whitetail Creek guests

Hunting here is pure Western, with rimrocks, deep canyons, gullies, and meadows. In addition to mule deer, though, you're hunting whitetails, which makes for a unique type of hunt in this kind of terrain. Owner Ray Hulse sends his guided hunters onto his own ranch, and also onto the surrounding acres. Much depends on weather, time of year, and whether his guides have located some good bucks worth pursuing. Hunters still-hunt, rattle, or hunt from blinds. Many bucks go in the 130 Boone and Crockett range, though a few stretch into the 160s. You never know what you're going to come across when you hunt this part of the state.

The lodge is comfortable, and can accommodate ten hunters — with eight more shacking up in adjoining cabins. Meals are buffet-style, and you'll hear no complaints here. Ray's wife is a culinary chef, and you'll eat like a king (or queen). Chicken, pork, shrimp, and fat, juicy steaks (Ray raises his own beef cattle) are all guaranteed to please.

To sum up, Hulse has this to say: "Trophy whitetail hunting is our specialty. We specifically manage crops to have green winter wheat or alfalfa growing in our valley during deer season. We realize that you pay for the trip, buy expensive equipment, take time off from work, have travel expenses, so we guarantee you a shooting opportunity or a free hunting trip that following year. That's how confident we are in our game management program."

With a deal like that, with good hunting, what can go wrong?

Vital Statistics

THE LODGE:

11 guest rooms, 38 beds total between the lodge and cabins; Hulse only likes to take a maximum of 16 deer hunters at a time, however; all rooms have private baths

SERVICES: Telephone, fax, copying, TV, laundry

HUNTS: Prices vary depending on region hunted and whether gun or bow

• $2,950 / 5 days regular deer hunt with rifle

• $1,550 - $2,950 / 3 days archery hunt, cost depending on time of year

• $3,950 / 5 days special trophy hunt, with guaranteed shot opportunity during the rut

PAYMENT: Credit cards, check

MEAL PLAN: 3 meals a day (buffet stye dinners of chicken, pork, shrimp, steak, with all the fixin's)

SPECIAL DIETS: Heart healthy, Kosher, vegetarian, salt/msg free

NEAREST AIRPORT: Rapid City, SD

TRANSPORTATION TO LODGE (110 miles): Rental car; van from lodge ($200 round trip)

CONTACT:

Ray Hulse
Whitetail Creek Outfitters
P.O. Box 279
Hulett, WY 82720
Ph: 307/467-5625
Fax: 307/467-5843

THE HUNT:

SEASON:

• bow: September 1 - 30

• rifle: October 1 - 21; November 1 - 30

• muzzleloader: October 1 - 21l November 1 - 30

BEST TIME TO HUNT: The rut, in mid-November

TERRAIN: "We go from rollng ponderosa pine hills to oak and cottonwood creek bottoms to mountain prairies."

LAND: Own 8,000 acres, lease 400,000 acres of private land

DRAW BLOOD POLICY? Yes ("Your hunting is finished if you braw blood and/or wound any animal. We find 99 percent of so-called 'missed' animals.")

HUNTING METHODS: Stand hunting (wooden ground blinds, tent blinds, two-man ladder stands), drives, still-hunting, vehicle, calling, rattling

YEARS IN BUSINESS: 8

STAFF OF GUIDES : 6

HUNTERS SERVED BY EACH GUIDE: 2

NONHUNTER CHARGE: $200 / day

LICENSES: Must apply ahead of season; leftovers after July

GAME CARE: Dress, package, freeze game for clients, no extra charge

OTHER ACTIVITIES: Other big game hunting (mule deer, elk, antelope, turkey), bird hunting, waterfowlng, fishing, horseback riding, fossil digging

BOONE AND CROCKETT

• B&C book bucks taken from property: 7

• Average B&C score: 140 to 150

• B&C bucks from this part of state: 20

CANADA EAST

MANITOBA, NEW BRUNSWICK, NEWFOUNDLAND/LABRADOR, NOVA SCOTIA, ONTARIO, PRINCE EDWARD ISLAND, QUEBEC

E ASTERN CANADA, from Manitoba to Nova Scotia, is a land of deep pine forests and innumerable lakes, vast plains, and sweeping grainfields. Such diverse habitat is perfect for the growing of trophy whitetails.

While you may find fewer deer in number in the forests and abandoned farmlands of New Brunswick, bucks grow large here, and carry heavy racks—especially in those areas where government forests abut agricultural development. And to the north, at the mouth of the St. Lawrence River, you can't beat Anticosti Island for a large, well-balanced deer herd (more than 100,000), trophy bucks, and unpressured hunting in a wilderness setting.

Big antlers are also the main draw where Manitoba's grainfields begin to give way to timbered areas. Look for big bucks along the central western border with Saskatchewan, particularly in the Duck Mountain region and along the Swan River drainage.

Deer herds thin out if you go north into the land of caribou and moose. But hunt in western Manitoba, or along the U.S. border across Ontario and into Quebec, along the St. Lawrence River area, and your chances of success increase remarkably.

Lodges

Manitoba
1 ARROW LAKE OUTFITTERS

New Brunswick
2 MALARKEY CABIN GUIDING SERVICE
3 NORTH VIEW HUNTING AND FISHING LODGE

Ontario
4 CRAWFORD'S CAMPS
5 HUBER'S LONE PINE LODGE LTD.

Quebec
6 FAIRMONT KENAUK
7 SAFARI ANTICOSTI INC. / ANTICOSTI OUTFITTERS INC.
8 SEPAQ - ANTICOSTI

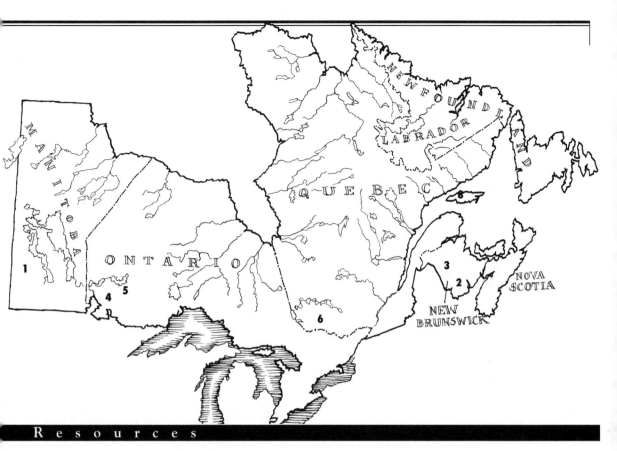

DEPT OF NATURAL RESOURCES
Rm. 333, Legislative Bldg.
Winnipeg, Manitoba
R3C 0V8 Canada
Ph: 204/945-3730

DEPT. OF INDUSTRY, TRADE AND TOURISM
Travel Manitoba
Dept. RHO, 7th Fl, 155 Carlton St.
Winnipeg, Manitoba
R3C 3H8 Canada
Ph: 204/945-3777, ext. RHO; 800/665-0040, ext. RHO
Fax: 204/945-2302
Web: www.travelmanitoba.com

DEPT. OF NATURAL RESOURCES AND ENERGY
Box 6000
Fredericton, New Brunswick
E3B 5H1 Canada
Ph: 506/453-2440

DEPT. OF NATURAL RESOURCES
Box 698
Halifax, Nova Scotia
B3J 2T9 Canada
Ph: 902/424-5935
Web: www.gov.ns.ca/natr

MINISTRY OF NATURAL RESOURCES
Fish and Wildlife Branch
300 Water St., PO Box 7000
Peterborough, Ontario
K9J 8M5 Canada
Ph: 705/755-1925

FISH & WILDLIFE DIV.
Dept. of Technology and Environment
Box 2000
Charlottetown, Prince Edward Island
C1A 7N8 Canada
Ph: 902/368-6083

DEPT. OF ENVIRONMENT AND WILDLIFE
Edifice Marie-Guyart
675 Blvd. Rene-Levesque Est.
Quebec City, Quebec
G1R 4Y1 Canada
Ph: 418/521-3860

TOURISM QUEBEC
1010 Sainte-Catherine St. W, Ste. 400
Montreal, Quebec
H3B 1G2 Canada
Ph: 800/363-7777, ext. 806
Web: www.bonjour-quebec.com

Arrow Lake Outfitters

Shoal Lake, Manitoba

ENJOY 17,000 ACRES of private land ideal for bow and rifle hunting. Arrow Lake Outfitters is located on the edge of Manitoba's Riding Mountain National Park — a one million-acre forest and game reserve with no fences, so game moves back and forth freely between the park and Arrow Lake's land.

Arrow Lake is a new operation for white-tailed deer. Riding Mountain National Park has had a no hunting policy since 1929. Add that to the fact that there has been no hunting on 99 percent of Arrow Lake's land for the past 25 years, and the result is that clients have the opportunity to hunt virtually virgin land.

There is a three-week hunting season for rifle, and a ten-week season for bow in Manitoba. White-tailed bucks in Manitoba frequently exceed 300 pounds.

The terrain in Arrow Lake's hunting area varies from gently rolling crop land with moderate bush cover, to deep ravines with heavily wooded areas. Arrow Lake has easy access to all of the hunt sites, and can accommodate any hunter regardless of age, shape, or any disability. Hunters will be placed in either tree stand or heated hutches.

All hunters are guided, with no more than two hunters per guide. The owners and guides have lived in the area for many years and know the whitetail patterns, and where to find the big bucks.

The lodge itself is located on scenic Arrow Lake. If you tag out early, you can go fishing for a few days while your buddies are still hunting. Each cabin is heated, with a washroom, two bedrooms, and a sitting area. Excellent meals are provided, including breakfast, dinner, and a hearty lunch packed for hunters daily.

As owner Ray Lazarak explains, "This is your hunt, and we will do our best to give you exactly what you want — the hunt of a lifetime, both in the field, and in the evening after shooting hours."

Arrow Lake is a top-notch lodge, with serious, good hunting. If you're interested, you should book early, as spaces are taken early.

Vital Statistics

THE LODGE:

Main lodge and cabins have 6 guest rooms, some have private baths; shower and bathroom in each cabin

SERVICES: Telephone, fax, TV, laundry

HUNTS:

- gun: $2,200 to $2,500 / week
- bow: $1,500 / week
- muzzleloader: $2,500 / week

PAYMENT: Check, other

CONFERENCE GROUPS: Yes

MEAL PLANS: All meals included (steak, meat balls, potatoes, roasts, salads, pastas, chicken dishes — "the works")

NEAREST AIRPORT: Winnepeg, MB

TRANSPORTATION TO LODGE (3 1/2 hours): Van from lodge, shuttle flight

CONTACT:

Ray Lazaruk
Arrow Lake Outfitters
Box 595
Shoal Lake, Manitoba
ROJ 1Z0 Canada
Ph: 204/859-3191
Fax: 204/859-2095
Web: arrowlakeranch.com

THE HUNT:

SEASON:

- bow: late August to late September
- rifle: late November to early December
- muzzleloader: late October to early November

BEST TIME TO HUNT: During the rut

TERRAIN: Varies from gently rolling cropland with moderate bush cover to deep ravines with heavily wooded areas

LAND: All private

DRAW BLOOD POLICY? Yes

HUNTING METHODS: Stand hunting (pie-shaped heated hutches raised 14' off the ground), still-hunting, calling, rattling

YEARS IN BUSINESS: n/a

STAFF OF GUIDES: 4

HUNTERS SERVED BY EACH GUIDE: 2

NONHUNTER CHARGE: $100 / day (U.S.)

LICENSES: Sold at lodge

GAME CARE: Dress, package, freeze and ship game (no extra charge)

OTHER ACTIVITIES: Bird hunting, waterfowling, fishing, biking, bird-watching, boating, canoeing, golf, hiking, skiing, swimming, wildlife photography

Malarkey Cabin Guiding Service

Keswick Ridge, New Brunswick

RAY DILLON, head of Malarkey Cabin Guiding Service, has the extreme good fortune to be situated in an extraordinary part of New Brunswick. Headquartered in Keswick Ridge, he's just north of the huge Mactaquac Dam on the St. John River. Due to Atlantic salmon low returns from the ocean in recent years, the St. John River system is no longer viable for, or open to, salmon angling. They do offer some top-notch smallmouth bass angling in the summer however. The country itself is primarily high country, dotted with apple orchards and dairy farms, prime habitat for white-tailed deer. To the north are huge areas of commercial forest, which would make anyone familiar with northern Maine feel right at home. As in Maine, the bucks here can run huge, with some monsters wearing heavy-beamed 10-point racks and tipping the scales at more than 200 pounds, field dressed. Also as in Maine, the hunting here can be somewhat frustrating to the uninitiated, as the terrain is thick, and the deer density low. Perseverance is the key: get into the woods every day, hunt likely areas hard, and sooner or later your chance at a monster will happen.

At the end of the day, hunters return to the Malarkey Cabin, a modern log structure with three guest rooms, 10 beds total, plus a comfortable living area. The food is excellent and varied, while the lodge, located right at the edge of the forest in a clearing, is within a stone's throw of hunting.

For hunters who tag out early, Malarkey offers excellent black bear, coyote, or upland bird hunting for ruffed grouse and woodcock. For the past four years, they've also enjoyed a 100 percent success rate on late September moose hunting (by lottery).

Vital Statistics

THE LODGE:

Modern log lodge has 3 guest rooms, all with private baths, 10 beds total

Services: Telephone, fax, TV, copying, laundry

Hunts:

• $1,200 for deer/bear/fishing / 6 nights, 5 days

Payment: Cash, check

Conference Groups: n/a

Meal Plans: 3 meals a day (dinners include roast beef, spaghetti and meatballs, roast turkey, lobster, steaks, fried chicken, ham, variety of vegetables, potatoes, 5 different desserts, all "home-cooked and delicious")

Nearest Airport: Fredericton, NB

Transportation to Lodge (45 minutes): Rental car; van from lodge $50

CONTACT:

Ray Dillon
Malarkey Cabin Guiding Service
1132 Route 616
Keswick Ridge, NB
E6L 2N9 Canada
Ph/fax: 506-363-2839
Email: dillonr@nbnet.nb.ca

THE HUNT:

Season:

• bow: first 3 weeks of Oct.

• rifle/muzzleloader: last week of Oct. - third week of Nov.

Best Time to Hunt: The rut (food supply and weather can affect the precise timing)

Terrain: Old farms, cedar swamps, power lines, clear cuts, logging roads, apple orchards, mixed growth and hardwood ridges, large and small woods

Land: 100 square miles of public and private land

Draw Blood Policy? Yes, whoever draws first blood claims the buck

Hunting Methods: Stand hunting (a variety are available, none heated), still-hunting, by vehicle, calling, rattling

Years in Business: 12

Staff of Guides: 2 - 4

Hunters served by each guide: 3

Nonhunter Charge: $400 / 6 nights, 5 days

Licenses: Sold over the counter at the lodge

Game Care: Dress, package, freeze and ship game for clients (cost varies)

Other Activities: Other big game hunting (bear, moose), bird hunting, fishing, hiking, skiing, wildlife photography

BOONE AND CROCKETT

• B&C book bucks taken from property: 4

• Average B&C score: 172

• B&C bucks from this part of state: 42

North View Hunting and Fishing Lodge

Plaster Rock, New Brunswick

ROUGHLY 20 MILES southeast of Grand-Sault, New Brunswick, and perhaps 45 miles northeast of Presque Isle, Maine, is the village of Plaster Rock, right in the middle of prime whitetail hunting in northwestern New Brunswick. Farms here provide green grasses and crops, while the hardwood ridges have plenty of mast. Stands of spruce and fir along stream drainages offer good cover. All combine to make ideal habitat for growing some mighty big whitetails. Few public roads invade the forests east of Plaster Rock, where logging operations result in plots of woods in various stages of regeneration. Terrain, while thick with vegetation and somewhat swampy and boggy, is not excessively high or difficult to negotiate.

Whitetail hunters in this area generally have a 25 to 35 percent success ratio. Owner Wayne DeLeavey qualifies that, however. "Our success rate was down to about 25 percent last year," he noted, " but our hunters missed two huge deer and passed up some smaller ones. One problem with listing a success rate is the fact that most of our deer hunters are repeat clients, which is not a problem, and will not kill anything smaller than what they have already shot."

Before dawn, you'll hike into the woods to reach a spot where you can sit and watch trails or rubs. Later in the day, you'll still-hunt the ridges, and when evening comes, you may work the edge of a field or head back to a well-used crossing on a game trail. Deer here have big bodies, dressing out at 200-pounds-plus, with 6- and 8-pointers dominating. The normal pattern is one guide serves three hunters, but for an additional fee, you can have a guide to yourself.

Hunters stay in the modern log lodge or in a log cabin nearby. All rooms have private baths. The lodge is equipped with hot water, showers, flush toilets, electric heat, and double and bunk beds. North View serves home-cooked meals (see the menu below — it's awesome, with plenty of it!) in the dining room, which has a big-screen satellite TV. For clients added enjoyment, there is also a game room complete with pool table, dart board and so on.

Vital Statistics

THE LODGE:

5 guest rooms, 15 beds total; all with private baths are in log cabins

SERVICES: Telephone, fax, TV

HUNTS: $1,200 / 5 days

PAYMENT: Cash or check

CONFERENCE GROUPS: Yes

MEAL PLANS: All meals included (Breakfast includes choice of eggs any style, cold or hot cereal, pancakes, potatoes, french toast, sausage, bacon or ham, toast, coffee or tea; box lunches of sandwiches, cheese, homemade sweet bread and cookies, coffee, tea; supper usually starts with hot soup, then main course of roast beef, pork chops, chicken, spaghetti, meat loaf or ham, potatoes, rice, vegetable, rolls or bread; dessert is usually pies (apple, blueberry, butterscotch, lemon meringue, coconut cream or banana cream), pudding, carrot or cheese cakes, tea, coffee)

NEAREST AIRPORT: Presque Isle, ME

TRANSPORTATION TO LODGE (45 miles): Rental car; van from lodge $75 round-trip

CONTACT:

Wayne DeLeavey
North View Hunting and Fishing Lodge
PO Box 1132
Plaster Rock, NB
E7G 4G9 Canada
Ph: 506/356-7212
Fax: 506/356-1800
Email: nvlodge@nb.sympatico.ca
Web: www.northviewlodge.com

THE HUNT:

SEASON:
• bow: October 2 - October 21
• rifle: October 23 - November 18

BEST TIME TO HUNT: Anytime

TERRAIN: Softwood valleys, hardwood ridges, clear-cuts; much of the property borders farm land, and early in the season, there is a fair amount of field hunting

LAND: Some private land, but mostly on controlled-access lumber company lands (totaling about one million acres); also some crown land (public land) but not much is hunted very often; there is usually snow on the ground the last 2 weeks of the season

DRAW BLOOD POLICY? No

HUNTING METHODS: Stand hunting, walking, still-hunting (depends on the weather and the hunter's preference)

YEARS IN BUSINESS: 17

STAFF OF GUIDES: 5

HUNTERS SERVED BY EACH GUIDE: 3

NONHUNTER CHARGE: n/a

LICENSES: Licenses are issued at camp

GAME CARE: Skinning; extra fee to have game cut and wrapped

OTHER ACTIVITIES: Other big game hunting (black bear, moose, coyote, wolf), bird hunting, bird watching, canoeing/rafting, fishing, waterfowling, wildlife photography

BOONE AND CROCKETT
• B&C book bucks taken from property: n/a (although last year, one North View hunter took a 29-pointer that field-dressed at 270 pounds)
• Average B&C score: n/a
• B&C bucks from this part of state: Many

Crawford's Camps

S i o u x   N a r r o w s ,   O n t a r i o

ATTACHED TO THE MAINLAND by an isthmus west of Crow Lake, the huge Aulneau Peninsula juts way out into the middle of sprawling Lake of the Woods. Named for Father Jean Pierre Aulneau, a Jesuit priest who explored the area in the 1730s, the peninsula's forests of spruce and fir were stripped in the late 1800s, leaving a dense second growth of poplar, birch and scrub oak mixed with stands of spruce, white pine and cedar. Elevations are not high, but the terrain is rugged. Grassy meadows and bogs serve to break up the dense forest here and there. This is perfect moose habitat, and the peninsula has one of the largest populations per square mile in Canada.

While moose and bear hunting are a major attraction at Crawford's Camp (located a few miles east of the peninsula at Sioux Narrows), big whitetails roam the mainland near camp, and draw more hunters to Crawford's than moose and bear combined. "We actually handle about twice as many deer hunters as we do bear hunters, and twice as many bear hunters as we do moose hunters," said Bob Rydberg, owner of Crawford's. "We have 82,000 acres leased for our bear hunts." On the other hand, as Rydberg notes, "All the land here is open to deer hunting. Millions of acres."

Hunters stay in one of the wooden, lakefront housekeeping cottages that dot the lakeshore for a quarter mile. Hunters generally get up each morning and either head to a stand overlooking a well-used deer trail, or slowly still-hunt along the edges of the forests. Guides are not generally used, though hunters can make special arrangements if they desire — not a bad idea, if this is the first time you've hunted this country. And while the Aulneau is restricted to primitive weapons for moose, deer hunters can take their pick of bow, muzzleloader or centerfire rifle to hunt the mainland and the islands.

Vital Statistics

THE LODGE:

17 cabins accommodate 2 to 7 each

SERVICES: Telephone, fax

HUNTS: $800 / week (Cdn), double occupancy

PAYMENT: Cash, check, credit cards

CONFERENCE GROUPS: No

MEAL PLANS: Housekeeping (bring your own), or eat at local restaurants

NEAREST AIRPORT: International Falls, MN

TRANSPORTATION TO LODGE (100 miles): Rental car; van from lodge ($100 round-trip for 4)

CONTACT:

Bob Rydberg
Crawford's Camps
Box 330
Sioux Narrows, Ontario
P0X 1N0 Canada
Ph: 888/266-3474
Email: Crawford@voyageur.ca
Fax: 807/226-5196
Web: http://crawfords-camp.com

THE HUNT:

SEASON:

• bow/rifle/muzzleloader: mid-Oct. to mid-Nov.

BEST TIME TO HUNT: November (during the rut)

TERRAIN: Dense second growth of poplar, birch, and scrub oak, mixed with stands of spruce, white pine and cedar; elevations are not high, but the terrain can be rough

LAND: Public land, limited access

DRAW BLOOD POLICY? No

HUNTING METHODS: Stand hunting, still-hunting, calling, rattling

YEARS IN BUSINESS: Since 1934

STAFF OF GUIDES: Available upon request

NONHUNTER CHARGE: Same as hunter

LICENSES: Sold over the counter

GAME CARE: Done by hunters

OTHER ACTIVITIES: Other big game hunting (moose, bear), bird hunting (grouse), waterfowling, bird watching, boating, fishing, swimming, wildlife photography

Huber's Lone Pine Lodge Ltd.

Dryden, Ontario

FOR MORE THAN 15 years, Huber's clients have been 100 percent successful on moose with good racks with 40-inch plus spreads. Huber's hunts more than 320 square miles of prime terrain, consisting of low brush, boggy stream channels, and thick timber.

You'll also find whitetails in this country — bucks that run in the 6- to 8-point range with live weights that often reach 250 to 300 pounds. Bring your own stand and pick a location (already scouted by one of Huber's knowledgeable guides) that overlooks active scrapes, rubs or game trails. Along with hunting from stands, stalking and limited drives also produce.

Huber's only books a limited number of hunters per year to ensure the continued trophy quality of the bucks on the property, as well as to give each hunter a quality hunting experience. Slots are often booked at least one year in advance, sometimes more, so hunters wanting to visit this prime property should call now for a hunt in a year or two.

Huber's also runs fall and spring bear hunts over baits. Fall bear and moose seasons overlap with grouse and duck hunting, and many hunters drive up with retrievers kenneled in their trucks.

Hunters stay in the base lodge, a well-kept, modern compound in a green glen by the lake. With a chef who is flown in each year from Munich, there's little doubt about the quality of the cuisine.

Vital Statistics

THE LODGE:

44 rooms with shared baths in the lodge; only 5 to 10 whitetail hunters are booked at a time

SERVICES: Telephone, TV

HUNTS: $1,225 / 6 days

PAYMENT: Cash, check or credit cards

CONFERENCE GROUPS: Yes

MEAL PLANS: German and Canadian cuisine; dinners include entrees such as chicken cordon bleu, chicken kiev, rinderbraten, roast beef, Muenchener turkey schnitzel, sauerbraten, surf and turf, New York steaks, and more, all with vegetables, potoates, soups, salads, and desserts (try the German rum cake — guaranteed you'll go back for seconds!)

NEAREST AIRPORT: Dryden International, ON

TRANSPORTATION TO LODGE (17 miles): Van from lodge ($35)

CONTACT:

Walter Huber
Huber's Lone Pine Lodge Ltd.
Box 546
Dryden, Ontario
P8N 2Z2, Canada
Ph: 1-800/665-2257
Fax: 807/938-6651
Email: whuber@dryden.lakeheadu.ca
Web: www.hearland.on.ca/hubers

THE HUNT:

SEASON: Mid-September - early October

BEST TIME TO HUNT: Anytime

TERRAIN: Low brush, boggy stream channels, thick timber

LAND: 320 square miles of leased land

DRAW BLOOD POLICY? No

HUNTING METHODS: Stand hunting, stalking, some drives

YEARS IN BUSINESS: 20

STAFF OF GUIDES: 10

HUNTERS SERVED BY EACH GUIDE: 2

NONHUNTER CHARGE: n/a

LICENSES: Sold over the counter

GAME CARE: Dressing and quartering

OTHER ACTIVITIES: Other big game hunting (bear, moose), bird hunting (grouse), waterfowl hunting, bird watching, fishing (walleye, smallmouth , northern pike), golf, snowmobiling, waterfowling, wildlife photography

BOONE AND CROCKETT

- B&C book bucks taken from property: 1
- Average B&C score: 201.5 (best typical), 250.1 (best non-typical)
- B&C bucks from this part of province: n/a

Fairmont Kenauk

Kenauk Montebello, Quebec

W HEN WHITETAIL HUNTERS think of Quebec, they usually think of Anticosti Island off the mouth of the St. Lawrence River. Justifiably so — with more than 100,000 deer, modern lodging, classic hunting opportunities, and a two-buck limit, Anticosti has a deserved reputation.

But another part of the province also deserves mention, and that's the Ottawa River Valley, an hour's drive west of Montreal. With a mix of field and forest, farmland and wilderness, and generally milder weather than regions to its east, this part of southern Quebec offers excellent whitetail hunting. The terrain is quite similar to that of northern New York and New England, making many deer hunters from the U.S. feel right at home.

One of the log chalets at Fairmont Kenauk in southern Quebec.

If you want to hunt this more accessible part of Quebec, look no farther than Kenauk Reserve. One of North America's largest and oldest private fish and game reserves, Kenauk is unfenced and is carefully managed with wildlife in mind. It offers more than 100 square miles of carefully protected and managed habitat, and boasts one of the highest hunter success rates on mainland Quebec. Hunters visiting Kenauk are assigned an exclusive territory averaging approximately 2,200 acres, meaning they'll have plenty of unpressured territory to hunt. Their chances of taking a buck are good, as the population averages 12 to 15 whitetails per square mile. Some of the bucks are huge, too, with 8- to 10-pointers, some topping 200 pounds, being taken each season.

Bowhunters get a bonus here if they hunt the early season, as Kenauk also offers a combination moose and whitetail hunt timed for when moose are in the peak of the rut. Stand hunting and driving are the preferred methods for whitetails here, although with a bit of prodding, you can probably convince your guide to let you still-hunt some of the more remote sections — if you can prove to him that your woods skills are up to it.

At the end of a day of hunting at Kenauk, you'll return to your own private cabin — there are 13 in all, some of which are on their own lakes. Recently renovated, the one- to four-bedroom cabins are cozy enough for a couple, but spacious enough for an annual hunting (or fishing) trip. Most feature fireplaces, and all have propane stoves, refrigerators, lights, screened-in porches and private docks. The kitchen and linen closet are both fully stocked.

Your stay at Kenauk also entitles you to full use of the extensive sports facilities at historic Fairmont Le Chateau Montebello, Fairmont Hotels & Resorts 4-star resort. And if you want to borrow their chef during your stay, just say the word. The management at Kenauk can easily arrange for your choice of a number of optional amenities, including full professional meal catering.

Vital Statistics

THE LODGE:

13 log chalets, 60 beds total; no main lodge

Services: None at the cabins

Hunts: $149 / day

Payment: Check, credit cards

Conference Groups: n/a

Meal Plans: Guests do their own cooking

Nearest Airport: Montreal or Ottawa

Transportation to Lodge (90 km): Rental car

THE HUNT:

Season:

• bow: Mid to late Sept.

• rifle: first Sat. in Nov. to the third Sat. in Nov.

Best Time to Hunt: Anytime

Terrain: 95% hardwood forest with hemlock and oak on mountaintops, cedar swamps, and beaver ponds in lowlands; lower Canadian Shield area with altitudes from 500 to 1000 feet, with many rocky outcrops, small streams, headwater ponds and beaver ponds; excellent whitetail habitat, with three major deer yards

Land: 65,000 private acres

Draw Blood Policy? No

Hunting Methods: Stand hunting (lock-ons with ladders and padded swivel seats), drives

Years in Business: 71

Staff of Guides: 5

Hunters served by each guide: Depends on the hunting party

Nonhunter Charge: $61 / night

Licenses: Sold over the counter

Game Care: Guide will assist with field care; butchering can be arranged locally

Other Activities: Bird hunting, fishing, bird watching, canoeing, hiking

CONTACT:

Bill Nowell
Fairmont Kenauk
1000 Chemin
KenaukMontebello, Quebec
J0V 1L0 Canada
Ph: 800/567-6845
Fax: 819/423-5277
Email: bill.nowell@fairmont.com
Web: www.fairmont.com

Safari Anticosti Inc. / Anticosti Outfitters Inc.

C a p - C h a t ,   Q u e b e c

EMERGING FROM THE prehistoric Champlain Sea, 3,200-square-mile Anticosti Island spreads across the entry to the majestic Gulf of St. Lawrence. The island remained uninhabited up until 1680 when Louis XIV Louis XIV, the Sun King, gave it to Louis Jolliet in acknowledgment of his discovery of the Mississippi.

Thereafter, several different initiatives to develop the island failed until the arrival of Henri Menier (1853-1913), the French chocolate magnate, who acquired the island in 1895 for the sum of $125,000. From then until 1913, Menier invested five million dollars in the island to turn it into an outdoorsman's paradise.

In 1926 the island passed into the hands of the Anticosti Corporation for 6.5 million dollars. The corporation later became subsidiary of consolidate Bathurst which, in 1974, sold the island to the Quebec Government for 26 million dollars. It was in 1984 that Anticosti Outfitters Inc. obtained a lease giving it exclusive hunting and fishing rights in the southeastern sector of the island.

Over this 400-square-mile area, Anticosti Outfitters Inc. has developed the most prestigious hunting and fishing grounds in the province of Quebec at a cost of 12 million dollars. Anticosti Outfitters' exclusive territory of 400 square miles has an estimated population of 15,000 whitetail deer.

This is classic deer hunting, with hunters heading out into the dense conifer forests early in the morning, following game trails, still-hunting quietly in areas where deer are known to live. Rattling and calling often work in this country, especially since the buck to doe ratio is about equal, and bucks are very competitive about finding does. If you choose to rattle, watch the area downwind of your position and be ready, as bucks can come in faster than you might suspect. Shots are often quick ones, generally at ranges less than 75 yards.

With a huge whitetail population, and an abundance of trophy bucks, Anticosti is the type of place that every deer hunter should visit.

Vital Statistics

THE LODGE:

Depends on type of hunt chosen — 2 housekeeping cabins can accommodate a total of 6 hunters; the 2 main lodges, Safari and Salmon, can accommodate up to 6 hunters in 3 rooms

Services: TV, VCR, laundry

Gun Hunts: From $900 - $3,200, depending on the package

Payment: Cash or credit cards

Conference Groups: Yes

Meal Plans: All meals included (French cuisine) with lodge plan; bring your own with housekeeping plan

Nearest Airport: Quebec City (on mainland); Salmon River Airport on the island

Transportation to Lodge (mileage depends on lodge or cabin): Van will pick you up for no extra charge

CONTACT:

Safari Anticosti Inc.
Anticosti Outfitters Inc.
Box/C.P. 398
Cap-Chat, Quebec
G0J 1E0 Canada
Ph: 418/786-5788 (Cap-Chat); 450/441-9560 (Montreal)
Fax: 418/786-2744 (Cap-Chat)
Email: antico@globetrotter.qc.ca

THE HUNT:

Season: Sept. - Nov.

Best Time to Hunt: Anytime, although the rut in November can be especially productive; some hunters like to hunt early, when the deer are in velvet

Terrain: Dense conifer forests, river drainages, swamps, coastal area

Land: Housekeeping plan hunters have more than 75 square miles to hunt; lodge hunters have more, with over 200 miles of new dirt roads and trails

Draw Blood Policy? No

Hunting Methods: Still-hunting, calling, rattling, vehicle

Years in Business: 16

Staff of Guides: Varies

Hunters served by each guide: 6 on housekeeping plan; one-on-one hunts for lodge-based hunters

Nonhunter Charge: n/a

Licenses: Sold over the counter at lodge

Game Care: Quartering, boxing of meat, and caping services are available

Other Activities: Fishing, bird watching, wildlife photography

SEPAQ-Anticosti

Quebec, Quebec

I F YOU'RE LOOKING TO HUNT whitetails in a natural setting where the deer are unpressured by hunters, you have to try hunting on Anticosti Island, located at the mouth of the St. Lawrence River just north of the tip of the Gaspé Peninsula. A 3,066-square-mile island with prime whitetail habitat, Anticosti was originally leased by chocolatier Henri Menier, who intended to develop its vast timber resources. In the process, Menier also decided to import some whitetails and see if he could grow a herd. That the deer survived, let alone thrived, is one of those coincidences of nature. Menier had no idea that the island lacked nut-bearing trees when he brought in his deer. Ever adaptable, the deer took to lichens and protein-rich seaweed, and with no natural predators on the island, they multiplied like crazy.

The population today is estimated to be in excess of 120,000. Two deer, either bucks or does, can be taken per hunter. The terrain is not difficult. The island is essentially a highland, part of the Cute-Nord region, broken intermittently by rivers such as the Jupiter that flows north, draining the center part of the island. Coniferous trees, firs, spruce and larch dominate, although you will also find occasional stands of birch and poplar, along with bogs full of lush, fresh grasses into fall. Just remember to bring a compass, as some of those fir stands are mighty thick and it's easy to get turned around.

A Crown corporation, SEPAQ operates a 1,700-square mile (more than half the size of the island) reserve where access is limited to guests who stay in one of the seven lodges or 20 housekeeping cabins. On average, each guest has eight square miles to hunt during the season, which runs from August into December. One guide serves four hunters maximum, and included is a 4WD, crew-cab pickup, an ATV, or horses if you prefer. Experienced hunters may seek little more than general direction from the guide, while first-timers to the island will receive personal attention. A typical hunt lasts four days. You'll spend the first two glassing and passing up deer that you'd ordinarily shoot were you back home. During the last two days, the heat's on. Will you find that 8-point-plus wall-hanger? Much depends on the weather, so be prepared for cold and damp or snow anytime from October on. Guests in the lodges live well. Meals are first-class with shrimp and oysters followed by smoked salmon and fine wines. With so much going for it, it's no wonder that Anticosti is generally booked solid at least a year in advance.

Vital Statistics

THE LODGE:

7 lodges (8 to 12 hunters per lodge), 20 house-keeping cabins (up to 6 hunters per cabin); Sepaq can accommodate up to 200 hunters at a time

HUNTS: Up to $1,759 (Cdn) / 4 days

PAYMENT: Cash, check, credit cards

CONFERENCE GROUPS: Yes

MEAL PLANS: Each lodge has a chef who creates his own menu, but all offer first-class meals; hunters in housekeeping cabins cook for themselves

NEAREST AIRPORT: Port Menier (from either Montreal or Quebec City)

TRANSPORTATION TO LODGE: You'll be picked up at the airport and driven to your lodge

CONTACT:

Gilles Dumaresq
SEPAQ-Anticosti
801 Chemin St. Louis
Quebec, Quebec
G1S 1C1, Canada
Ph: 800/463-0863
Fax: 418/682-9944
Email: lavallee.francine@sepaq.com

THE HUNT:

SEASON:

• bow/rifle/muzzleloader: Aug. 25 - Dec. 19

BEST TIME TO HUNT: Anytime, although the rut in mid-November is always prime

TERRAIN: Coniferous trees, firs, spruce and larch dominate, with stands of birch and poplar, and bogs

LAND: 1,700 acres of Crown land

DRAW BLOOD POLICY? No

HUNTING METHODS: Still-hunting, calling, rattling, vehicle

YEARS IN BUSINESS: Since 1985

STAFF OF GUIDES: 50

HUNTERS SERVED BY EACH GUIDE: 4 maximum

NONHUNTER CHARGE: 50% of regular price; special hunting rates for children aged 12 - 21

LICENSES: Sold at the lodge

GAME CARE: Field dress, butcher, pack for shipping with lodgeplan; do-it-yourself with housekeeping plan

OTHER ACTIVITIES: None during hunting season; salmon fishing in summer

CANADA WEST

ALBERTA, BRITISH COLUMBIA, SASKATCHEWAN

T HE WESTERN PROVINCES of Canada offer something for everyone. With the cold winters and less sunshine than areas to the south, whitetails here on the northern fringe of their range grow on the average to a much larger body size than southern deer. With this increased body mass comes larger antlers as well.

Whitetail hunters would be wasting their time looking to the Yukon or Northwest Territories, where they would find elk, sheep, bear, lions, and mule deer, but few if any whitetails. Whitetails instead are found in the Fort St. John region and Peace River drainage of British Columbia. In Alberta, hunters should concentrate on the major river valleys of the central agricultural region. Most of the bigger bucks are taken from an area that extends from Edmonton east to Cold Lake on the Saskatchewan border, then south to Empress and west to Cochrane, about 20 miles west of Calgary, then back up to Edmonton.

Saskatchewan is justly famous for the world-record typical whitetail, scoring 213 5/8, which was taken by Milo Hanson on his farm near Biggar in November 1993. There are big bucks throughout much of the province, especially in the agricultural areas bordered by hardwood forests, and hunters booking a hunt in this province can expect to have the hunt of a lifetime.

L o d g e s
A l b e r t a
1 D & S GUIDING LTD.
2 DON AYERS OUTFITTERS
3 LEGEND OUFITTING
S a s k a t c h e w a n
4 MAKWA RIVER OUTFITTERS LTD.

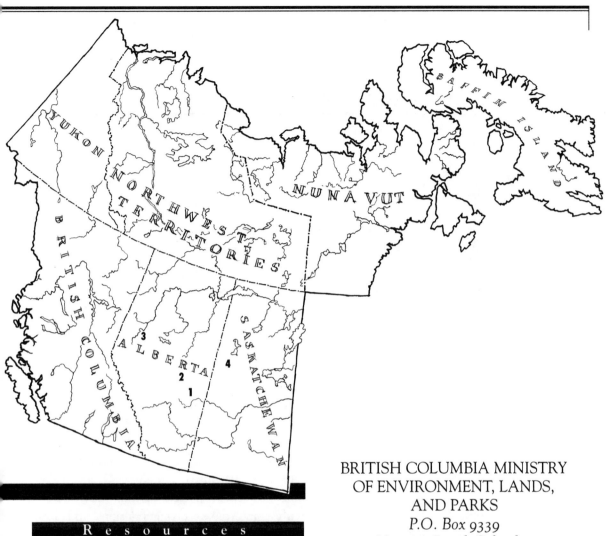

ALBERTA DEPT. OF
ENVIRONMENTAL PROTECTION
Main Fl., Petroleum Plaza, North Tower
9945 108 St.
Edmonton, Alberta
T5K 296 Canada
Ph: 403/427-7381
Web: www.gov.ab.ca/env/
TRAVEL ALBERTA
10155 102nd. St.
Edmonton, Alberta
T5J 4G8 Canada
Ph: 800/661-8888
Web: www.explorealberta.com

BRITISH COLUMBIA MINISTRY
OF ENVIRONMENT, LANDS,
AND PARKS
P.O. Box 9339
Victoria, British Columbia
V8W 9M1 Canada
Ph: 604/387-9422

SASKATCHEWAN ENVIRONMENT
AND RESOURCE MANAGEMENT
3211 Albert St.
Regina, Saskatchewan
S4S 5W6 Canada
Ph: 306/787-2930
Web: www.gov.sk.ca/govt/environ/

TOURISM SASKATCHEWAN
1900 Albert St.
Regina, Saskatchewan
S4P 4L9 Canada
Web: www.sasktourism.com

D & S Guiding Ltd.

Viking, Alberta

THE ULTIMATE CHALLENGE for the serious whitetail hunter is a trophy deer, and Alberta is unquestionably one of the best places in the world to go after a trophy. Mild winters and light pressure contribute to the province's claim of being the "Whitetail Capital" of the world. A large percentage of the hunting consists of drives, a productive method for bagging a deer. But D&S Guiding also hunts from stands, uses deer calls, rattles antlers and stalks; they use whatever method is necessary to take a deer. Pre-season scouting by the guides is also critical, as it gives D&S a chance to pattern the big bucks, figure out their preferred escape routes, and plan their tactics accordingly.

D&S Guiding hunts three separate areas in Alberta, covering a variety of different terrain: open farmland, rolling hills, heavy bush, and the famous Battle River area, a hard-wood laced riverbottom mixed with pasture. Good habitat and climate combined with excellent food availability help to produce good densities of mature bucks with massive antler growth.

D&S Guiding Ltd. has a large number of repeat hunters each fall due to consistent hunting success, mixed with comfortable accommodations and excellent camp food. This hunt can be booked by itself or combined with a mule-deer hunt.

Mulies are hunted in the same general area as the whitetails. High densities of trophy mule deer are found in the parkland area of Alberta. The habitat to find the big monster bucks is a patchwork design of interwoven hayfields, cultivated lands for cereal crops, pastures, and stands of willows and poplars along the Battle River coulee. The size of the mule deer is notable, continuing to impress both guides and hunters.

Vital Statistics

THE LODGE:

Hunters stay in a local motel, which can accommodate 6 - 10 people; all rooms have private baths

SERVICES: Telephone, fax, copying, TV, laundry

GUN HUNTS:

- $4,000 / 6 days one-on-one
- $3,500 / 6 days two-on-one
- $4,500 / 10 days one-on-one
- $4,000 / 10 days two-on-one

mule deer/whitetail combo hunts are also available

PAYMENT: Cash, check

CONFERENCE GROUPS: Yes

MEAL PLANS: All meals included (healthy and hearty; menu includes bacon, eggs, hash browns, toast and juice for breakfast; sandwiches, cookies, fruit, juice or soda for lunch; full- course meals with meats, vegetables, soups, potatoes, desserts and drinks for dinner)

NEAREST AIRPORT: Edmonton International, AB

TRANSPORTATION TO LODGE: Van, no extra cost

CONTACT:

Dean Cumming
D & S Guiding Ltd.
Box 447
Viking, Alberta
T0B 4N0 Canada
Ph: 780-336-2390
Fax: 780-336-2397
Email: dcumming@telusplanet.net
Web: www.dsguiding.ab.ca

THE HUNT:

SEASON: November 1 - 30

TERRAIN: Farmlands, rolling hills, pasture land, heavy bush, Battle River area

LAND: n/a

DRAW BLOOD POLICY: n/a

HUNTING METHODS: Stand hunting, calling, rattling, stalking

YEARS IN BUSINESS: n/a

STAFF OF GUIDES: n/a

HUNTERS SERVED BY EACH GUIDE: One

NONHUNTER CHARGE: $100 / day

LICENSES: Outfitter pre-buys licenses

GAME CARE: Packaging, freezing and shipping of game is available at an extra cost

OTHER ACTIVITIES: Other big game hunting (mule deer, coyotes), waterfowling, antiquing, wildlife photography

Don Ayers Outfitters

Edmonton, Alberta

WHILE SASKATCHEWAN has gotten most of the press in the past decade, thanks in large part to Milo Hanson taking the No. 1 all-time typical whitetail near Biggar in 1993, Alberta has been quietly racking up book bucks throughout that time. In fact, many hunters in the know are predicting that the next No. 1 buck will come from Alberta. In the Boone and Crockett record book, Alberta's entries are numerous and impressive, with its best typical buck scoring 204 2/8 and its top non-typical entry measuring a whopping 279 6/8s! With good feed, good genetics in much of the herd, plus relatively light hunting pressure, Alberta could very well be the source of the next world record.

Hunters must have a guide to hunt in Alberta. One outfit that's smack in the middle of Alberta's prime whitetail country is Don Ayers Outfitters. Ayers mostly hunts the zones just outside of the Bow Zone around Edmonton, which is well-known for its trophy-class deer. This is farmland with a lot of patch spruce and poplar that provides great deer habitat. Ayers has the rights to hunt on more than 12,800 acres in this territory.

Ayers also holds all the whitetail allocations in an area bordering the beautiful Athabasca River, west of Whitecourt, Alberta. Classic whitetail habitat covers some 500 square miles. This is woods hunting at its best, with a lot of clear-cuts offering the deer an abundance of feeding opportunities. The hunter can expect to be hunting the cut lines or watching the open clear-cuts, and must be prepared for long shots.

The camps are varied, depending on which of Ayers' territories you hunt. They range from a modern-style farmhouse with downstairs bedrooms to lodging in heated log cabins. Great meals are prepared and served by outstanding cooks. In some areas, Ayers will house clients in a hotel or motel with a restaurant. Ayers supplies all meals and rooms. In some instances, you may also be housed at a guide's home in the hunting area.

No matter where you hunt with Ayers, the general drill is to use ground blinds and tree stands for the mornings and late afternoons. The blind can be heated to keep you more comfortable if the weather turns extremely cold. This is his most successful style of hunting. During the middle of the day, he'll drive you around in his truck, stopping in likely areas to glass and perhaps do some rattling. Although methods are varied, they all have proven successful.

Vital Statistics

THE LODGE:

Primary lodge, a rustic farmhouse, houses 2-6 hunters; depending on where you hunt in his territory, you may stay at a hotel, motel or private home

SERVICES: Depends on where you stay

GUN HUNTS:

• $3,250 / week, two hunters with one guide

• $3,750 / week, one-on-one

• $4,500 / 9-day hunt, two hunters with one guide, mule deer and whitetail

PAYMENT: Credit cards, check, other

CONFERENCE GROUPS: No

MEAL PLANS: All meals included (dinners include roast beef, chicken, roast pork hamburgers, veggies, breads, desserts)

NEAREST AIRPORT: Edmonton, AB

TRANSPORTATION TO LODGE: Rental car; van from lodge

CONTACT:

Don or Tuffy Ayers
Don Ayers Outfitters
3015-109 Ave.
Edmonton, AB
T5W 0G2 Canada
Ph: 780/479-4433
Fax: 780/474-9068
Email: info@donayers.com
Web: www.donayers.com

THE HUNT:

SEASON:

• rifle and muzzleloader: Nov. 1 - Nov. 30

BEST TIME TO HUNT: Last three weeks of November

TERRAIN: Most of the terrain is farmland with woods, but Ayers does have all the whitetail allocation near the Athabasca River, so there is much variety, including bottomlands

LAND: 30 square miles of private and public land

DRAW BLOOD POLICY? No

HUNTING METHODS: Stand hunting (heated, enclosed stands), still-hunting, calling, rattling

YEARS IN BUSINESS: 27

STAFF OF GUIDES: 4 - 8

HUNTERS SERVED BY EACH GUIDE: 2 maximum

NONHUNTER CHARGE: $1,000 / week

LICENSES: Sold through Ayers

GAME CARE: Dressed only

OTHER ACTIVITIES: Other big game hunting (mule deer, coyote, wolf)

BOONE AND CROCKETT

• B&C book bucks taken from property: n/a

• Average B&C score: 140 to 160

• B&C bucks from this part of state: n/a

Legend Oufitting

Wanham, Alberta

IKE WHITE'S got a good thing going. Hunting a 40 by 50 mile area in the heart of Alberta's big buck country, White knows where the trophy bucks are — he knows their travel patterns, their bedding areas, and where they go to feed. Once he patterns a big buck in the pre-season, he sets up lock-on stands overlooking well-used trails — most go from the thick timber to agricultural fields. Then it's just a matter of placing a hunter in one of those hot stands, and seeing what happens.

What happens, of course, is that the rut starts, the bucks go crazy, and all that patterning goes out the window! But not entirely, because even if a buck is running all over the territory looking for estrus does, White still knows his approximate location. If a hunter is willing to wait it out, sooner or later that buck is going to come down one of his favorite trails. Correctly used grunt calls can help make it happen. In some cases, White takes his hunters still-hunting, especially when he knows a specific buck is back in the timber and probably isn't going to come out.

Hunting Alberta can be tough, but there are some huge bucks there. In fact, many people predict that the next record-book whitetail is going to come from this province, surpassing the Milo Hansen buck that set the record back in 1993. That huge typical scored 213 5/8, and was taken near the town of Biggar in Saskatchewan. White knows there are bucks as big in his territory. One of his hunters took a monster non-typical a few years ago that scored 206 1/8.

A 218 B&C gross non-typical taken out of Alberta's woods.

© Legend Outfitting

The weather can be extreme in this country during the fall. It can get God-awful cold, but then, like anywhere else in the whitetail's range, it can get downright hot during hunting season — which is just what you don't want, because then all of the deer will lie down and not move until the cool after-dark hours. White tells his hunters to bring layered clothing; be ready for anything from 0°F to 60°F.

Vital Statistics

THE LODGE:

4 guest rooms, one with private bath, 5 beds total

Services: Telephone, TV, laundry, gym

HUNTS:

• $4,500 / 10-day one-on-one hunt, plus license fee and tax

PAYMENT: Cash, travelers checks, money orders

MEAL PLANS: All meals included (breakfasts of eggs, bacon, sausage, pancakes, waffles; lunches of sandwiches, soups, small meals, pastries; dinners of elk, moose, deer, steaks, chicken, pork, pastas)

SPECIAL DIETS: Can accommodate any special diet upon advance notice

NEAREST AIRPORT: Grande Prairie, AB

TRANSPORTATION TO LODGE: Lodge van at no extra cost

CONTACT:

Mike White
Legend Oufitting
Box 174
Wanham, Alberta
T0H 3P0 Canada
Ph:780/618-2033.
Email: Levellok@Levellok
Web: Levellok.com

OFF-SEASON

105 512 Street
Pittsburgh, PA 15203
Ph: 412/431-5440
Fax: 412/431-1569

THE HUNT:

SEASONS:

• rifle: September 17 - November 30

BEST TIME TO HUNT: November 1 - 30

TERRAIN: Primarily agricultural land surrounded by large amounts of timber; generally the terrain is flat, but very hilly near the riverbottoms

LAND: A combination of private farm land bordered with government public land

DRAW BLOOD POLICY? No

HUNTING METHODS: Stand hunting (climbers, lock-ons, and permanent enclosed stands), still-hunting, calling

YEARS IN BUSINESS: 6

STAFF OF GUIDES: 3

HUNTERS SERVED BY EACH GUIDE: 1

NONHUNTER CHARGE: $100 / day

LICENSES: Outfitter pre-purchases licenses

GAME CARE: Dress, package, freeze and ship game (cost varies, but the average cost for butchering and shipping is $150)

OTHER ACTIVITIES: Elk and mule deer hunting, bird hunting, waterfowling

BOONE AND CROCKETT

• B&C bucks taken from property: 3

• Average B&C score: 155

• B&C bucks from this part of state: 15

Makwa River Outfitters Ltd.

M a k w a ,   S a s k a t c h e w a n

YOU CAN NEVER BEAT OLD-FASHIONED, down-home hospitality, and you can bet that the Dopko family — Ken, Kathy, and two sons Walker and Connor — will give you just that. Owners of Makwa River Outfitters Ltd., they provide comfort galore in a fully modern cabin. Leave your bulky sleeping bags and camping gear at home; it's all provided here.

The hunting here is special — big-bodied, big-racked whitetails often make the records books. All hunting is done from stands that overlook wooded areas and clearcuts that dot the 70,000-plus acres the Dopkos hunt. Bucks can move at any time of day, especially during the rut or when the temperature drops, so hunters have to be ready at any time. Shots can be long — up to 300 yards and more across clear-cuts — but can also be close in. You never know when a buck will turn up, or where.

At the end of the day, you'll head back to the lodge to share stories of the hunt around the kitchen table, then take a hot shower and sink into a soft bed to dream about more hunting excitement the next day.

Big whitetails from northern Canada are at the top of most hunters' dream lists. Here you can make it happen at a lodge that aims to please.

Vital Statistics

THE LODGE:

3 guest rooms in lodge, 8 beds total, 1 private bath

SERVICES: Telephone, fax, copying, TV

HUNTS: Prices available upon request

PAYMENT: Cash, travelers checks

MEAL PLANS: Full course meals, complete with desserts

SPECIAL DIETS: Can accommodate upon advance notice

NEAREST AIRPORT: Saskatoon, SK

TRANSPORTATION TO LODGE (180 miles): Rental car

CONTACT:

Ken Dopko
Makwa River Outfitters
Box 89
Makwa, Saskatchewan
S0M 1N0 Canada
Ph:306/236-4649
Fax: 306/236-4716
Email: k.dopko@sk.sympatico.ca
Web: www.makwariveroutfitters.com

THE HUNT:

SEASONS:

• rifle: Nov. 6 - Dec. 9

• bow and muzzleloader: Oct. 30 - Nov. 4

BEST TIME TO HUNT : Anytime

TERRAIN: Wooded areas with swamps and clear cuts

LAND: Approximately 110 square miles, or 70,400 acres, all leased

DRAW BLOOD POLICY? Yes

HUNTING METHODS: Stand hunting (lock-ons, enclosed and heated metal stands with break-up camo, ladder accessible)

YEARS IN BUSINESS: 10

STAFF OF GUIDES: 2

HUNTERS SERVED BY EACH GUIDE: 2

NONHUNTER CHARGE: n/a

LICENSES: Sold at the lodge

GAME CARE: Makwa Outfitters will dress and cape the animal; if client wants, he may cut, wrap and freeze meat to take home.

OTHER ACTIVITIES: Bear hunting (many color phases), waterfowling, golf

BOONE AND CROCKETT

• B&C bucks taken from property: 10 - 12

• Average B&C score: 145 - 150 (if a hunter is patient)

• B&C bucks from this part of state: n/a

Alphabetical Listing of Lodges